Rediscovering Eve

Rediscovering Eve

Ancient Israelite
Women in Context

CAROL MEYERS

OXFORD
UNIVERSITY PRESS

OXFORD
UNIVERSITY PRESS

Oxford University Press is a department of the University of Oxford. It furthers the University's objective
of excellence in research, scholarship, and education by publishing worldwide.

Oxford   New York

Auckland   Cape Town   Dar es Salaam   Hong Kong   Karachi
Kuala Lumpur   Madrid   Melbourne   Mexico City   Nairobi
New Delhi   Shanghai   Taipei   Toronto

With offices in

Argentina   Austria   Brazil   Chile   Czech Republic   France   Greece
Guatemala   Hungary   Italy   Japan   Poland   Portugal   Singapore
South Korea   Switzerland   Thailand   Turkey   Ukraine   Vietnam

Oxford is a registered trademark of Oxford University Press
in the UK and certain other countries.

Published in the United States of America by
Oxford University Press
198 Madison Avenue, New York, NY 10016

Library of Congress Cataloging-in-Publication Data
Meyers, Carol L.
Rediscovering Eve : ancient Israelite women in context / Carol Meyers.
p. cm.
This work was published in 1988 under "Discovering Eve : ancient Israelite women in context".
Includes bibliographical references and index.
ISBN 978-0-19-973455-9 (hardcover : alk. paper)—ISBN 978-0-19-973462-7 (pbk. : alk. paper)
1. Jewish women—Palestine—History.   2. Women in Judaism.   3. Women in the Bible.
4. Palestine—Social life and customs—To 70 A.D.   I. Title.
HQ1172.M49 2013
305.4'862—dc23
2012008782

ISBN: 978-0-19-973455-9

9 8 7 6 5 4 3 2 1
Printed in the United States of America

For Eric

Contents

Preface

MORE THAN TWENTY years ago, with the encouragement of many col-leagues and friends, I published a book—*Discovering Eve: Ancient Israelite Women in Context* (Oxford, 1988)—that I hoped would enlighten read-ers about women in the biblical past. My goal was twofold: to provide new ways of understanding the Eve of the Genesis narrative, and also to reconstruct the everyday lives of women in the earliest period of ancient Israelite existence. The second goal would presumably contribute to the first. The book drew on biblical texts, archaeological data, and social sci-ence materials.

Much has changed since the 1980s in all of the areas that were my resources for that book, and I was thrilled when Oxford seemed inter-ested in publishing a revised version that would take into account those changes along with my own subsequent work on women in the world of the Hebrew Bible. Having agreed to update the 1988 book, I soon found that a revision was not possible. I would not be merely correcting or improving or updating a few points; I would not simply be adding some references. The changes I found myself making were too extensive and too profound for the result to be considered a second revised edition. At every step of the way, I found myself able to retain very little of the pre-vious book. It is my hope that the new title, *Rediscovering Eve: Ancient Israelite Women in Context,* acknowledges my indebtedness to its anteced-ent but also represents the fact that there are substantial differences. The present book is similar in structure and goals to its predecessor but also differs in many ways.

Most obvious is the scope. Readers who are familiar with the 1988 book will notice that I no longer restrict my observations about women's lives to the earliest period of ancient Israel (Iron Age I, ca. 1200–1000 BCE). Rather, I believe that the agrarian life that obtained in that period continued throughout most of the Iron Age for most people.

Also, the ensuing decades of anthropological and archaeological research, at least some of which has been directed to understanding households, have provided a sounder basis for reconstructing the context of women's lives. I believe that this research has enabled me to draw a richer portrait of their daily experiences than before. Similarly, when I began my work on biblical and Israelite women in the 1980s, the literature on the subject was rather limited. Now it is enormous, as is the general literature in the study of sex and gender by anthropologists, literary critics, and others. The possibilities for interpreting gender relations as well as for understanding Israelite society have expanded, and this book has been the beneficiary. Before, I struggled to find worthwhile scholarly resources; here I struggled to judiciously represent or incorporate scholarly trends without overwhelming the reader with references to every pertinent study.

Finally, my views have changed or been refined, not only by all the literature I have consulted but also because of the many more opportunities I have had to teach, lecture, and write, in academic settings and in the wider community, about various topics relevant to this project. Over the years the questions and comments of students, teaching assistants, colleagues, editors, and the many other people who have heard me talk about Eve and Israelite women have challenged, supplemented, and otherwise altered my views. I also took seriously the published reviews of the predecessor book—sometimes agreeing with a reviewer's criticism and revising my exposition, and sometimes sharpening (I hope) my arguments.

My gratitude to the people who provided direct assistance as I researched and wrote this book is enormous. The librarians at Duke University were unfailingly cooperative in helping me obtain the materials I needed. Colleagues at other institutions were graciously willing to provide advance copies of work not yet published. The staff in the Religion Department at Duke cheerfully assisted me in technical matters. A Duke graduate student, Sean Burrus, enthusiastically helped me with proofreading and reference checking; he also offered many astute observations about the content, enabling me to improve the manuscript. As for Oxford University Press, a deep expression of thanks goes to Cynthia Read, who took on my 1988 book and was willing to let me try again in 2011. Her assistant, Lisbeth Redfield, graciously provided answers to my many questions about manuscript submission. The copyeditor, Gary Berleth, improved the manuscript in countless ways. Finally, the production manager, Sravanthi Sridharan, patiently responded to my many queries as she expertly moved the manuscript through to production. To all these people I am extremely grateful.

Finally, I could hardly have completed this project without the deep interest, loving support, professional encouragement, and scholarly advice of my husband, Eric. Moreover, his patience has been nothing short of phenomenal, considering how often I spent evening and weekend hours working on this book instead of enjoying time together with him.

Carol Meyers
Duke University
Durham, North Carolina
December, 2011

Note on Translations, Transcriptions, and Documentation

THE SCRIPTURE QUOTATIONS contained herein, unless otherwise noted, are from the New Revised Standard Version Bible (NRSV), copyright 1989, Division of Christian Education of the National Council of the Churches of Christ in the United States of America. Used by permission. All rights reserved.

The chapter and verse numbers used in citing the Bible are those appearing in the NRSV and most English translations. These references sometimes diverge from those found in Hebrew Bibles; in such cases the Hebrew reference is provided too, preceded by "Heb."

Because the Bible is an important source for this study, the examination of certain texts in the original Hebrew has been an essential part of the task. Discussion of a number of Hebrew terms and phrases, especially those that lack exact English equivalents and those that have not always been accurately translated, appears in several chapters. I have chosen to simplify the standard scholarly system of transliteration by omitting diacritical marks over vowels. In doing so, my intention is to preserve the technical aspect of this enterprise while making it accessible to the nonspecialist.

Similarly, with respect to documentation, I have tried to satisfy the needs of both the scholar or student and the general reader. The notes contain full documentation of the sources I have consulted. However, with few exceptions, the notes contain no additional discussion or technical details. Thus the text of this book can be read straight through without looking at the notes except when the reader might be interested in the references cited. The reader should also be aware that the scholarship on many aspects of this book is vast and that I have not referred to every possible source; rather, I have tried to choose representative ones that contain references to many other relevant works.

Rediscovering Eve

I

Eve and Israelite Women: Understanding the Task

EVE. WE ALL think we know her and understand what she represents. Few come of age in Jewish and Christian cultures, and perhaps Muslim ones too, without having heard of Eden and the primeval couple, Eve and Adam. Most of us have read, or have had read to us, the simple and powerful narrative of Genesis 2 and 3. It is no wonder, then, that when scientists proposed on the basis of sophisticated DNA research that all humans evolved from a single female, they dubbed her Mitochondrial Eve. Moreover, when *Newsweek* reported on this development in the study of human origins, its cover featured a depiction of a woman and a man; an apple and a serpent in the drawing made the biblical allusion clear.[1] Eve clearly has iconic status. As the first woman, Eve symbolizes all women, signifying for many the essence of female existence. But what do we really know about biblical Eve and the women she represents?

Searching for Eve

So well known is the Eden narrative of Genesis that it is somewhat surprising to find that the story of Eden is not a prominent theme elsewhere in the Hebrew Bible. Neither are the actions of Eve and Adam ever mentioned as examples of disobedience and punishment, although the long story of Israel's recurrent rejection of God's word and will provides ample opportunity for citing the Eden case. Only in the writings of early Judaism and Christianity, in the last centuries BCE and the first centuries CE, do Eve and Adam emerge into the mainstream of religious literature and theological discussion. By then, well after the original shaping of the Eden story, Eve's role is recast by the beliefs and the needs of the nascent Jewish and Christian communities in the Hellenistic-Roman world. So compelling are the views of Eve portrayed in the New Testament, in rabbinic lore, and in the Apocryphal and Pseudepigraphical books that it is difficult to examine the Eve story without being influenced by the dominant Jewish and Christian interpretations of that story. These interpretive traditions are considered briefly in chapter 4 and the epilogue of this book.

What would Eve look like without the overlay of later perspectives? How different would she be? Rediscovering the Eve of the Genesis narrative itself is the task of this book. It will try to recover the Eve of the Hebrew Bible, who may be radically distinct from the Eve depicted by the unsympathetic, if not misogynist, writings of influential figures like Paul or Rabbi Yohanan or the anonymous author of the first-century Books of Adam and Eve. Chapters 4 and 5 will deal directly with the first woman and the story of Eden.

But Eve is not simply a literary figure. She is a link to the experience of the Israelites in the ancient Near Eastern world. Not only does Eve represent Israelite women, she is also a product of the way of life of women in that world. The realities of everyday life provided the raw materials from which the biblical narrator forged this now famous tale. The artful crafting of the simple yet powerful narrative is inextricably linked to the life experience of the ancient author. The world around him (or her? or them?) contributed to the choice of words, characterizations, and motifs—to the shaping of the narrative's multiple and multifarious messages.

The grounding of the Eden tale in the ancient Israelite world can readily be seen in some features of the garden itself and in the outcome for the male figure. The abundance of water in Eden, for example, is well suited for the lush setting of a tale that emerges from a land so poorly endowed with water resources as was ancient Israel. Furthermore, two of its flowing streams are the Mesopotamian rivers, the Tigris and the Euphrates. These great rivers were surely known to many Israelites, whose ancestors—the matriarchs and patriarchs of Genesis—are said to have come from Mesopotamia. The appearance of these rivers in the Eden tale indicates that it is rooted in the larger cultural world of the ancient Near East. Also, God's mandate to Adam at the end of the tale, which sets forth the difficulties of eking out a living, reflects and sanctions the conditions of agricultural life in the Palestinian highlands.

God's words to Eve similarly reflect and sanction the life context of most Israelite women. To comprehend women's way of life in ancient

Israel is to recognize the reality that shaped the literary figure Eve. In this sense, "Eve" is Everywoman—every woman who lived in ancient Israel, or at least every ordinary woman. Understanding the Eve of Genesis entails situating her in the context of Everywoman Eve. The reality of daily life in ancient Israel informs the reality biblical Eve faces as she leaves the garden. Chapter 3 explores that world, identifying its conditions and constraints.

At this point it is necessary to distinguish between "Israelite woman" and "biblical woman." Few would dispute the overwhelming orientation of the Hebrew Bible toward men and the male world. Male authorship is assumed, even though a few fragments of women's writing may be preserved. Named men outnumber named women by a factor of about twelve to one, and a similar ratio can be assumed for the numerous unnamed figures.[2] To be sure, women are prominent in Genesis and several other narrative books. Also, although they are virtually nonexistent in most poetic books, notably Psalms and many prophets, they at least make cameo appearances in all but five books.[3] But these female figures tell us little about ordinary Israelite women. The narrative figures are the most visible; yet, almost to a woman, they are exceptional. They are women who rose to positions of prominence, were the spouses or offspring of notable men, or were the victims of some horrendous deed. As such, can they be considered representative of their gender? Can information about the daily existence of most women be extracted from what we read about a Deborah or a Miriam, an Athaliah or a Huldah, or a Dinah? Exceptional women, at least those with community roles, are not ignored here; but they are relegated to the excursus in chapter 9.

The focus instead is on their ordinary sisters, who are largely invisible in the Hebrew Bible. To presume they can be found there is to commit a fundamental methodological error. Assuming that the countless women inhabiting the villages and hamlets of ancient Israel can be seen in the several exceptional biblical ones is to believe we can see an entire structure when only a fragment is visible. It would be to succumb to the Everest fallacy—an error in logic in which the visible extreme and the invisible normal are assumed to be the same. The exemplary case is to believe that the highly visible Everest is representative of all mountains. The term "Everest fallacy" was coined by a historian to draw attention to the fact that what survives in literary sources is usually exceptional and hardly represents the ordinary.[4] Similarly, anthropologists note that features of the everyday life of women and men in traditional societies often differ from conventional notions or images in their literature.[5]

In short, women in the Hebrew Bible are not representative of women in ancient Israel. To put it bluntly, there is a disconnect between the textual representation of female figures in the Hebrew Bible and the lived experience of real women. Thus the purpose of this book is not only to examine the Eve of the Eden story but also to bring to light the lives of Everywoman Eve, the ordinary women of ancient Israel. All who read the Bible or who are affected by its role in religious, community, or national life—whether students or scholars, feminists or the faithful—are directly or indirectly affected by the Eden story. An awareness of the invisible lives of Israelite women that form the background for the outcome of the Eden narrative can inform in new ways, in addition to the many that already exist, our understanding of this foundational and influential cultural tale. For centuries we have looked at Eve through the distorting lenses of male-dominated, Judeo-Christian tradition. Now perhaps we can see her in the direct light of her own world. Chapter 6 looks at the physical and social features of that world, chapters 7 and 8 present the many activities of Everywoman Eve, and chapter 10 reconstructs Israelite gender relationships.

A clearer view of Israelite women may also provide a fresh perspective on women in passages of the Hebrew Bible besides the opening chapters of Genesis. Because of the fundamental role of biblical texts in Judaism and Christianity, any information that can contextualize passages that are difficult or controversial in the contemporary world becomes relevant beyond the academy.

Approaches in Biblical Studies

The motivation and the means for this quest to elucidate the Eve narrative and examine its context come from the impact of two disciplines on biblical studies. One is the importance of feminism on the study of religion and religious texts. First-wave feminism of the nineteenth century accompanied the suffragist movement, and second-wave feminism arose from the civil rights and antiwar movements in the 1960s and 1970s. Both those political movements produced feminist biblical scholarship, which is often divided into a similar first-wave and second-wave sequence.[6] Now a third wave of feminist biblical scholarship, beginning in the 1990s, is linked to cultural studies; it is grounded in literary criticism and critical theory and is concerned with political issues. Women-centered analysis is combined with factors of race, social class, nationality, and sexuality in relation to current readers of the text.[7]

The other is the engagement of biblical studies with social science research. Sociological and anthropological theories, which have their roots in nineteenth-century scholarship and are discussed again in chapter 10, have long been used in biblical studies to investigate the origins and development of ancient Israel. Social science theory provides the means to understand the gender roles and dynamics of ordinary Israelites. The specific kinds of social science research useful for this project are described in the next chapter.

Because this study of Eve and of ancient Israelite women is indebted to both feminist biblical scholarship and social sciences approaches in biblical studies, each deserves closer scrutiny.

Feminism and Biblical Scholarship

Defining feminism is not easy, for the term can be understood in a variety of ways.[8] For some it is a specifically political term, referring to enterprises like the women's movement in the United States and other countries. For others it is a broader concern for identifying and ending the injustices, inequalities, and indignities experienced by women in all areas of life. In this sense, it can be considered antisexist, that is, concerned with eliminating sexism (the idea that one sex or gender is superior in one or more ways to the other) and the accompanying and limiting stereotypes about both women and men. Feminism has derived its strength and energy from recognizing gender inequities in the modern world.

The impact of feminism on many academic disciplines has been significant, especially in the development of women's studies (or gender studies) courses and programs.[9] Studying women's social, economic, and political roles and identifying women's cultural contributions are understood to be basic for addressing feminist concerns. Some feminist scholars find fault with the depth or breadth of the impact of feminism on various disciplines. Yet few would deny that it has become an essential part of the academic enterprise in hundreds of institutions of higher learning in the United States and elsewhere.

Closely related to feminism and women's studies is the category of gender, which has similarly entered many academic disciplines. Gender is recognized as a distinct mode of experience and also a system subject to analysis. Indeed, the very nature of the term "gender" and its relation-ship to "sex" have become subjects of considerable discussion in the larger academy and in biblical studies.[10] Defining gender and sex is as fraught with difficulty as is defining feminism, and the extent to which biolog-ical characteristics affect social roles and identity is a subject of ongo-ing debate. In general, however, the term gender denotes the culturally constructed, not innate, aspects of human life that differentiate females and males (or women and men). As such, it is not fixed but varies from group to group and also can change over time within a group. Moreover, a group's ideas about appropriate gendered behavior do not always coin-cide with actual practice. Sexuality is somewhat harder to characterize, for many theorists challenge the biological essence or immutability of sexu-ality as a category and insist that, like gender, it is socially constructed. Others contest the binary understanding of sex that sees only two catego-ries (female and male) and thereby marginalizes humans whose sexuality doesn't seem to fit one of those categories. Decades ago gender and sex were typically understood as separate dimensions of human beings; now each is perhaps better understood as part of a continuum of features.

When it comes to biblical studies, women along with gender and sex-uality are not simply topics of academic concern. As in many other fields, feminist research is important because there is more at stake than just intellectual inquiry. Many institutional and theological issues in Judaism and Christianity involve the interpretation of biblical texts dealing with women. What is the relationship of those texts to the evolving stance of synagogue and church on the role of women? In its broadest sense that question affects many vital concerns, such as the legitimacy of leadership roles for women in formal structures of Judaism and Christianity and the nature of the relationship between women and men in the informal set-ting of home and family. Thus it affects the ways in which decisions are made for continuing or changing tradition-based patterns in both formal and informal situations related to religious life. Arguments for maintain-ing gender inequality in religious contexts (especially Catholicism) still draw on biblical texts as well as denominational traditions.[11]

But there's more. General attitudes toward women in many coun-tries, apart from the perspectives and practices of institutional religion, are often rooted in the traditional understanding of biblical texts. This is especially true in the United States, a country that is "by world stan-dards...a highly religious country," where about one-third of its popula-tion, according to recent surveys, say they read the Bible daily.[12] Views permeating the national religious culture can perpetuate discriminatory aspects of the political culture.[13] Too often, emotional justification for the existence and continuation of present unacceptable gender roles or behaviors is embedded in religious texts that shape our collective psyche. It is no wonder that the popular media frequently feature news reports and documentaries on women, gender, or sexuality in relation to the Bible.

The great interest of both the media and the academy in the relationship of the Bible to women's issues arises from the fact that the Bible poses thorny problems for people with feminist and human rights concerns. Although the Bible can serve as a resource in the struggle for human rights, it can also have the opposite effect. As a leading feminist theologian and biblical scholar notes, "From the nineteenth into the twentieth and now twenty-first centuries, the bible has been used…as a weapon against wo/men's emancipation to equal citizenship in society and church."[14] Examination of biblical texts and their role in the theoretically secular facets of modern life seems essential, especially because of the serious conceptual and institutional difficulties involved. A recent overview of feminism in relation to the Hebrew Bible lists at least seven different problematic areas for feminists who read the Bible.[15] Its androcentrism (domination by men and male perspectives) and the paucity of female figures are among the problems. So too is male God language. Persistent male bias in the two millennia of biblical interpretation often makes matters worse.

Other Bible-related issues raised by feminists are in my opinion less clear. For example, violence directed toward women in the Hebrew Bible is often cited as a problem by those who condemn current abusive behavior.[16] But is the Bible really advocating spousal abuse? The problem is not always with the biblical text itself but with interpreting it out of context. Biblical passages depicting sexual abuse are not approving it; on the contrary, these horrific human misdeeds call dramatic attention to a flawed society.[17] Another problem is the attribution of patriarchal domination to ancient Israel, the society that produced much of the Bible. But this too is less straightforward than is usually assumed (see chapter 10). Aspects of current Western sexual politics may be rooted in the Bible or its interpretive tradition, but that does not mean they originated in the social realities of ancient Israel.

Whether or not all of the problems of the Hebrew Bible for the modern world are equally valid, there is no question that acceptance of the authority of the Bible, which is at the core of Judeo-Christian religion, is the basic issue. It has become clear that one cannot simply apply a biblical text to a current situation in a straightforward manner. How then can one deal with an authoritative text that asserts something apparently antithetical to feminist concerns? A wide spectrum of responses has emerged.[18] At one extreme are feminist scholars who reject the Bible outright as an authoritative text, perhaps the most famous example being the radical theologian Mary Daly.[19] Most others accept biblical authority but find ways to modify passages relating to women by using historical, cultural, or theological analysis. The more constructive interpreters—sometimes labeled reformists—focus on positive texts; they resign themselves to inequities or claim that difficult texts are largely descriptive rather than prescriptive. Some feminist critics consider these strategies flawed and strive to find other meaningful and responsible ways to understand the gender dynamics of the Hebrew Bible. Perhaps the most hopeful approach is one that looks to the trajectory of the interpretive tradition, including ongoing theological struggles within institutional religion, as well as to the text itself for an authoritative stance.[20] Still, I think it is fair to say that feminist hermeneutics—meaning an interpretive strategy that is mindful of feminist belief in the full humanity of all persons—is evolving and will always be as diverse as its practitioners. At the very least, whether one accepts some or none of the plethora of viewpoints found in feminist biblical scholarship, it is clear that gender is now on the radar screen of most mainstream biblical scholars.

Aside from their different responses to problems stemming from biblical authority, feminist biblical scholars engage in diverse ways with the variety of methodologies found in academic biblical study. Within that variety, two basic approaches dominate feminist biblical research.[21] Some scholars follow a historical-critical path, attempting to analyze specific texts in relation to their ancient context and even endeavoring to reconstruct that context. Because the biblical world is so different from the modern world, they believe that any attempt to understand what the Bible *means* for today's reader must be preceded by an effort to discover what it *meant* for ancient ones. Several aspects of this book would be considered historical criticism.

Others are more concerned with the literary nature of biblical texts. Many of the literary approaches found in feminist biblical scholarship challenge the notion that the Bible can be read objectively. Acutely aware that texts can have multiple meanings and values, postmodern feminist critics analyze literary features of texts, especially narratives, with the goal of identifying and critiquing the ideologies embedded in them. Interested more in how readers—especially modern ones—might understand the text than what the ancient authors may have meant, practitioners of this approach are not concerned with the complex history of the text and the dynamics of the ancient (supposedly patriarchal) society that produced it. Because this approach focuses on how an ancient text "reads" today, its interpretations tend to be highly critical—not only of the Hebrew Bible, often considering it a problematic manifestation of a patriarchal ideology oppressive to women, but also of both traditional historical-critical and "neo-liberal" approaches.[22]

However, to be fair, not all feminist literary approaches find the Hebrew Bible irredeemably sexist. Many, perhaps the majority, find value in the representations of women in the Hebrew Bible. Some insist on literary readings that do acknowledge and take into account that the texts are products of an ancient, very different society. This approach has been called a "culturally cued literary reading."[23] Others see "countertraditions" in biblical narratives, claiming that women's voices can be discerned within, behind, or even in opposition to the prevailing androcentrism of the text.[24] Similarly, even some postmodern critics insist that more subtle readings, especially of narratives, can find women's resistant voices and avoid the trap of looking at the Hebrew Bible monolithically.[25]

All told, literary approaches now dominate feminist biblical scholarship. The surge in popularity of this approach in the academy since the late twentieth century is certainly one factor underlying the emphasis on literary analysis in biblical scholarship in general, not only in feminist biblical studies. But there are other reasons too.[26] Sociohistorical approaches—which examine the nature of women's lives, not just the nature of the biblical text alluding to their lives (or failing to do so)—are inherently interdisciplinary. As described in the next chapter, they involve the use of archaeological materials, comparative literary and sociohistorical data, and social science models and theories in addition to the many traditional tools of biblical interpretation. Yet the typical location of biblical studies—in religion departments within humanities programs in colleges and universities, or in theological seminaries and divinity schools—tends to isolate biblical scholars from gender-related research in the social sciences. Moreover, many biblical scholars have theological or divinity degrees as part of their graduate training; and this usually means minimal exposure to social science disciplines.

Overall, perhaps feminist biblical scholars may find it too daunting a task to attempt to use the resources of so many disciplines, some unfamiliar to them, and integrate them into a feasible reconstruction of women's lives in biblical antiquity. Nonetheless, the project of discovering Israelite women in some ways resonates with the goals of current feminist biblical study in that it involves "stepping outside the Bible's androcentric ideology" and asking "questions about what it says and doesn't say about gender roles."[27]

Looking at the ancient context of Israelite women also resonates with general trends in feminist studies. The second-wave feminists of the 1970s, especially the influential radical feminists, were concerned with universals.[28] Believing male dominance to be universal, they sought economic and social explanations for its origins. By the end of the 1980s many feminist scholars recognized that the search for universals was problematic and also objected to the judgment of women's traditional roles in comparison to traditional male roles. They thus turned to more specific issues. Feminist anthropology in particular (described in chapter 2) insisted that gender differentiation is a salient feature of any cultural system but that one must seek to understand past communities on their own terms. That perspective is important for the approach of this book.

In sum, feminism entered the various humanities and social science disciplines, including the study of religion and the Bible, with the intention of analyzing gender dynamics in order to advocate changes that would end discrimination against women and also, now, against any dominated group. Although effecting current social change is not a central goal here, the search for the life experiences of Israelite women has an indirect role to play in understanding biblically based inequities in the contemporary world. As such, it must deal with cultural relativism and the problem of making value judgments about a different culture, issues considered in chapter 10. At this point, suffice it to say that by identifying the roles of women and the interaction of women with each other and with men in their own cultural contexts, many erroneous assumptions, unfounded stereotypes, and other misconceptions about Israelite women that continue to limit or threaten the full humanity of women today can be exposed and thereby perhaps lose their negative impact on women's lives.

Social Sciences and Biblical Scholarship

Using social science methods in feminist biblical studies is, as just noted, relatively rare. But those methods do appear elsewhere in biblical studies.

Indeed, biblical scholarship has a long history of engagement with the social sciences, going back to the work of the Scotsman William Robertson Smith in the late nineteenth century.[29] Smith drew on his extensive research on Middle Eastern tribal groups to theorize about various customs and social structures of the Israelites. His proposals have since been modified or discarded, but his ideas about the relationship of the realities of the material world to a people's beliefs and practices have had enduring significance. Similarly, one of the giants in the establishment of modern biblical scholarship, Julius Wellhausen, used social science concepts in his reconstruction of the religion and society of ancient Israel.[30] Like Smith's, Wellhausen's theories about Israelite society have been largely discredited; yet his reconstruction of the literary development of the Hebrew Bible remains a prominent, albeit controversial, part of biblical studies. One of the founders of modern sociology, Max Weber, also wrote about the Israelites.[31] Problematic aspects of his work too have since emerged, but the basic social types he identified and the questions he raised about connections between beliefs and socioeconomic organization continue to influence biblical studies.

Although there have since been ebbs and flows in the engagement of biblical scholars with the social sciences, important studies drawing on social science data and theories appeared sporadically throughout the twentieth century.[32] A notable example came in the 1970s and 1980s, when biblical scholars sought to understand Israelite origins in nontheological ways. They dared to step outside the Bible's own theological rhetoric, in which Israel's existence and beliefs were commanded by God, in order to identify the social, economic, and political forces leading to the beginnings of ancient Israel and its beliefs.[33] Several cultural and sociopolitical forms found in ancient Israel—such as tribes, monarchy, and prophecy—have also been subjected to sociological rather than theological analysis.[34] The results have been illuminating. Not every biblical scholar may be convinced by the results of these social science approaches, and some even find them sacrilegious; but few are immune to the process of thinking in these ways about the history and institutions of ancient Israel. At the least, a social science approach can relieve biblical scholarship of the problematic notion that the Israelites were a people specially chosen and ultimately cast aside.

Social science methods continue in biblical studies in the twenty-first century. After all, ancient Israel was first and foremost a community, a social entity. That its literary creation, the Hebrew Bible, was to become an authoritative *religious* document should not blind us to the fact that what we call *religion* was but one mode—albeit the most enduring and influential one—of ancient Israel's existence as a *society*. Social science appraisals of ancient Israel are based on the fundamental premise of its social existence. To understand the living community of ancient Israel means examining it in the context of its own multidimensional environment, including its social and political prehistory, its ecological environment, and its agrarian-pastoral economic base. Using a variety of resources (discussed in chapter 2), scholars have made significant strides in reconstructing the social history of ancient Israel.[35] Our knowledge of the people of the Book is thus no longer limited by the information contained in that Book.

The starting point for studying Israelite society, well into the last century, was the Hebrew Bible. But by the 1970s scholars realized that biblical information can be misleading, for Israel's biblical self-description does not appear in categories readily useful for social science analysis. The ancestor stories in Genesis were no longer considered a reliable account of the pre-national period. Still, the broad outlines of the national story were accepted: sojourn in and departure from Egypt, followed by settlement in the "promised land," establishment and division of a monarchy, conquest by Assyrian and Babylonian imperialists, exile from the land and then restoration as a small Persian and then Greek province. Other Near Eastern documents, which reflected customs and institutions similar to ones found in the Hebrew Bible, gave scholars confidence in the Bible's basic veracity. Similarly, archaeological discoveries seemed to verify biblical accounts.

All this began to change in the closing decades of the twentieth century.[36] Newer methods of archaeological excavation and interpretation challenged facile correlations between texts and *tel*. (The Hebrew word *tel* denotes an artificial mound created by the successive destruction and rebuilding of ancient settlements; the Arabic equivalent is *tell*.) Biblical scholars have become even more acutely aware that Israel's formation and history are presented largely in theological language; that is, the Bible describes human events in terms of God's actions, compromising its use as a compendium of historical facts. Moreover, they have seen how information in other ancient documents about peoples or events mentioned in the Hebrew Bible shows that biblical narratives are often highly selective, sometimes including apparently trivial or mundane matters while omitting information of great political or social importance. Also, scholars began to accept that most biblical writings were formalized many centuries after the events they purport to describe. Later materials are so artfully inter-twined with older ones that separating them is difficult at best.

In short, although many biblical books read as history, they are not his-torical records. Like most "historical" narratives before the Enlightenment, their purpose was edification. Telling a story to transmit key ideas was more important than presenting factually accurate information. Yet the Hebrew Bible does preserve at least some authentic information about Israel's beginnings and development. Scholars interested in the emergence and development of Israelite society struggle to discern those authen-tic historical details. Because of these methodological problems in using the Bible as a source of information (and others described in chapter 2), social science methods offer a fresh approach in the study of ancient Israel. Sociology and anthropology have identified sets of social phenom-ena that can be linked to particular social settings. When those settings are analogous to the conditions of Israel's existence, some of the gaps in our knowledge can be filled inferentially.

This procedure is not without risks and has aroused its share of criti-cism, yet there can be no doubt that it offers many valid insights not otherwise possible. For example, research data on tribal groups, with their clan and family subdivisions and their characteristic uses of resources and establishment of leadership, help biblical scholars understand the dynam-ics of Israelite tribal beginnings. Similarly, cross-cultural studies of forces leading to state formation and the growth of bureaucracies contribute to a better appreciation of the Israelite shift from tribal organization or chieftaincy to kingship. They also allow us to comprehend why, despite the social and economic stratification it introduced, the monarchy is so highly regarded in the Bible. Underlying all these analyses is acknowl-edgment of the sensitive relationship between economic-ecological fac-tors and the adaptive nature of group behavior and organization.

The progress made in the social science investigation of ancient Israel has obvious implications for the study of gender in Israelite society. Better conceptions of the social world of the biblical past mean more effec-tive investigations of the gender dynamics in that world. Social science approaches make the social actors—the women, men, and children of ancient Israel—more discernible as figures in the ancient landscape. Eve and the women she represents, as the subtitle of this book indicates, must be understood in their own context: Israelite society. Thus this book is indebted to the engagement of biblical studies with the social sciences, especially anthropology.

THIS BOOK WILL use a multifaceted, interdisciplinary, integrative approach. As such, although it might be situated among the sociohistorical approaches of feminist biblical study, in reality it is an anthropological project—more specifically, a project of sociocultural anthropology (also called social anthropology or cultural anthropology), which draws heavily on data supplied by ethnography (the study of particular groups). Because anthropology has developed ways to recover data about and to theorize aspects of people who no longer exist, its integrative procedures are particularly congenial to reconstructing the lives of Israelite women. To be sure, biblical texts are an important part of this enterprise, which includes a detailed examination of Genesis 2–3. But it stands outside the confines or rubrics of biblical studies and tries to take a fresh look at ordinary Israelite women apart from the Hebrew Bible, which tells us so little about them. In this way it is aligned with new views of the relationship between social sciences and biblical studies—views that insist on resisting the temptation to depend on biblical depictions.[37]

That being said, this study of Israelite women differs in one important respect from most anthropological studies of premodern peoples that are no longer in existence. Those studies are typically carried out by anthropologists who are archaeologists whose fieldwork focuses on prehistoric or ahistoric peoples—that is, groups who have left behind no written documents that would aid the work of researchers. In contrast, studies of Israelite society do have textual evidence: the Hebrew Bible and other documents from the ancient Near East. The importance of those written materials is enormous, perhaps too enormous, for the information they contain is often magnified or generalized in ways that distort the community it presents. (The limitations of biblical evidence are described more fully in the next chapter.)

In its focus on the women of a past society, this project is indebted to the way feminist anthropology helps determine the questions and models pursed by ethnographers. Both aspects of social science research—ethnography and feminist anthropology—along with textual and archaeological materials, provide the resources for this book and are discussed in chapter 2.

Note on Terminology

Several of the terms used in this book may be ambiguous, unclear, or unfamiliar and deserve clarification.

Hebrew Bible is used in reference to the first part of the Christian Bible, where it is labeled "Old Testament" or sometimes "First Testament," terms that imply a "New Testament" as a successor scripture. Hebrew Bible is a more neutral term because it does not imply fulfillment in a subsequent document. Because it doesn't privilege a Christian interpretative tradition, it is usually the preferred term of biblical scholarship and academic study. It also reflects the fact that its original language is mostly ancient Hebrew. (The book of Daniel, parts of Ezra, and several other passages are written in a closely related Semitic language, Biblical Aramaic.)

A similar desire to use neutral language underlies the common academic use of BCE (Before the Common Era) as an abbreviation for dates otherwise labeled BC (Before Christ) and of CE (Common Era) instead of AD (Year of Our Lord).

Iron Age is an archaeological designation representing the era in which iron gradually replaced bronze for making most tools and weapons.[38] Keyed to Israelite history, it designates the last two centuries of the second millennium BCE and the first five and a half centuries or so of the first millennium BCE. That is, it begins ca. 1200, which is when the people ultimately called Israelites first appear in the eastern Mediterranean. (An Egyptian inscription of ca. 1207 BCE contains the first mention of "Israel.") And it ends in 586 BCE, when the Babylonians conquer Jerusalem. The Iron Age itself is divided into the Iron I or premonarchic period, ca. 1200–1000, and the Iron II or monarchic age, ca. 1000 to 586.[39] The subsequent period of exile and then restoration under Persian domination is critically important for the formation of the canon of the Hebrew Bible and the emergence of the Jewish people, but the basic lifeways of those periods are somewhat less well known and are beyond our purview.

The terms *Israel* and *Israelite* can be used in various ways. In the Hebrew Bible Israel appears as: an alternative name of the patriarch Jacob; the name of the land or country associated with the people of the same name; a designation for the entire people of Israel, represented by the twelve tribes said to be descended from Jacob; the name of the northern kingdom, after the united monarchy associated with Saul, David, and Solomon splits into a northern and a southern kingdom; and, after the northern kingdom was conquered by the Assyrians (in 722 BCE), as an occasional designation for the southern kingdom, Judah, which survived until the Babylonian conquest (in 586 BCE). In this book the name "Israel" and the gentilic "Israelite" are used in a general cultural, rather than a specific political sense. Although scholars are skeptical about whether the ethnic, social, or political identity of the inhabitants of Palestinian sites can be established, especially for early Iron Age settlements, most find compelling evidence for mapping out the territory that can be identified as Israelite throughout the Iron Age.[40] The discussion of Israelite settlements in chapter 3 accepts the majority consensus.

Palestine today designates a political entity; however, it can also be used, as in this book, as a geographic designation for the area of the southern Levant or southern Canaan occupied by the Israelites.[41] Literally meaning the "land of the Philistines," a biblical designation for the southwest coastal area, it became a conventional name for the broader territory between the Mediterranean Sea and the Jordan River as early as the fifth century BCE. Several different biblical concepts of that area are noted in the next chapter.

2

Resources for the Task

CONVINCED THAT ORDINARY Israelite women can become more visible than they currently are, how can we proceed with the task of increasing their visibility? Developments in feminist biblical study and the socio-historical analysis of ancient Israel have paved the way for rediscovering Eve and her Israelite sisters. This interdisciplinary project clearly requires the integration of several kinds of materials: ancient texts, archaeological information, and anthropological studies and interpretive strategies. Indeed, those who investigate gender in past societies are well aware that "the most convincing and nuanced readings of gender...[involve the use of] multiple lines of evidence."[1] Even so, the information for reconstructing life in the past is inevitably incomplete, leading us to wonder if the integration of different kinds of data can provide reasonable hypotheses about the past.

An analogy from imaging technology—the hologram—can help allay such concerns. The three-dimensional imaging of holography can represent the three basic kinds of evidence used together for reconstructing the past: "Literary, archaeological, and comparative sociological interpretations interact in ways similar to the three laser beams used to create a holographic image [that] is analogous to the interpretations offered as hypotheses by biblical historians."[2] Similarly, the three main kinds of evidence brought together in this project—texts, archaeological materials, and anthropological studies—can converge to bring life to otherwise lifeless data and produce an image of Everywoman Eve. Each kind of evidence poses difficulties, however, and this introduction to them considers their problems as well as their potential.

The Hebrew Bible and Other Ancient Writings

Written sources are an important resource. Primary texts originating with the people being studied or coming from roughly the same time period are virtually always preferable to other data. The textual evidence for this project includes not only the Hebrew Bible but also some inscriptional materials from ancient Palestine and the literatures of Israel's ancient Near Eastern neighbors. However, using primary texts does not mean taking them at face value, especially when probably only a fraction of the documents produced by ancient Israel has survived and when relatively few parts of the Hebrew Bible, at least in their final form, date to the Iron Age (ca. 1200–587 BCE).

The Hebrew Bible

The usefulness of the Hebrew Bible is complicated by several issues already noted in chapter 1: the difficulty in identifying material that is historically reliable, the relative invisibility of ordinary women, and the text's androcentric perspective. But more must be said. Other factors contribute to the distorted view of Israelite women that can result from using only biblical data.[3] To begin with, three features of biblical authorship underlie biblical androcentrism and are of particular importance: the *gender*, *social position*, and *geographic location* of those who wrote, collated, and edited much of the Hebrew Bible.

With respect to *gender*, it is widely accepted that male authors produced much if not all of the Hebrew Bible. The final form of the Pentateuch (the first five books of the Bible) is the work of priestly activity. (The priesthood was an all-male, hereditary group that excluded women—and also men who did not belong to the priestly tribe.) Virtually all of the narratives from Joshua through 2 Kings probably drew from documents or traditions circulating among male courtiers or scribes. The second narrative account, 1–2 Chronicles through Ezra and Nehemiah, likely took shape in male leadership circles in the postexilic period. All the prophetic books bear male names. The remaining biblical books—even the two bearing women's names (Ruth and Esther)—were probably written by men. A female voice may be detected in the Song of Solomon and perhaps in Proverbs, and female authorship or voices can be posited for other biblical passages.[4] Yet these traces of women's words are embedded in an overarching structure formalized and finalized by men.

The male gender of the authors and editors of the Hebrew Bible is not the only problem, and it may not be the major one. Their *social position* is also a serious factor. Most of the male authors and editors were part of a literary elite, a tiny and unrepresentative minority. Even in modern societies with high literacy rates, less than one percent of the population actually writes books.[5] The alphabetic script of the Hebrew language, which was easier to learn than the hieroglyphs and cuneiform of the surrounding cultures, perhaps made substantial literacy possible. However, analysis of epigraphic (written) remains from Iron Age Palestine indicates that literacy was virtually nonexistent except for professional scribes and perhaps a few other members of the religious, political, and perhaps mercantile elites.[6] Even functional literacy—the ability to write one's name well enough to sign a document—was limited; most people could neither read nor write. Thus the written form of the Hebrew Bible was produced by a tiny segment of society and could be read by relatively few.

This shouldn't surprise us, in light of what we know about low literacy rates in medieval Europe, when literacy did not extend to the peasantry comprising the bulk of the population, and even later. Similarly, biblical writings were hardly accessible to all Israelites. This is hard to fathom, given that today the Bible is one of the most printed and best-selling books: in the United States more than 90 percent of households have Bibles, often multiple copies.[7] Its accessibility is taken for granted. Not so in the biblical world. Furthermore, and this may even be harder to absorb, there was no Hebrew Bible at all, at least not as a canonical whole, until centuries after the Iron Age, long after Israelite culture had morphed into its successor, early Judaism. Moreover, it was not until late in the history of ancient Israel that some of the materials comprising the Hebrew Bible were collected and deemed authoritative. To be sure, many tales, aphorisms, and other genres would have circulated orally before then and may have been widely known. Yet, for most of the hundreds of years of Israelite existence in the Iron Age not only was the Bible not accessible, but actually there was no such thing as the Bible in anything close to the form we now take for granted.

Related to the social position of biblical authors is the matter of their intended audience. Largely written and produced by elite males, it was addressed, first and foremost but not exclusively, to male heads of households. (Households are described in chapter 6.) Hebrew grammar alerts us to this. Hebrew is a gendered language: its nouns are either masculine or feminine, and there is no gender-neutral pronoun like English "it." Reading the Bible in English—no matter how good the translation—masks the fact that, for example, the second person singular and plural "you" in Hebrew is nearly always grammatically masculine. Of course, masculine pronouns and other grammatically masculine terms are sometimes used inclusively to denote both genders. Moreover, the social gender of a word is often inclusive even when the grammatical gender is masculine.[8] Women were not always excluded. Every case must be considered in its own textual context, and one instance of inclusive social grammar is considered in chapter 4. However, as often as not, men and not women are addressed by grammatically masculine terms.

The *geographic location* of biblical authors is relevant too. Priestly leadership, beginning with the monarchy and continuing when Judah was a province of imperial powers (Babylonians, Persians, and then Greeks), was based in the temple in the capital city, Jerusalem. Virtually no major shrine existed outside of Jerusalem once the temple was constructed there.[9] Even without regional temples, cultic activity other than the household practices described in chapter 8 likely took place at shrines outside Jerusalem in the early centuries of the monarchy; but coteries of priests would have been few and far between. In the seventh through fifth centuries BCE, when the Hebrew Bible was taking shape, priestly activity was almost certainly limited to Jerusalem. Similarly, the "historical" narratives of the Bible are based in part on the records of court chroniclers based in the Jerusalem palace. These are probably the records, no longer extant, mentioned in biblical narratives and bearing titles like "Book of the Annals of the Kings of Judah" (e.g., 1 Kgs 22:45).[10]

But Jerusalem was hardly an ordinary place. By the time the Pentateuch and major parts of the books from Joshua to 2 Kings were taking shape in the late eighth century and afterward, Jerusalem had become considerably larger than any other settlement in the land and was the only true urban center. If frequency of appearance is any indication, it also dominates the Hebrew Bible, where "Jerusalem" appears almost 700 times—far more often than Samaria (capital of the northern kingdom), mentioned barely more than 100 times. Jerusalem probably had markets and technologies available nowhere else. And there were differentials of wealth, family size, and work patterns that set it apart, in ways related to gendered life, from the rural settlements and fortified towns (described in chapter 3) in which most people lived. Conditions in Jerusalem did not necessarily obtain elsewhere. For example, the biblical mention of male potters and a bakers' district in Jerusalem (Jer 18:3; 37:21) gives the impression that only men made ceramic vessels and that bread was commercially available. But the situation was different elsewhere. Images of the countryside are common in the Hebrew Bible, especially in prophetic oracles, for agriculture was the economic basis throughout the Iron Age. Yet the daily life of country folk, especially women, remains mostly obscure.

In short, much of the Hebrew Bible was produced by the literary activity of a small, unrepresentative segment of the Israelite population: literate elite men in an urban context. Biblical information about non-urban women comes from sources hierarchically and demographically removed from them. This gendered, social, and geographic distance between women and the shapers of sacred tradition is reflected in the androcentrism of the Hebrew Bible. At the same time, it should be noted that literate, urban, elite men were unrepresentative of the population as a whole. Priestly officials, kings, officers, scribes, and bureaucrats were distinct from the rest of the people, both male and female.

The omission of details about the daily lives of most women (and men) is, to be fair, not simply the concomitant of the gender, status, and location of the shapers of the Hebrew Bible. Their overall interests must also be taken into account. Most of their writings concern national, collective institutions and events. They sought to convey their beliefs about the emergence and existence of a corporate entity—the people Israel. Once we leave the family stories of Genesis, we enter the public world of national leaders. A few of them are women: Deborah the judge, Miriam the prophet, several prominent queens, two wise women. But mainly we see male figures: judges and warriors, kings and sages, prophets and priests. Only occasionally do we have a glimpse of the daily lives of ordinary folk, male or female.

Another consideration relates to the social structure of ancient Israel, in which land and other property were transmitted across generations along male descent lines. Biblical genealogies, which rarely include female names, reflect this concern for male lineages, or patrilineages. These genealogies were not entirely records of social reality. To a certain extent they were literary constructs meant to establish "blood" connections among neighboring groups in order to secure stable intergroup relationships. Biblical genealogies thus connect all the disparate tribal groups and sub-groups into a symbolic family tree. Omitting women accommodated the patrilineal principle and also gave the formation of genealogies the flexibility they needed to accommodate out-of-group marriages and thus new connections. Women are critical for these lineages because of their biological function of producing the necessary heirs to maintain the lineage, but they rarely appear in the genealogical structures. Even in the book of Genesis, where the matriarchs are characters in their own right, the narrative emphasis is on their biological role in overcoming infertility and producing offspring to establish the ancestral lineage.[11]

Another important issue is the relevance of materials in the legal sections of the Pentateuch. Stipulations concerning women are often cited as examples of the oppression of women in ancient Israel. Indeed, reading about men indenturing their daughters or selling unwanted female servants to foreigners (Exod 21:7-8) gives the impression that women were little better than chattel, despite the accompanying measures for benign treatment of servants and slaves (both male and female). Biblical legal texts—some because of their presumed harshness, and others (like Exod 22:25, which prohibits the charging of interest) because they seem incredibly idealistic and economically impossible—inevitably evoke two important questions.

One is whether the legal stipulations of the Pentateuch are only a theoretical set of regulations, never meant to function in social reality. That is, are they really laws? This question is difficult to answer. Long-held assumptions that biblical laws were the law of the land for ancient Israel are now considered problematic. A textbook examining *Everyday Law in Biblical Israel* puts it this way:

> We cannot be sure to what extent the laws set out in the Bible were actually put into practice during the Iron Age—the time of ancient Israel and Judah....Some of them may have been purely utopian; some were rules of practice transfigured by ideology; and others, although pragmatic in content, were most probably the product of academic circles, that is, of groups of scribes engaged in a theoretical endeavor.[12]

Biblical laws were anything but law codes in the modern legal sense. They cannot be taken en masse as normative for all Israelites in the Iron Age. However, careful study of the practice of law from other ancient Near Eastern societies, in which documents of court cases have survived, provide relevant information. It seems that some of the stipulations in the Pentateuch, but certainly not all, were related to real-life jurisprudence.[13] Each stipulation must be considered on its own.

The second question may be even more important: if at least some of the stipulations do emerge from actual practice, what social setting do they reflect? Addressing this question means recognizing that the Pentateuch has three discrete groups of legal materials: (1) the Covenant

Code in Exodus 21–23 (called the Book of the Covenant in Exod 24:7); (2) the Deuteronomic Code of Deuteronomy 12–26; and (3) Priestly regulations in Leviticus and parts of Exodus and Numbers. The origin of the Deuteronomic and priestly materials in urban social settings seems likely; like other ancient Near Eastern laws, they pertain to members of elite families living in urban or palace contexts and tell us little about the lives of average folk.[14] But the Covenant Code is generally considered a collection of legal materials of small Israelite communities. However, analysis of the Covenant Code in light of what is now known about village society disputes that understanding. Very little in this corpus can be linked to the handling of disputes in small, relatively isolated settlements.[15] Those settlements were not without rules to govern behavior and help village leaders resolve problems; but, given the virtual absence of literacy beyond the palace and temple, those rules were customary regulations that circulated orally. Moreover, village laws deal with issues concerning their own economic and social arrangements, which tend to be different from those of cities. All told, relatively few biblical rulings reflect the legal framework of village life.

Moreover, if at least some of the biblical regulations *were* intended for the general populace, they may have had little impact outside the capital. The laws of a central authority in an urban center do not always reach into rural communities, even in the modern world. One informative example comes from South Africa. Among the national laws established to promote women's equality is one that forbids the virginity testing of young girls. However, according to a local politician, laws like this "do not necessarily have any impact on the lives of people."[16] Similarly, although female genital cutting in Guinea and elsewhere has long been illegal, violations are rarely prosecuted. In rural areas villagers still follow local traditions; a dual law system is the de facto reality. These examples show that customary village rules can exist separately from the rulings of national governing bodies. If this happens in the twenty-first century, it shouldn't surprise us that Jerusalem-based legal materials would not have reached into the countryside, especially settlements far from the capital. Most people lived according to local customs appropriate for their small-scale communities.

One further consideration, alluded to in chapter 1 and revisited in chapter 10 and the epilogue, is the disconnect between the ideology and the social reality of a premodern people. Near the end of his distinguished career, British anthropologist Sir Edmund Leach cautioned that:

"The observer must distinguish between what people actually do and what people say that they do; that is between normal custom as individually interpreted on the one hand and normative rule on the other.... [The anthropologist] must distinguish behavior from ideology."[17] Biblical scholars do not have the methodological option of observing behavior. Only the ideology is available, and it can diverge from the normative practices of daily life.

A good example of this comes from a study of the women of Jeme, a small Coptic town of the seventh-eighth centuries CE in Egypt.[18] A treasure trove of documentary evidence uncovered there has been mined for information about women's lives. The male "literary ideals" for proper female behavior, revealed in a homily by a local monk and in other similar texts, have been examined in relation to women's activities as recovered from economic and legal texts and letters. The religious texts are in line with the general negative conceptions of women in late antique Christianity (discussed in chapter 4 and the epilogue) and would lead one to believe that women's activities were limited to their households. In contrast, the secular documents show women functioning in economic, social, and religious matters: "They were active on many levels in the public life of Jeme and environs: in their immediate neighborhoods, in their communities, in the western Thebes area in general, and even outside the region."[19]

A more recent example comes from a small east Mediterranean village studied in the mid-twentieth century. In observing women's roles in community life, the researcher was "struck by the disparity between the formal structure and the manner in which decisions are actually made. With respect to the political sphere, the variance between the ideal and the real is such that local political life bears very little resemblance to what a reading of the laws and codes of the political institutions would imply."[20]

In sum, the Hebrew Bible is a problematic source: it rarely names or describes ordinary women and their lives, and what it does say may distort or mask social reality. Does the fact that it has its own agenda, one not congenial to recovering Everywoman Eve, render it useless?

Despite all the obstacles, the Hebrew Bible remains an invaluable resource for identifying general aspects of life in Israelite times. Material details of daily life are often part of the imagery or circumstantial background that the biblical storytellers and poets use to advance their messages. These details provide important information, whether or not one accepts the story line as history or the theological claims as valid. For example, we cannot know if the rainfall anticipated at certain seasons was the result of God's will, as the Bible asserts (Deut 11:14); but we can learn from biblical references that rain at certain times of the year was essential for the cropping patterns of Israelite farmers. Similarly, the account of Rebekah providing bread and savory food for her son Jacob to give to his father (Gen 27:17) may be a folktale about inheritance issues; but it nonetheless indicates the importance of bread in a meal. This kind of incidental or background information in the Hebrew Bible is useful, no matter what the date of the text in which it appears, because the economic basis of Israelite society (see chapter 3) remained relatively constant over the many centuries of Israelite existence. Using biblical texts containing these details has made it possible to determine the patterns of agriculture and animal husbandry that were the mainstays of the economy.[21] Other aspects of daily life relevant to this book, such as identifying women's tasks, are similarly informed by biblical passages (see chapter 7); and women's community roles (see chapter 9) are known mainly through biblical references.

Other Ancient Writings

In addition to the Bible, other ancient documents—written by Israelites as well as by other peoples of the ancient Near East—provide relevant information. Most Israelite documents were written on perishable materials and have not survived. Portions of the biblical text itself are available only from copies or fragments found among the Dead Sea scrolls, and they date to hundreds of years or as much as a millennium after composition. And the earliest complete Hebrew copy of the Hebrew Bible (the Leningrad Codex) comes from about 1008 CE.

The only Israelite texts that actually date to the Iron Age and exist in their original form are several kinds of inscribed objects—mainly ostraca (potsherds with inscriptions, usually brief, written in ink) and stamp seals (small inscribed stones, sometimes set into rings or worn on a chain) or their impressions. The former usually have an economic function or convey brief messages; the latter bear their owner's name and serve to mark documents or pottery vessels. Many of the seals are "unprovenanced"; that is, they turn up on the antiquities market and their place of origin is unknown, which means that their authenticity is uncertain. Fortunately, at least some come from legitimate excavations.

Sizeable groups of ostraca have been recovered from Israelite sites, notably Arad, Lachish, and Samaria. And stamp seals, bullae (the images produced when seals are impressed on wet clay), and jar handles that have been stamped occasionally are unearthed at Iron Age sites. Most of these inscriptions contribute little to an understanding of women's lives. However, several ostraca and a small group of seals bearing women's names inform the discussion in chapter 9 of women's business dealings.

In contrast to the relative paucity of written remains from Iron Age Palestine, hundreds of thousands of inscriptions on enduring substances, such as stone or clay, have been discovered in other parts of the ancient Near East. Legal, cultic, and economic documents abound. Many (e.g., the Gilgamesh Epic and Hammurabi's Code) contain parallels to biblical materials and are consulted by biblical scholars. There is no doubt that comparative information plays an important role in biblical scholarship. And with their frequent references to women, these documents are a rich source of information about women in the societies that produced them.

But are they valuable for understanding the lives of ordinary women in ancient Israel, let alone in Egypt or Mesopotamia? Probably not. Like the Hebrew Bible, Egyptian and Mesopotamian texts come from elite, urban settings and reflect the lives of the upper classes in stratified societies. In the introduction to a book on women in the ancient Near East, Egyptologist Barbara Lesko notes that "ordinary women hardly show up in the historical records left by the great civilizations of the past."[22] If those records are of little value for studying ordinary Egyptian or Mesopotamian women, they surely are of little relevance for studying ordinary Israelite women.

This is particularly true in that they reflect life in complex cities with extensive royal and cultic precincts, all much larger than Israelite settlements. For example, the Assyrian capital Nineveh covered almost 2,000 acres, whereas Jerusalem for most of the Iron Age was a modest regional center of little more than 12 acres. Even during its brief period of expansion late in the eighth century BCE, it was only about 150–175 acres in extent. (For comparison, Central Park in New York is 843 acres.) The documents of the ancient superpowers reflect life in sprawling, densely populated, metropolitan centers quite different from ancient Israel's few cities and many small settlements.[23] In general, they have little value for considering Israelite women, even urban ones; yet sometimes they provide relevant information about wide-ranging ancient Near Eastern cultural patterns.

All told, the inadequacy of the Hebrew Bible and ancient writings as sources of information about ordinary women means that other kinds of information are important. An interdisciplinary approach demands the use of other sources, and archaeology is one of them.

Archaeological Data

The land of the Bible has probably been excavated more than any other place of comparable size on earth. For almost two centuries, archaeologists and explorers have been drawn to the landscapes and locales mentioned in the Bible. As independent witnesses to the lives of the ancient Israelites, material remains have enormous potential—potential that has been realized to a great extent in the study of Israel's national history. However, as witness to the daily lives of ordinary folk, especially women, archaeological data present difficulties no less daunting than those involved in using texts. Two problems loom large: (1) excavation strategy: the kind of sites selected, and the areas of those sites chosen for excavation; and (2) recording and publication strategy, especially the way the recovered artifacts are documented.[24]

First, the problem of excavation strategy, beginning with site selection. The archaeology of ancient Palestine, or Syro-Palestinian archaeology, is often called "biblical archaeology."[25] This popular but misleading designation indicates that excavations frequently are undertaken because they might shed light on the Bible or the biblical story. The old image of the excavator with spade in one hand and Bible in the other has not disappeared; a prominent excavator recently invoked that image in describing her work: "I work with the Bible in one hand and the tools of excavation in the other."[26]

Most archaeologists today recognize the difficulty of making secure links between the biblical account of an event and the material remains of the site said to be involved. Yet possible biblical correlations often hover in the background and influence research goals, sometimes for the pragmatic function of attracting attention and funding. For example, the website of the expedition working at Megiddo, a major site in northern Israel, proclaims that "Megiddo is the jewel in the crown of biblical archaeology" and that "Megiddo is widely regarded as the most important biblical period site in Israel."[27] A large percentage of the remains from Megiddo predate ancient Israel, yet the Bible figures prominently in the face the excavators present to the public.

Archaeology is still enamored of and elated by its intimate contact with objects and structures of the biblical past. Fieldwork has thus concentrated disproportionately on sites with a biblical pedigree—places mentioned often in the Hebrew Bible or associated with key events or important figures. Because those sites are mainly the larger walled settlements, smaller settlements—villages and hamlets, farmsteads and country estates—in which most people lived are too often ignored.

The kind of work carried out at those biblically connected sites is also significant. The excavators seek to expose the full series of occupation levels that form a *tel* in order to establish a site's overall chronology and history. The Iron Age levels, especially destruction layers, are then typically connected if possible with references to battles mentioned in the Bible or other ancient sources. The material evidence sometimes authenticates biblical information but also sometimes contradicts it. Either way, the overall concern is usually with political history or regional economy and with associated change over time, not with social or economic aspects of household life at the site. To put it another way, the archaeological enterprise has generally favored the "macro" level of human society with its large-scale political and religious institutions. Of less interest is the "micro" level, the settlements and structures representing small-scale life processes.

The propensity to favor the macro level also means a focus on monumental architecture—fortification systems (walls, towers, and gates), palaces and villas, temples, and other large edifices—rather than domestic buildings. Monumental structures and the distinctive artifacts they may contain (e.g., weapons, sumptuous vessels, cultic objects, and perhaps even inscriptions) are a powerful draw. And as the settings of military personnel, governing authorities, and the cultic establishment, they illuminate the communal affairs of a select, male segment of the population.

The archaeological focus on large sites and communal structures has resulted in a general inattention to the spaces inhabited by the women and men comprising the Israelite peasantry (a term explained in the next chapter). Large settlements and political history have been favored over small settlements and social history. Like the Hebrew Bible, most archaeological projects have had an urban elite bias or even a gender bias. Because archaeology is "a highly constructed form of knowledge seeking,"[28] decisions about where and how to excavate are not completely objective, value-free, and inclusive.

The same can be said about the recording and publication strategy of many field projects with respect to the artifacts uncovered, especially

ones from domestic structures. (Yes—some dwellings are usually excavated too, even when monumental buildings are preferred.) The artifacts
include pottery vessels, stone and metal tools, bone and ivory implements, articles of personal adornment, and other items. The remains of
food (grape and olive pits, seeds and grains, fragments of animal bones)
also occasionally survive. Knowing exactly where each object was discovered in a domestic structure is critical for understanding the use of space
and for reconstructing gendered work patterns. Unfortunately, because of
the traditional chronological interests of archaeological projects, artifacts
are often saved and sorted according to their development and change
over time rather than by focusing on the physical or spatial context of
their use.

This is especially true for pottery. The cumulative knowledge of a century of ceramic analysis has made it possible for archaeologists to date
pottery types fairly closely. Potsherds are thus invaluable for dating the
levels in which they are found. Consequently, the publication of ceramic
remains tends to follow typological rather than spatial considerations. The
stratum, or level, in which a vessel or sherd was found may be meticu-
lously recorded, with its exact find spot noted. Yet the final publication
of a site typically groups pottery by type and date and does not always
indicate exactly where the sherds were found. To be fair, many sites have
been so badly disturbed in antiquity, with successive settlements repeatedly built over destroyed ones, that many artifacts are no longer in their
"original" position. The find spot would then be meaningless. But occasionally artifacts are found as they were left when a building was destroyed
or abandoned millennia ago. With some notable exceptions,[29] the reports
of those buildings are not always conducive to reconstructing household
activities.

The recording and publication of other household items is also problematic. Again, the dominant focus on typological groupings means that
excavation reports often feature the best examples of each kind of artifact
but don't indicate how many other examples of this type were discovered
or where they were found. Moreover, it is difficult or impossible to determine where objects were found in relation to each other. Such information is essential for recreating assemblages of artifacts and determining
the various uses of household space. The same is true for organic materials. The remnants of ancient foodstuffs are identified and are typically
published in catalogues that provide insufficient details about where and
in what quantity they were found. Moreover, most projects collect only

visible organic materials and neglect the data provided by micro-analysis
of soil samples.

In short, publications too often decontextualize artifactual and organic
remains. Traditional publication strategies are ideal for establishing change
over time in relation to sociopolitical history, but they have limited value
for understanding living spaces and associated activities. Many archaeological publications are not user-friendly for research on women's lives.

But the situation is far from hopeless. The publications of some older
projects do provide appropriate data for reconstructing household life.[30]
Others can sometimes be reexamined in order to ascertain aspects of
household activities.[31] Also, projects interested in Israelite beginnings in
the Iron I period, when there were no Israelite cities, concentrated on
exposing village sites and their domestic structures.[32]

Just as important, developments in the wider discipline of archaeology have influenced the archaeology of Israelite sites in significant ways.
The New Archaeology or "processual archaeology" beginning in the
1960s mandated detailed attention to a settlement's environment and
to its faunal and floral remains; these data were critical for the emphasis of processual archaeology on cultural systems and change.[33] Although
archaeologists working at Palestinian sites had little use for the ahistorical
aspect of processual archaeology,[34] its multidisciplinary character led many
of them to become more multidisciplinary in their research designs. Then
"post-processual archaeology," with its acknowledgment that artifacts are
clues to the dynamics and meaning of human experience, emerged in the
1970s and 1980s.[35] Both developments required attention to all details of
an ancient site and thus increased attention to households and all aspects
of their artifacts.

The emphasis on detail in both processual and post-processual
approaches has been important for the emergence of "household archaeology," a small but significant part of the archaeology of ancient Israel.
Attention to households and their activities is just as important as attention to political history and communal institutions in the study of an
ancient society—for the household is where most people lived. Household
archaeology looks at a society from the bottom up instead of the typical
top-down way, thus providing a window into daily life and an important
perspective on the nature of that society.

When it comes to gendered aspects of daily life, household archaeology is the only option. It enables researchers to reconstruct gendered
activities, thereby mitigating the general cultural biases and specifically

male ones in research on past societies. In short, it can overcome the invisibility of women in traditional forms of research.[36] Household archaeology is essential in the quest to recover women's lives. In that respect it is closely aligned with "gender archaeology," or the archaeology of gender.

Gender archaeology emerged as part of second-wave feminism in the late 1970s as a way to remedy the gender bias—the tendency to see everything through male eyes—in archaeology.[37] Men and women were seen as polar opposites, and women were viewed mainly in terms of their maternal roles. Gender archaeology contests those notions by recovering the activities and identities of women and men, by recognizing that they are different but not oppositional, and by establishing that both are integral to household and communal life. It overcomes the traditional focus on male activities by concentrating on those of women. Gender archaeology is closely related to feminist archaeology, which in turn is part of feminist anthropology (see below); and some see them as virtually identical or consider one a sub-discipline of the other. Although feminist archaeology is more inclined toward engaging epistemological considerations, both are adamant about discovering the full range and importance of women's activities and about refusing to apply modern Western gender norms to premodern societies.[38]

In its search for the gendered aspects of household life, gender archaeology is fundamentally a project of "social archaeology." This sub-discipline of archaeology goes back to the 1970s and has many facets.[39] Especially important is its recognition of the human dimension of ancient technologies and economies and its insistence on seeking to understand the "social contexts and lived experiences" of premodern peoples.[40] Because feminist or gender archaeology focuses not only on finding women in the archaeological record but also on finding out about their relationships with each other and with men, it can be considered social archaeology.

Foregrounding the social interactions of everyday life in Israelite households is critical to understanding women's experiences. Identifying their activities is important (see chapters 7 and 8), but so too is recognizing their interactions with others and interpreting the meaning of their relationships (see chapter 10). That is, archaeological data must be interpreted. Doing so is impossible on the basis of the material culture itself, for archaeologists dig up dwellings and artifacts, not social units. It can only be done by using analogies and models provided by anthropological research.

Anthropological Materials

Anthropology—the study of human beings—is a broad discipline with multiple subfields and diverse interests. However, two main kinds of anthropological research are essential for investigating the lives of Israelite women. One is ethnography, a subfield of sociocultural anthropology. In documenting observable societies, ethnography provides analogies that are indispensable for reconstructing Israelite lifeways and women's activities. The other is the work of feminist anthropologists. Feminist approaches have permeated the entire spectrum of archaeology, but their research as archaeologists studying past societies and as ethnographers studying recent ones suggests ways to evaluate the roles and relationships of Israelite women.

Ethnography

In providing empirical observations of living premodern societies, ethnographic research helps us fill in many of the gaps that are inevitably present in the data about ancient ones. By looking at the material practices and social patterns of an observable culture, we can infer that similar practices and patterns obtained in an ancient culture with a similar set of environmental conditions. Ethnographic data are important for ascertaining both functional and social aspects of what excavators uncover; the process is sometimes called "ethnoarchaeology."

The functional aspect deals with basic questions of interpreting material culture. When archaeologists uncover an object, how do they know what it is and how it was used? After all, artifacts don't come out of the ground neatly labeled. For example, the many different kinds of pottery vessels unearthed are given names—such as water jug, storage jar, cooking pot, goblet, etc.—in archaeological publications. Similarly, small perforated stone discs are identified as spinning whorls. These designations may seem intuitive, but they come from noting how similar vessels or objects are used in observable traditional cultures. Other functional aspects include determining how long it takes for a particular task to be performed and whether a standard household task tends to be done by people working alone, in tandem, or in groups. These are among the features of household life that can be reconstructed only by consulting ethnographic reports. The discussion of women's household activities in chapter 7 draws on these kinds of observations.

Ethnographic data are also used in multiple ways for determining social aspects of an ancient society. One that is critical for this book is the gender attribution of artifacts, which are not themselves "gender noisy." Not only do artifacts lack identifying labels, they also have no tags informing us who used them. The division of labor by gender is nearly universal, with some tasks more likely performed by men and others more often by women. Yet, a landmark cross-cultural study of the basic economic activities has shown that not all tasks are universally performed by the same gender.[41] We cannot assume that women everywhere are responsible for the same household tasks. Ethnographic data, along with texts (such as a biblical reference to a woman performing a certain task) and iconography (such as the depiction of a woman performing that task in ancient Near Eastern representational art) when available, make gender attribution of artifacts possible.

Another kind of social interpretation involves information needed to assess the value of women's work. How do we determine the place of women's tasks in the household economy? Does a woman's role in producing a certain foodstuff represent a major or an insignificant contribution to the survival of her household? Feminist anthropology (or gendered ethnoarchaeology) helps us answer these questions (see below). But the answers depend on first knowing the basic economic system of ancient Israel. Clues in the Bible are important, but so are the cropping patterns of peoples living in similar ecological environments before the appearance of modern agricultural machinery and chemicals. Much of the discussion in chapter 3 relies on data collected in Middle Eastern or Mediterranean countries before widespread modernization changed traditional practices.

Ethnography also makes it possible to determine family size, which is an essential factor in assessing women's roles in bearing and caring for children. Archaeologists can usually determine a domicile's size, but that alone can't tell us how many people lived there. Without information about population density in traditional societies, it would be virtually impossible to estimate the number of people living in individual dwellings and in settlements of various sizes in biblical antiquity.

One other kind of social interpretation is critical for studying Israelite women, namely, the social context of their activities and its significance. If the location of women's tools in a domicile can be determined, how can that help us understand women's interactions with others within their household and outside it too? Answers to these and similar questions can be suggested only by considering ethnographic data about women's work patterns.

Lest this seem to be a completely rosy picture of the value of ethnography, some problems must also be noted.[42] Using ethnographic information to interpret archaeological remains is an analogical process, and its validity depends on the degree of similarity between the cultures being compared. Some scholars worry that the reasoning involved—in social interpretations more than functional ones—may be too subjective. To be sure, no two societies are exactly alike; but it is also the case that similarities are more likely when the two societies exhibit many of the same basic economic, environmental, technological, and demographic features. In fact, ethnographic studies show "a large degree of consistency" in "technical details, daily life patterns, and living conditions" of societies from all over the Middle East.[43]

For this reason, ethnographic information about Middle Eastern peoples from records and observations made before the impact of modernization are used in analyzing material remains from ancient Israel. For example, research on small Iranian mountain villages has been enormously important in reconstructing the ancient Israelite use of household space.[44] Documents from Mandatory Palestine (1923–1948) help us understand the ancient economy. The accounts of female travelers in the Ottoman Empire in the late nineteenth and early twentieth centuries provide valuable information about women's economic and religious activities. Studies of village life in Mediterranean countries in the Aegean area and on the islands of Sicily and Cyprus—places with ecosystems similar to those of the Palestinian highlands—are also useful. In addition, data from further afield may be relevant under certain conditions.

Used with caution, ethnographic data provide a legitimate and invaluable resource for understanding the material remains of an ancient society and for interpreting the behavioral correlates of those remains. Without them, investigating the lives of ordinary Israelite women would be virtually impossible. In short, although using data from a recent premodern society to understand an ancient one entails the risk of invalid comparison, the value of gaining insights possible in no other way outweighs the risk.

As important as ethnographic data are, a further kind of interpretation is necessary—one that helps us understand the meaning and value of women's activities. How can we evaluate the importance of women's various activities in their households and communities? Did women's responsibility for certain household processes contribute to how they were perceived in their communities and also in their self-perception?

Developments in feminist archaeology have contributed substantially to the interpretive processes needed to answer these and similar questions.

Feminist Anthropology

Many of the ethnographic studies used in this book are ones whose research goals and analytic processes are those of feminist anthropology. Like feminism itself, feminist anthropology is defined in various ways. Simply said, it seeks to understand female-male differentiation and to correct male bias in the study of human societies. Feminist anthropologists focus on women as subjects of study and, just as important, as figures who are rendered invisible, silenced, or otherwise misrepresented in traditional approaches. Some feminist anthropologists study contemporary industrial societies, but most are ethnographers who investigate past cultures or premodern societies surviving in the present. Their work counters and corrects interpretations of the past that see men as the chief actors and agents in social groups. They discover the active roles women hold/have held in their communities and recover the ways women serve/have served as agents of social and economic production. Their studies have produced a wealth of materials concerning a wide variety of societies. They have made women visible. They have shown that women's roles as actors and agents may differ from those of men but are no less significant.

Like feminism and feminist biblical study, feminist anthropology has experienced several waves of development, with each later wave signaling a change in emphasis rather than a displacement of its predecessor.[45] First-wave feminist anthropology accompanying the nineteenth-century suffrage movement was concerned with retrieving basic information about women's lives in traditional societies. Influential second-wave feminist anthropology in the 1970s saw the development of diverse interpretive emphases.[46] More recently, since the 1990s, third-wave feminist anthropologists (and archaeologists) are forming theoretical constructs as they strive to understand the myriad patterns of gender distinction and valuation that occur throughout the world. They recognize that gender is one of many elements—including age, wealth, ethnicity—that operate together to construct identity. And they realize that these factors are not static; they are fluid and flexible, changing over time and in relation to daily activities.[47]

Feminist anthropological study and analysis of premodern cultures is thus relevant to the investigation of ancient Israelite women, whose world was fundamentally different from our own in many ways—including its physical environment, its economic constraints, and its social and political systems. Israelite gender identities and valuations were different from ours because they were embedded in a very different way of life. Yet we inevitably tend to be "present-minded" in our thinking about Israelite women. That is, because the Hebrew Bible is relevant to many Jews and Christians today, people feel a sense of continuity between contemporary life and the biblical past. As a result, there is a tendency to assume that modern ideas about private and public life, the value of women's work, and other similar issues were the same in biblical antiquity. (See the discussion of "presentism" at the end of chapter 6.) The ethnographic work of feminist anthropologists in examining traditional cultures helps us resist that tendency by providing evidence that our assumptions about gender in the past are all too often misconceptions. Their work shows that women in traditional societies can serve as agents and exert power in household life in ways that are hardly trivial. It not only helps us reconstruct the dynamics of the daily life of Israelite women; it is also invaluable for evaluating their activities, interactions, and relationships (see chapter 10).

All told, in providing both comparative data and theoretical models drawn from their ethnographic research on premodern societies, feminist anthropologists provide invaluable materials for the investigation of ancient Israel, which, after all, was a premodern society. Indeed, without the lens of anthropological research, ordinary Israelite women would remain barely visible. Traditional approaches to the study of the past, especially of societies like ancient Israel that have left written records, have tended to focus on the prominent religious, political, or social events and institutions visible in texts and usually associated with men, thereby ignoring or misunderstanding what women did. The ethnographic study of traditional cultures developed by feminist anthropologists thus is essential for recovering the otherwise indiscernible aspects of the lives of women in past societies, including Israelite women, and also challenging and correcting existing suppositions about them and their communities. This use of ethnography to reconstruct and interpret past societies, sometimes called "gendered ethnoarchaeology," has produced important theoretical discussions as well as significant studies of individual societies.[48]

Anthropological research—ethnography (ethnoarchaeology) and feminist anthropology (in archaeology and ethnography)—is thus a critical component of the multidisciplinary approach of this book. Together with archaeological materials and information from the Hebrew Bible and

other ancient texts, it provides the data needed to render Everywoman
Eve visible.

UNLIKE MOST ANTHROPOLOGICAL studies of past societies, this
one uses textual data as well as archaeology and ethnography. Its anthropological approach can thus be considered an *ethnohistorical* one. That
term is usually used to designate the study of a particular people or culture that uses historical (written) records in addition to other kinds of
data. Ethnohistory is an appropriate designation for the study of Israelite
women for several reasons.[49] One is its insistence on integrating data from
every possible source, including material culture, and not just the texts
that mention the people being studied. Using multiple sources can produce more accurate and complete information than would otherwise be
possible. Another is the assumption (like that of ethnoarchaeology) that
the cultures of living peoples can provide insights into those no longer
visible.

In addition, a prominent feature of ethnohistory, which derives from its
own history as an anthropological discipline, makes it especially attractive
for studying Israelite women. Ethnohistory developed in the second half
of the twentieth century in the United States to study Native Americans.
Ethnohistorians recognize that indigenous peoples are sometimes absent
from written records about the settlement of North America or, just as
important, that the documents that mention them contain strong cultural biases—the colonial perspectives of the white Europeans who took
over and sometimes destroyed the indigenous peoples. Thus they seek to
understand Native American peoples on their own terms, using material
culture (including archaeological data, photographs, maps, paintings, etc.)
and ethnographic observations along with a judicious use of the information in written documents. Anthropologists as well as ethnohistorians call
this an *emic*, or insider, perspective.[50]

Because of their low visibility and largely marginal appearance in the
Hebrew Bible, a text reflecting the bias of its elite male authors, Israelite
women are in a position similar to that of indigenous Americans. Studying
Everywoman Eve in her Israelite context can similarly benefit from the
circumspect use of written sources and by a concerted effort to use every
other possible kind of information.

3

Setting the Scene: The Ancient Environment

EDEN EVE AND Everywoman Eve can become visible only by looking at them in their own context; we must attempt to enter their world. This is no easy matter because of the millennia that separate us from the Iron Age. Yet the distance in time is the symbol but not the substance of the problem. Our contemporary way of life sets us apart from any premodern people. Most of us live in or near cities in a postindustrial, highly technological world. We leave our homes to work in offices or stores, schools or factories; or we even work at home. We have instant and constant communication with others. The weather may be a recurrent item of news and conversation, but for most people in developed countries environmental constraints rarely impinge directly on central aspects of daily life. The experiential distance between us and biblical antiquity is vast, but we must attempt to bridge it if we are to see Israelite women.

Women's roles, responsibilities, and relationships vary considerably across cultures; but in premodern societies, they are related to the environment. One of the pioneers of gender anthropology insisted that a group's subsistence technology—the way they procure their food—is a critical determinant of its patterns of gendered life.[1] Subsistence patterns in turn depend largely on environmental variables. Thus, examining the material context of ancient Israel is essential for understanding its gendered activities and interactions.

Entering the world of Israelite women means asking where and how they lived. Were most Israelites city dwellers, or did they live in rural settings? What kind of natural resources were available to them? What was the basis of their economy—that is, were they pastoralists or farmers or some combination of these modes? What environmental risks did they face, and what were their strategies for survival?

Many of us today are concerned about the environment. We want to change policies and practices that have produced global warming and pollution. Yet only in the event of catastrophic natural events does the environment have a direct, life-death impact on our lives. An early frost may destroy our flower beds and disrupt the aesthetics of our neighborhood landscapes, but it hardly threatens our survival. Do we ever look at the sky on a late fall morning and wonder when the first rains of winter will begin, awakening life in the seeds we have placed in the parched ground, seeds that will produce grain for feeding our families in the long months ahead? Do we fear that the rains will be sparse and that the seeds will crumble into the dust around them, leaving our families hungry and our storehouses lacking seeds for the next planting? Can we ever understand what it means to live in a world in which existence is intimately, immediately, and inextricably bound up with environmental features?

Far removed as we are from the landscapes of ancient Israel, becoming familiar with the constraints of daily life there is the first step toward making Eve visible. Doing so also helps transcend the barriers separating us from the world of our biblical ancestors. Three aspects of the Israelite environment are relevant: the location and type of their settlements, their mode of subsistence, and the risks and problems inherent in their way of life.

Highland Settlements

Where did Everywoman Eve live together with her husband, sons and daughters, and perhaps one or both of her husband's parents or other near kin? (See chapter 6 for a discussion of family size.) Answering that question means first delineating the land of ancient Israel and then describing its settlement patterns.

The Hebrew Bible has several different visions of the extent of Israelite territory. The most realistic one, based on geography and archaeology as well as the Bible, locates Israelite territory in the highlands west of the Jordan River, stretching from the headwaters of the Jordan in the north to the northern Negev in the south: "from Dan to Beersheba" (e.g., 2 Sam 3:10). The "Land of Israel" may loom large in our imagination because of its biblical role, but it occupies a very small part of the larger Fertile Crescent extending from Egypt to the Persian Gulf. The Dan-to-Beersheba territory of the biblical text is no more than about 90 by 150 miles.

But if they have any veracity, those dimensions represent only a brief period in Israelite history. Except for a possible tenth century BCE expansion, ancient Israel's core until the end of the northern kingdom in the late eighth century BCE was the highland area of central Palestine—the mountainous spine west of the Jordan (including the foothills, or Shephelah) from the Beersheba basin in the south up to and including the Galilean uplands in the north. Afterwards, only the southern highlands and Shephelah area were Israelite. For most of its existence, the Israelites occupied a circumscribed fraction of the biblical ideal. Moreover, most of its territory was hilly or mountainous. That terrain figures prominently in the agricultural potential of Israelite territory (see the next section of this chapter).

A variety of settlements dotted the landscape.[2] Extensive surveys and excavations have located and analyzed hundreds of sites of various sizes. But determining the size of a settlement in a specific period is a daunting task. Archaeologists use sophisticated techniques to calculate ancient populations, but the results remain reasonable approximations.[3] Still, the estimated sizes of Israelite settlements mentioned below—both their acreage and their population—may seem shockingly small in relation to our own experience living in densely populated cities and sprawling suburbs.

Bible translations lead us to believe that most Israelites were city dwellers. The Hebrew word 'ir appears more than 1,000 times and is usually rendered "city," an English word denoting a relatively large, permanent settlement with public or communal buildings and a range of goods and services. But the Hebrew word often designates settlement types that were not really cities. What were those types? Archaeological surveys and excavations have been helpful in identifying the hierarchy of settlement types in ancient Israel.

Immediately before the beginnings of Israel, the highland core of Palestine was sparsely settled, probably because its harsh landscape and poor water sources (see the last section of this chapter) were less congenial to settlement than the coastlands, lowlands, and broad valleys. But in the period of Israelite beginnings (ca. 1200–1000 BCE) those highlands were dotted with over 300 settlements.[4] The character of these sites is as remarkable as the number. Most were new settlements, indicating an influx of people generally identified as Israelites. And they were unusually small, often less than an acre; only a few were as large as four or five acres.[5] They were tiny villages or hamlets, most with several dozen dwellings, housing fewer than several hundred people. And they are all agricultural settlements, as was the case for most settlements throughout the Iron Age.

The settlement pattern changed significantly in the Iron II period (ca. 1000–586 BCE), with increased population and the establishment of a monarchy. Many tiny settlements disappear and larger ones, with fortification walls, appear on the landscape. Several settlements were regional administrative or military centers—notably Megiddo, Hazor, and Gezer (see 1 Kgs 9:17-19). Yet they averaged less than 20 acres in size and 1,700 in population at the beginning of Iron II.[6] Although they had some urban features—denser population, communal or public structures, and some commodity producers, many of their inhabitants were agriculturalists.[7] None of these regional centers were like the sprawling cities of Egypt or Mesopotamia. Only about 2,000 people lived in Jerusalem before the end of the eighth century BCE, when, as noted in chapter 2, its population increased enormously, probably because of refugees from the conquered northern kingdom. Only then did Jerusalem become a true urban center, at least eight times larger than any other city in the kingdom.[8]

A group of smaller walled settlements of the Iron II period can also be identified, especially in the southern kingdom, although not all survived throughout the period.[9] Some were 7–12 acres in size with 200 to 2,000 inhabitants; but many were in the 2–7 acre range, and 38 percent were less than an acre in size. Except for having walls, these settlements were similar to the tiny agricultural settlements of the Iron I period. An assortment of rural settlement types—small unfortified villages or hamlets and isolated farmsteads—have also been identified for the Iron II period. All told, the average nonurban settlement might have between 75 and 150 people, or less.[10]

Biblical terminology also reflects a variety of sites.[11] There are separate terms for

- large walled settlements with citadels (*qiryah*, e.g., Deut 2:36);
- tiny hamlets surrounding walled settlements or isolated farmsteads (*haserim*, e.g., Josh 21:12; Lev 23:31);
- satellite settlements called "daughters" (*banot*, e.g., Num 21:25; NRSV "villages") around larger ones called "mothers";
- other unwalled settlements (*perazot*, e.g., Ezek 38:11; *kafar*, e.g., Josh 18:24);
- walled settlement (*'ir*), that is, any concentration of dwellings surrounded by a wall.

The last type, the one often translated "city," thus denotes a fortified settlement of any size but not necessarily a truly urban site.

Biblical terms also designate land use.[12] An open space (*migrash*) for pasturage or limited agriculture extended about 300 meters (nearly 1,000 feet) immediately around the wall of a fortified settlement. Beyond this space agricultural fields (*śadot*) extended some 2–5 kilometers (ca. 1–3 miles). This land-use pattern reflects the farming and pastoral components of the Israelite economy and indicates that both walled and unwalled settlements were inhabited by agrarians who worked the surrounding fields. A similar situation existed in Europe until the last few centuries: in fourteenth-century England over 94 percent of the population was agrarian, and 97 percent of Russia's population was agrarian in the eighteenth century.[13] In the classical world no more than 10 percent of the population lived in true cities.[14] In Palestine itself most people lived in rural villages in the early twentieth century.[15]

In short, relatively few Israelites experienced urban life, and even in the larger walled towns most people were agrarians. Thus calling the Iron II period "markedly urban"[16] is misleading. The Iron II settlement pattern included a variety of sites, with their configuration changing over the centuries. But only 4 percent were larger than 12 acres,[17] and even those retained their agricultural economic base throughout the Iron Age. Ancient Israel was predominantly both rural and agricultural.

A Farming People

As the preceding discussion indicates, the Israelite economy was an agrarian one that included both crops and livestock. It is an example of the "agrarian mode of production," in which sustenance is acquired by exploiting cultivable land.[18] Yet that mode typically involves large fields, irrigation, and the production of surpluses, none of which characterize Israelite agriculture. The Israelite economy thus resembles an advanced horticultural mode, which refers to small-scale subsistence production of a variety of crops, and also domesticated animals, and is typical of highland regions. The importance of kinship in its political system is another feature of advanced horticultural societies that was present in ancient Israel.[19] The small-scale level of production was related to the considerable environmental challenges, which are described in the next section, followed by a summary of the basic foodstuffs of the Israelite diet.

Environmental Constraints

Perhaps the best-known biblical description of ancient Israel is "a land flowing with milk and honey." Milk represents animal husbandry, and honey (probably date or grape syrup, not bee's honey) represents the products of the land. The phrase, found twenty times in the Hebrew Bible (e.g., Exod 3:8; Jer 11:5), symbolizes plenitude and promise even today, having entered the public imagination as the name of a John Lennon–Yoko Ono album entitled "Milk and Honey" (a 1980s New York phrase for a mixed white and Asian couple, and also a sign that Lennon and Ono considered America a land of opportunity).[20]

"Flowing with milk and honey" connotes agricultural abundance. But how realistic is that image? How prosperous were Israelite farmers? Studies of the topography, climate, and ecology of Palestine indicate that the imagery of a bountiful land reflects an ideal more than the reality. The milk-and-honey phrase represents the covenantal perspective of biblical authors, who saw a cause-and-effect relationship between disobedience and difficulties. The harsh reality of life on the land is understood as punitive, the result of disobeying God's teachings/covenant, with the idyllic image obtainable only through obedience.[21] The land of divine promise may be fertile, but the core of the Israelite homeland was not conducive to consistent agricultural prosperity for reasons considered below.

Why then did the Israelites settle there? The Bible offers a theological explanation—it is the promised land, pledged by God to the ancestors and their descendents (e.g., Gen 12:1-2; Deut 6:3). A social science perspective sees the Israelite emergence in the highlands as the convergence of a variety of social, political, and economic factors.[22] Either way, it is clear that Israelites endured in Palestine for more than a half a millennium, largely independent of the neighboring superpowers that eventually overpowered and dominated them. And they endured in a territory with limited resources.

Availability of Water

Sufficient water, the sine qua non for human habitation, was not always available. Relatively few natural springs produce water year-round, and few streams flow throughout the year. Rainfall was the chief source of water, as the Hebrew Bible explains: "the land you are about to enter to occupy is not like the land of Egypt…where you sow your seed and irrigate...the land which you are crossing over to occupy is a land of hills and valleys, which drinks water by the rain from the sky" (Deut 11:10-11). Israelite agriculture is called dry-farming—also known as dryland farming or rainfall agriculture—a system found in areas with significant water constraints. Moisture for crops came mainly from seasonal rains rather than from springs, rivers, or irrigation. The amount of rainfall varies greatly in the small overall area of Palestine, but rainfall amounts in most areas are near enough to the 200–300 millimeters (ca. 8–12 inches) per year necessary for dry-farming.

The rainy season lasts about six months, from late October to late April, with 70 percent of the annual total falling between November and February.[23] This may have been sufficient for crops, although droughts were not uncommon (see below); but Israelites needed water all year for themselves and their animals. The dearth of perennial water sources in much of the hill country and adjacent lowlands was a problem solved only by human intervention. The most common solution was to dig cisterns into the bedrock of the hilltops or hillsides where most settlements were situated.[24]

Cisterns are underground shafts usually up to 6 meters (20.7 feet) deep and 6–10 meters (20.7–32.8 feet) in diameter at the bottom. Unlike wells, which go down to the water table, cisterns were filled by channeling surface runoffs into them during the rainy season. Or water collecting in nearby shallow pools was scooped into jars, carried to the cisterns, and emptied into them. Cisterns made water available for household use during months when no rain fell; without them, many Israelite settlements would not have been viable. They have been excavated at many sites.[25] And biblical texts mention them occasionally, with several passages indicating cisterns in each household (2 Kgs 18:31; Prov 5:15).

Yet having cisterns was not without problems. For one thing, they were labor intensive. Digging them required considerable initial labor, and afterwards cisterns and the channels leading to them had to be periodically cleaned of the silt that inevitably accumulated. Moreover, they held adequate water for the dry season only if enough rain fell in the winter months; and this did not always happen (see the last section of this chapter). Other strategies for procuring permanent water supplies, which meant digging down to the water table through deep shafts and long tunnels, were sometimes implemented. Costly to excavate and maintain, these water systems are found mainly at the largest sites.

Arability of the Land

Israelite agriculture depended not only on water but also on the terrain and soil quality, both of which vary considerably across the subregions of Palestine, with some areas more conducive to farming than others.

Much of Israelite territory was mountainous or hilly. Most valleys were relatively narrow, except for the broad Jezreel separating the Galilean mountains from those of Samaria and, to a lesser extent, the Nablus (biblical Shechem) basin in the Samarian mountains. Galilee in the north has the most rugged terrain—relatively steep slopes crisscrossed with small narrow valleys—although Lower Galilee is less fractured. The Samarian highlands in the center of the land are also craggy and uneven but less than their Galilean counterparts. The Judean highlands in the south feature a succession of steep slopes and narrow valleys that give way to the rounded foothills of the Shephelah on the west and to the plateaus and ravines of the Negev highlands on the south.

This overall geomorphology, with few broad plains or valleys, poses problems for cropping. Grains, which were the mainstay of the Israelite diet (see below), are most efficiently grown on level ground where plows can easily turn the soil and rainwater can penetrate evenly. The problem of uneven terrain, like that of scarce year-round water supplies, was solved by technology: terracing. Workers dug into the rocky slopes to create flat surfaces and then piled the stones they collected along the outer edge to retain the soil. These narrow, tiered strips of land were used for planting cereal crops and also trees and vines.[26] Terraces were used extensively throughout the Iron Age, with some still in use today. Although Israelite agrarians probably did not invent terracing, they developed it into a prominent agricultural strategy mentioned in several biblical texts: the "terraced fields" of Judges 5:18 (NRSV "heights of the field") and 2 Samuel 1:21 (NRSV "bounteous fields").[27] Several other terms, including the common word for "field" (*śadeh*), sometimes denote terraced fields rather than flatland ones.[28]

Terracing made all the difference for the Israelites. It made dry-farming possible on lands otherwise too steep or rocky for anything but thorns and scrub oak and thus maximized the marginal agricultural potential of the highlands. It was an ingenious solution to several problems: it provided level surfaces for crops; the stones littering the hillsides were used to construct terrace walls; and removing stones to build terrace walls exposed cultivable soil. Moreover, terrace walls slowed the runoff of rainwater cascading down the hillsides in winter downpours, thus retaining *the joys of sex!*

essential moisture on each terrace level—otherwise rainwater would be lost to agriculture and would also contribute to soil erosion. Achieving the benefits of terracing, however, had human costs. Though simple in concept, terraces are a labor-intensive technology. Their construction was a "complex operation demanding a staggering investment of time and labor."[29] Once built, terrace walls had to be continuously and vigilantly maintained to forestall or correct the potential destructiveness of driving rain and rushing water. The labor requirements of ancient Israel's cropping system were increased significantly when a household's agricultural holdings included terraced slopes.

Like terrain, soil types were an important feature of the arability of Israelite lands. Several soil types, with varying suitability for agriculture, can be identified.[30]

The dominant soil throughout the highlands is the well-known Mediterranean *terra rossa* ("red soil"), so called because of its characteristic deep red color. These soils are probably the best highland soils, but their fertility is impaired by several factors. Sometimes they are too shallow for root systems to form, and they are often stony. Also, they have high clay content and become very hard during the long dry summer, making it difficult for early winter rains to penetrate them. Plowing requires considerable effort, and surface runoff during winter downpours erodes terracing. In short, the most fertile soils in Israelite territory are the ones that require the most effort to exploit successfully for agriculture.

Several other soil types are less common but occasionally exploited. Grey-white or yellow-brown *rendzinas* are found in some highland areas interspersed with terra rossas. Rendzinas are deeper than terra rossas and are less likely to harden in the dry summer months; but they are relatively nutrient poor, don't hold water very well, tend to be stony, and are often on slopes too steep for terracing. Overall they are less well-suited to agriculture than the terra rossas. The dark *basaltic* soils in the southeast Galilean hills are similar and can sometimes be used for farming, but overall they played a minor role in highland agriculture. Finally, fertile *colluvial* soils, formed by particles washed down from the hills, accumulated in basins and valleys, few of which were controlled by the Israelites.

ISRAELITE FARMERS FACED considerable environmental constraints. Their lands may have been part of the Fertile Crescent, but they lacked the reliable year-round water supplies, level terrain, and thick silt deposits that made the Nile valley and the Tigris and Euphrates plains so productive. Ancient Israel's highland terrains provided limited arable land and fertile soils, and rainfall was often scarce. Yet, by using the technologies of the day and expending considerable effort, Israelite farmers were able to establish an agricultural regime. Conditions were perhaps best in the Samarian hills in the center of the country, which is probably why the northern kingdom of Israel, centered there, was more prosperous than the southern kingdom of Judah.

Given the many constraints, the agricultural regime can be characterized as subsistence farming in which most households were self-sufficient at a minimal level. Israelite agrarians produced what they needed for their own consumption, leaving little to trade in the marketplace.[31] They were "peasants," a term used in this book to designate small-scale, independent agriculturalists who produce for their own needs and not for profit.[32] (This differs from the terminology used, usually by Marxists, to describe feudal societies, in which peasants are exploited by the landholding aristocracy.) Israelite households were the basic unit of consumption as well as production. They were not isolated from larger social or political structures (see chapter 6, pp. 113–117), but their agricultural production integrated them only minimally into those structures. The productivity of their own landholdings was the economic basis of life for most Israelites.

The Israelite Food System

What did the Israelites eat? Their food system has already been described as an agricultural (or advanced horticultural) mode. More specifically, it was a "Mediterranean mixed system," meaning that grain was central but that crop diversity was important.[33] The cropping pattern was related to environmental variables, including varied terrains and unpredictable rainfall.

The Israelite diet can be determined from biblical texts, analysis of paleobotanical remains, and ethnographic observation of current dietary patterns in the less modernized parts of the region.[34] The Israelite food system had three mainstays—grain, wine, and (olive) oil—that appear together in many biblical texts. For example, Yahweh promises to bless "your grain and your wine and your oil" if the people are obedient (Deut 7:13) and chastises them for forgetting that "it was I who gave her the grain, the wine, and the oil" (Hos 2:8). (*Yahweh* is the biblical name for Israel's one God; in the polytheistic world of biblical antiquity, deities had proper names to distinguish one from the others, hence the revelation of God's name in Exod 3:13-16.)

Grains were by far the most important of this Mediterranean triad. Until industrialization changed the food consumption patterns of the developed world, cereals provided 70 percent or more of the daily calorie intake for most people.[35] In Sardinia in the 1930s bread was 78 percent of the daily diet by weight.[36] In ancient Israel grains were probably about 75 percent.[37] So important were they that the word for bread, *lehem*, sometimes designates "food" more generally in the Hebrew Bible. For example, Jacob invites his kin "to eat bread," that is, to "have a meal" (Gen 31:54; cf. Acts 2:46). Similarly, in traditional Greek villages the typical way to say "to eat a meal" is "to eat bread."[38] For millennia, "to break bread" has metaphorically meant "to eat." Bread (or other grain products) was clearly the staff of life. (The important role of women in bread production is discussed in chapters 7 and 9.)

The oil mentioned in the Bible is olive oil, a product of the olive trees indigenous to the east Mediterranean, where they thrive in the shallow soils and hot summers of the highlands and can endure years with below average rainfall. Olive oil was the major dietary fat for the Israelites and also provided fuel for oil lamps; olives themselves were probably not eaten.[39] Grapes too were grown more for their products—wine and also raisins and syrup—than for the fruit itself, which is available only during grape harvest. Mentioned frequently (185 times) in the Hebrew Bible, wine was the most common beverage. Adult men consumed as much as a liter of wine a day in the postbiblical period;[40] consumption was probably less but still substantial in Iron Age settlements.

Other foods were less common. Barley was grown in the drier areas and was a supplementary grain source. Lentils and beans were also important, although they are barely mentioned in the Hebrew Bible. Few other fruits and vegetables were eaten. Figs, dates, and pomegranates are included in the "seven species" (along with wheat, barley, olives, wine) representing the land's fertility (Deut 8:7-8). But dates grow mainly in the Jordan Valley and were not generally available elsewhere, and pomegranates symbolized fertility but were probably not widely eaten. Figs, mostly in their dried form, were more important judging from their frequent mention (more than 50 times) in the Hebrew Bible. Vegetables barely appear in the Bible; they required considerable amounts of water and at best would have been available only seasonally. Seeds and nuts of various kinds were also of minimal importance.

As in all ancient Near Eastern societies, the Israelite agricultural regime included animal husbandry.[41] Sheep and goats were by far the most common livestock; cattle had a limited role; the presence of chickens is uncertain; and fish were available mainly near the Sea of Galilee. Pigs were largely absent, although attributing this to religious interdiction or ethnic identity before the end of the Iron Age is problematic. Dairy products and meat were consumed, but not so often as plant-based foods. Milk was available only during the months when sheep and goats gave birth; and even then, most of it was processed into cheese or ghee. If biblical references (e.g., Job 21:24) are any indication, fresh milk was a luxury.

Meat too was a special foodstuff, consumed at festal events (see chapter 8) more than at daily meals in contrast to today's developed world, where animal protein often occupies a large part of the dinner plate. The limited amount of arable land in ancient Israel was needed to produce food crops for humans, not to grow fodder for large flocks or herds. And the natural pasturage on the hillsides was limited in its capacity to sustain grazing animals. Thus meat consumption practices in biblical antiquity were probably like those in contemporary developing countries where plant-based diets predominate.[42] In short, the diets of most Israelites depended little on animal protein.

The importance of animals, however, transcended their use as a food source. Although relatively few in number, cattle served as draft animals. The more numerous goats and sheep were essential sources of hair and wool for the textiles produced in each household. Just as significant, they were a resource in years of insufficient crop yields, as the next section explains.

The Struggle to Survive

Technological developments and careful cropping patterns compensated to a certain extent for the relatively limited environmental resources of the Palestinian highlands and allowed for population growth during the Iron Age.[43] The population of the central highlands was about 54,000 at the end of Iron Age I and reached about 165,000 in the mid-eighth century BCE at the height of Iron Age II expansion and before Assyrian and Babylonian invasions reduced the population. The population had increased significantly, but the overall rate of growth of about 0.4 percent/year over two centuries was nowhere near the rates recorded in many contemporary populations, even in countries with minimal medical resources. In 1995, for example, the annual growth rate of Afghanistan was 3.5 percent.[44] Premodern populations could never achieve that rate because famine and disease (discussed below) as well as war caused significant and recurrent population loss (as did infant and maternal mortality; see chapter 5). In fact, famine and disease were often more lethal than armies in decimating premodern populations. For example, dysentery during the Crimean War (1854–1856) claimed ten times more British soldiers than did battle wounds.[45]

Ancient Israel's modest population increase thus did not necessarily signify prosperity. Landholdings were inevitably subdivided among heirs as the population grew, which somewhat reduced the resources of each household; and people were forced to move into the more marginal lands on the drier fringes of the highlands. Moreover, as the political structure changed, governing institutions expanded and taxation inevitably claimed a portion of the already tenuous subsistence productivity of many households. Life in the highlands was never easy, and it arguably became progressively more challenging over the centuries of Israelite existence. Producing sufficient food required hard work. In addition, droughts and other environmental factors periodically led to food shortages, causing hunger and sometimes famine; and recurrent disease also affected the well-being of the household unit.

Labor Demands

The modest variety of foodstuffs grown by Israelite peasants often (but not always, as the next section indicates) offset the problems caused if one crop failed. Diversified cropping also helped spread out the labor requirements, for different crops were planted and harvested at different times.[46] Even so, highland farming required the labor of more people than the members of a simple nuclear family (see chapter 6). The labor variant is as important as the environment in considering the difficulties facing Israelite agriculturalists. Productive labor is, in a sense, a demographic issue that affects family size and gender roles. For the Israelites, the hard work of both women and men and the reproductive capacity of women were the necessary responses to considerable labor needs (see the discussion of Gen 3:16 in chapter 5).

In addition to the strenuous and time-consuming work of maintaining terrace walls and cleaning silt from cisterns, the annual agricultural cycle—sowing, weeding, harvesting, and processing crops as well as tending animals—entailed other arduous and tedious tasks.[47] Moreover, the particular combination of crops, climate, growing season, and harvest times precluded an even distribution of agricultural tasks throughout the year. Some seasons of the year required concentrated efforts.

The sowing of the all-important grain, for example, took place within a rather limited time period at the onset of the rainy season. And grain had to be harvested in the few weeks or sometimes only several days between when it ripens and when the "latter rains" (sudden downpours in late spring) begin. These cloudbursts could rot or destroy unharvested grain.[48] The subsequent processes—threshing, winnowing, and sieving—must also be carried out immediately so that late rains would not drench the harvested grain. Similarly, summer fruits had to be gathered and sun-dried before fall rains began. Grapes especially offer a short window of opportunity for harvest: the ripe fruit must be picked before it falls to the ground and rots.

Given the climate and geomorphology of the highlands, Israelite farmers could do little to stagger sowing or to spread out the harvest. Production cycles inevitably created labor-intensive periods. Community efforts were perhaps initiated to accommodate the labor demands at particular times of the year. For example, threshing floors (e.g., 1 Sam 23:1; Ruth 3:2-6) may be examples of communal cooperation at harvest time.[49] Similarly, olive and grape processing, which required equipment too expensive for most individual households, took place in shared installations in rural settlements (see chapter 6, p. 116).[50] Terrace construction may also have involved pooled labor. Yet cooperative efforts only partially offset the demands of a labor-intensive agricultural system; the hard work of *all* household members was essential.

Women (and children too) were thus a vital part of the labor force of Israelite households, especially at harvest time. Women and men may have performed different tasks in the harvesting process, but all participated according to ethnographic data collected from Mediterranean societies before harvesting was mechanized.[51] In one Greek village men climbed olive trees and shook them to knock the olives to the ground, where women gathered them; and women used sickles to cut wheat, which men gathered into bundles.[52] A similar division of labor was observed for olive harvesting in early twentieth-century Palestinian villages; but the opposite labor pattern obtained for the wheat harvest, with men cutting the grain and women collecting it into bundles.[53] In Cyprus women sometimes tied up sheaves while men cut the grain and sometimes vice versa.[54] Women's harvesting tasks were in addition to their arduous regular work load.

Older people also helped according to their abilities, and children worked in age-appropriate ways. In traditional subsistence societies, children as young as five were part of the everyday labor force as well as at harvest time.[55] Children were an "integral part of the labor force in most rural societies" not only for agricultural work but also to support elderly parents unable to care for themselves.[56] Having children to supply labor and other needs, as well as for the pleasure they might bring to parents, was a fundamental aspect of peasant society. The labor of children accordingly appears in several biblical texts (e.g., Prov 10:5; Jer 7:18).

Because many working women today face the competing demands of jobs and of children, one might wonder if there was tension in biblical antiquity between women's many subsistence tasks and their reproductive role. Probably not. The idea of work and motherhood as oppositional alternatives for women is a relatively recent phenomenon, a product of industrialization and the separation of the workplace from the home. It is not normally found in preindustrial societies where the household *was* the workplace (as chapter 6 explains). A prominent sociologist puts it this way: "In the long evolution of the human species, women have always engaged in productive labor along with child-bearing and -rearing. Hence women in industrial societies are not departing radically from the past when they combine childrearing and employment."[57] Ancient classical sources concur—Strabo, Diodorus, and others report that certain tribeswomen bear children and feed them while working.[58] Similarly, women in a mid-twentieth-century Greek village worked throughout pregnancy. If a woman was out gathering firewood when labor began, she would rest until giving birth, then pack up the infant and the bundle of firewood and return to her home.[59]

Israelite women in agricultural households—like women in traditional peasant societies everywhere—performed an endless succession of tasks (see chapters 7 and 8) along with bearing children. Everywoman Eve would have been astonished at our contemporary career-family dilemmas. Even elite women were rarely relieved of a significant number of tasks. Women in well-to-do families in a Sardinian highland village before modernization worked very hard even if they had servants.[60] If the multitasking affluent woman of Proverbs 31:10-31, idealized as she may be, is any indication, the same was true for many elite Israelite women.

The labor needs of an agrarian family meant hard work for all; and for women, having children was also important. However, nutrition and health problems affected women's (and men's) lives and interfered with labor needs and reproductive success.

Nutrition and Health Problems

In describing the Mediterranean agricultural regime and foodways of the Israelites, I have avoided the term "Mediterranean diet," for it would give the erroneous impression that the semi-vegetarian Israelite diet was nutritionally sound. The highly regarded, heart-healthy Mediterranean diet of today approximates the traditional Greek diet of the 1950s when Greeks already had technologies (refrigeration, pest-control chemicals, etc.) and markets that assured the availability of diverse seasonal foods.[61] It is not the diet of peasants in the ancient Mediterranean basin, where nutritional deficiencies were all too common.

Those deficiencies—inadequate calories and also the lack of a varied enough set of foods to provide adequate nutrients—are the result of agricultural problems that have been alluded to but not specified. Estimating types and quantities of available foods for ancient populations is difficult, but archaeological materials and ancient texts (including classical sources) present a grim picture. Grapes and olives do not grow equally well in all parts of the hill country, and it is possible that not everyone had access to sufficient amounts of oil and wine. The Israelite diet included relatively few fruits and virtually no vegetables. To be sure, the grains that were the main supplier of calories are an excellent food source; they provide important protein for people who ate little meat as well as adequate amounts of vitamin E and some B-vitamins. Yet they lack certain nutrients, which are supplied by other foods in healthy diets. But the Israelite diet was not always sufficiently varied.

Thus many people, especially in the more marginal environments, likely suffered nutritional deficiencies. Even if the available foods supplied sufficient nutrients, recurrent food shortages (discussed below) frequently meant the lack of key nutrients, especially iron, calcium, vitamins A and C, and other trace elements and vitamins. Deficiency diseases (e.g., eye ailments, anemia, bladder stones) caused by inadequate amounts of essential nutrients affected many people, but probably peasants more than elites.[62] Not fatal in themselves, deficiency diseases reduce energy levels and also resistance to infectious diseases.

Pregnant or lactating women are especially vulnerable to dietary deficiencies, particularly insufficient iron and calcium.[63] Physically active pregnant women typically require three times more iron than men; otherwise they become anemic. The characteristic fatigue, weakness, and diminished energy of anemia would have been unrecognized as a deficiency problem and would have gone untreated. Similarly, pregnant or lactating women require twice as much calcium as men; and the weakened bones, high blood pressure, and general malaise accompanying calcium deficiency would also have been unrecognized and untreated. Today pregnant women often take iron and calcium supplements. In biblical antiquity pregnant women all too often suffered the consequences of dietary deficiencies.

Life-threatening infectious diseases were also a persistent menace. Vaccines and medical treatments have dramatically reduced these diseases in the modern world, making it difficult for us to grasp their ubiquitous presence and deadly consequences in antiquity.[64] The ancient Israelites were subject to the periodic outbreak of epidemic infectious diseases (plagues) as well as endemic parasitic disease, that is, infections that occur more or less all the time without much change over years or even centuries.[65] Frequent biblical references to plague and pestilence indicate that the outbreak of disease was a terrifying and ever-present possibility. Catastrophic "plagues" (*maggepot*) could decimate a community (e.g., Num 25:9; 2 Sam 24:15). And "pestilence" (*deber*), perhaps a general term for infectious disease, was a life-threatening condition often mentioned together with war and famine (e.g., Jer 14:12; cf. Deut 28:21-28).

Food shortages, when crop yields were too small to provide enough calories, were just as problematic as inadequate nutrition in affecting the well-being of Everywoman Eve and her family. Insufficient yields were caused by several factors, including inadequate water. The mean average rainfall in Palestine suffers a 25 percent decrease in four out of twenty years.[66] Moreover, even if total precipitation is adequate, crop yields drop unless it is distributed between the early and later rains; and this does not always happen. Also, much of the winter rains are lost to agriculture because of their intensity and the high evaporation rate.[67] Grain yields in Palestine were thus highly variable, with lean years five to seven times less productive than good years.[68]

Biblical authors were attuned to these problems. The seasonal rains have specific designations: God promises "rain (*meṭar*) for your land in its season, the early rain (*yoreh*) and the later rain (*malqoš*), and you will gather in your grain, your wine, and your oil" (Deut 11:14). The frequent inadequacy of sufficient rain is associated with human flaws, as in this prayer attributed to Solomon: "When heaven is shut up and there is no rain [it is] because [the people] have sinned against you [God]"; but God will "grant rain in the land" if the people obey God (1 Kgs 8:35-36). The inevitable rainfall deficits, which caused periodic agricultural shortfalls and inadequate calories, were understood in theological terms. Other conditions—hail, violent storms, insects, and blight—frequently exacerbated the problem and were similarly perceived as divine punishment. Solomon's prayer also associates "blight, mildew, locust, or caterpillar" with sin (1 Kgs 8:37; cf. Amos 4:9; 7:1). Political factors such as warfare, with the resulting loss of crops or stored products, and taxes would have further compromised the sufficiency of yields.

Because of all these factors, food shortages were probably widespread and frequent in ancient Israel; chronic hunger and poor nutrition likely affected much of the peasant population. This conclusion is supported by data about ancient societies in the Aegean area, with cropping patterns and resources similar to those of the Palestinian highlands. The picture there is every bit as dire. Crop yields varied greatly, and food shortages were chronic.[69] Ethnographic data show similar dietary problems: in a Greek mountain village in the early 1970s, because little fresh food was available in the winter, the monotonous diet consisted mainly of bread and oil.[70] The same was true in a Palestinian village in the 1950s, where most people had a very poor diet.[71] Peasant Mediterranean populations experienced endemic, persistent deprivation and hunger—so common that it seemed like the norm.

No wonder, then, that "hunger" appears frequently (more than 100 times) in the Hebrew Bible. Often paired with "thirst," it represents the endemic insufficiency of calories and sometimes denotes famine, that is, unusually severe food shortages resulting in starvation and death. Famine is a recurrent theme, playing on the audience's familiarity with food shortages (e.g., Gen 45:6; 2 Sam 21:1; 2 Kgs 8:1). Some texts, especially in Jeremiah (e.g., 14:16), are explicitly theological in "explaining" why devastating famines occur.

This theological understanding of famine, as well as disease, military defeats, and other natural disasters, is characteristic of ancient cultures.[72] The Mesopotamian hero Atrahasis, for example, tells how the gods resort to famine, drought, plague, and flooding when the political strife of humans disturbed their repose.[73] How else could the ancients deal with the apparently inexplicable spread of devastating natural disasters and lethal illness? Even in more recent times, some perceive the onset of certain diseases (such as AIDS) or the devastation of hurricanes and earthquakes as divine punishment.

Whether or not all Israelite peasants shared the Bible's view about the cause of hunger and disease, like most agriculturalists they developed strategies for coping with persistent food shortages and periodic famines. (They also tried to treat disease; see chapter 8). Some advance measures might minimize difficulties in the event of poor yields, and some mechanisms dealt with crisis situations.[74] To prevent food shortages, peasant farmers characteristically try to produce surpluses in a good year. These surpluses are rarely marketed (see chapter 6, p. 116); rather they are stored for the inevitable lean years. The importance of stored grains is mentioned in a biblical text about the ideal of plenitude when stored grain can be cleared out (Lev 26:10). And the high percentage of storage jars among the pottery forms recovered in the excavations of some dwellings suggests the storage of more grain and oil than would be needed for a single year.[75]

Biblical texts indicate practices for augmenting food supplies in dire situations. Some wild animals, especially fallow deer and gazelle, were considered suitable for consumption (Deut 12:15, 22); and their bones are occasionally identified at Iron Age sites.[76] Birds were hunted or trapped (Prov 6:5; Amos 3:5), or their eggs were collected for food (Deut 22:6; Isa 10:14). Leafy greens, fruits, seeds, and nuts that grew in the wild provided some nourishment for desperately hungry people when food supplies diminished (Job 30:3-4), and wild plants were used for a barely edible stew during a famine (2 Kgs 4:39). Classical sources and ethnographers similarly report the use of these "famine foods" by agrarians living in marginal environments.[77]

However, perhaps the most important resource for dealing with crop shortages came from the animal husbandry component of the Mediterranean agricultural regime. Because pasturage growth does not suffer as much as field crops do in dry years, animals can survive on marginal lands under drought conditions. Serving as a fallback mechanism when crop yields are insufficient, animals are the "classic stored food"; they can be slaughtered for food in times of extreme shortages. As Hopkins puts it, "Animals are a mobile resource subject to a different set of environmental constraints than fixed fields of crops."[78]

One other measure, described in chapter 7 in relation to women's roles, is the human one—people helping each other. Despite the ingenuity Israelite agrarians may have shown in finding ways to compensate for inadequate food supplies, the members of one household often survived because people in other households provided assistance. The great variability in land forms, soils, and rainfall patterns across short distances meant that not all households always experienced the same degree of deprivation. Resources contributed by kin, neighbors, friends, and perhaps even patrons to desperate families would have formed a last resort for coping with food shortages and famine. No less than "famine foods," the social fabric of Israelite settlements, often woven by women, would have contributed to the survival of struggling households.

ANALYSIS OF THE setting of ancient Israelite life presents a less than glowing picture. One scholar reports that subsistence agriculture took place in "a generally harsh environment," another that "scarcity rather than abundance played a critical role in the lives of the ancient populations."[79] Moreover, the varied vocabulary for *poverty* in the Hebrew Bible suggests its prevalence in Israelite society.[80]

These assessments are echoed by ethnographic data. Life in a Greek mountain town with environmental constrains similar to those in the Israelite highlands is described in these poignant terms:

> Of all the villager's crops wheat is the most vital...but the winning of bread from the rocky fields is, as the villagers say, "an agonizing struggle" (ἀγωνία). For the greater part of the year nature, if not actually hostile to man, is at least relatively intractable. Day after day the farmer wears himself out in clearing, burning, ploughing, double-plowing, sowing, hoeing, weeding; all through the year there are risks from hail, floods, drought, locusts, diseases, any one of which could, particularly in the past, reduce him to debt and hunger.[81]

As in ancient Israel, grain is all important. The struggle to survive, presented from the male perspective but no doubt echoed in women's experience, marked the rhythms of life. Another ethnographic account of a Greek mountain village indicates that men's struggles had their parallel in women's:

> [A feature of women's lives is] the severity and apparent inevitability of their labor. Women bear heavy burdens...they work unceasingly....Their stouthearted exhaustion communicates...how to struggle well....The woman's drudgery parallels the men's burdens....The counterpoint of women's work to men's work shows that drudgery is systemic and spread throughout the society.[82]

In describing the hardships facing Israelite peasants, I have focused on environmental constraints and attendant health problems, all with consequences for women's lives, and have only alluded to the political factors (i.e., taxation) that would also have contributed to the hardships of agrarians, making them more vulnerable to food shortages. The taxation issue is considered in chapter 6. At this point, the fact that the survival of most Israelite agrarians required the strenuous effort of all members of a household provides the relevant context for looking at the Eve of the Genesis tale.

4

Eve in Eden: Genesis 2–3

EVE IS ARGUABLY the major character in the Eden story. She has a larger speaking part than her male counterpart. She is certainly the more active character—in the fateful scene where they eat of the forbidden fruit, she is the subject of five active verbs while the man is the subject of only one ("he ate").[1] Eve is the protagonist; her perception of the quality of the fruit and her subsequent actions, and only secondarily those of Adam, are critical to the narrative plot.[2] Moreover, she alone has a bit part in the immediate sequel to the Eden episode, when she bears Cain and Abel at the beginning of Genesis 4; Adam has no role in that narrative except to impregnate her.

Eve's role in the biblical story is clear and twofold: Eve in Eden; and Eve as Everywoman, foreshadowed in the details of Genesis 2–3. These two aspects are best considered separately—the woman *in* Eden in this chapter, and the woman *out* of Eden in the next. The use of the pair *in-out* rather than *in-after* is deliberate, for my emphasis is on the depiction of differences between the imagined Eden place and the reality of the outside-the-garden place rather than on a temporal contrast, which might imply a historicity to the Eden tale.

Before proceeding, I want to note that the names of the first couple do not actually appear throughout the narrative. The first woman is called "Eve" only as they are about to leave the garden (Gen 3:20). The first man is not called Adam in the Eden episode at all; his name apparently first appears near the end of the next chapter (Gen 4:25) or at the beginning of Genesis 5 (v. 1).[3] However, for convenience I will occasionally use the names Eve and Adam when referring to their story or to passages that precede their being named.

Also, I hope that this reading of the Eden tale comes close to discovering its "original meaning." I acknowledge that the very concept of an original meaning is problematic and that other perspectives on what the storyteller meant and how Israelite audiences understood this tale cannot be discounted. Still, looking at its context can perhaps take us closer to discerning its intent than would be otherwise possible. The general context of agrarian life is described in the preceding chapter, and contextual issues are integral to several points in this chapter and the next.

The Eden tale presents special challenges for determining its meaning for an Israelite audience. As one of the most familiar of biblical narratives, it is prominent in post-Hebrew Bible traditions. It has influenced post-Israelite notions of gender roles and relationships perhaps more than any other Hebrew Bible text. But is it really the biblical tale itself that has such influence? Or is it the traditions it has spawned? We must remember that these chapters antedate by hundreds of years, perhaps almost a millennium, the religious traditions that accepted them as normative statements about human nature. The earliest Jewish and Christian communities drew on the story of Eden, among many other parts of ancient Israel's sacred literature, to help them deal with their own social and theological concerns. Biblical interpretation is as old as the formation of the biblical canon itself, and interpretations of Genesis 2–3 abound.

The earliest Jewish and Christian sources, followed by the rabbinic sages and church fathers who were the leaders of postbiblical religion, interpreted and emphasized certain features of Genesis 2–3 in expressing their views of creation and gender, of sex and sin. Their comments tell us more about their world than about the meaning of this tale in its Israelite context, centuries before it became canonical. Many of their prolific writings became authoritative for many Jews and Christians, giving their writings about the Bible a canonical status and dogmatic force of their own, and influencing virtually all later interpretations of the Eden tale. Consequently, we inevitably look at it through their interpretive eyes without realizing that translations and expositions of Genesis 2–3 may distort or misrepresent the meaning and function of the tale in its Israelite context. Our assumptions about the story based on later tradition and not on the ancient Hebrew tale itself can distort our view of the Eve of Eden. Thus a brief look at those traditions is in order. (They are also discussed in the epilogue.)

The Interpretive Tradition

An example unrelated to gender is a good place to begin. Ask yourself: What was the forbidden fruit? Ancient traditions identified it variously as a pomegranate, grapes, or a fig, among others; but chances are that, like most others, you would say apple. The dominant apple tradition probably derives from a play on words in the Vulgate (the fourth-century CE Latin translation of the Hebrew Bible), which calls the tree of knowledge (Gen 2:17) a tree of *boni* ("good") *et mali* ("evil"). *Mali* is the genitive of *malum*, which can also mean "apple." (One would say something like *malum malum* for "a bad apple" in Latin.) Another possibility is that Renaissance artists depicting the Eden story drew on the story of the golden apples in Greek mythology. Whatever the reason for the popular view that the forbidden fruit was an apple, it has endured. Many later writers, including Milton in *Paradise Lost*, have the first couple err by eating an apple. But the Hebrew simply says "fruit."

Other lasting misinterpretations have become entrenched in our literary, artistic, and religious culture. It is virtually impossible for today's readers to consider the first family without preconceived notions, especially with respect to gender, that may change or distort the Hebrew tale. To be fair, the authors of those dominant postbiblical traditions were probably not concerned with how their own context may have differed from that of the Israelites in ways that would affect their reading of biblical texts. Nor did they possess our current interpretive tools. That said, it remains that the misrepresentations of the ancient interpreters with respect to gender often became the repressive norm (to be discussed further in chapter 10).

What are some prominent misconceptions in the interpretive traditions?

As already noted, Eve is not mentioned in the Hebrew Bible after the beginning of Genesis. Her first post-Hebrew Bible appearance is in the book of Tobit, a popular work of historical fiction dating to the fourth or third century BCE. (Tobit is part of the Apocrypha, which is included in Catholic and Orthodox bibles but not Jewish or Protestant ones.) In a prayer offered as they consummate their marriage, a newlywed couple recalls the first couple: "You made Adam and for him you made his wife Eve as a helper and support" (Tob 8:6). Notable is the absence of the word "sin," given the tendency to connect Eve with sin in other early works. But Adam as the first human and Eve as a supportive helper are problematic concepts and are discussed below.

A more explicitly negative portrayal of Eve appears in Ecclesiasticus (Sirach, or Ben Sira), an early second-century BCE Jewish work also in the Apocrypha. An apparent allusion to her appears in this verse: "From a woman sin had its beginning, / and because of her we all die" (25:24).[4] Although it may have been a minority position at the time—for some other early sources blame Adam or the fall of evil angels and their cohabitation with women (Gen 6:1-4)[5]—Ben Sira's assertion that a woman brought sin and death into the world is the earliest example of a tenaciously dominant interpretation.

Another negative appraisal appears a century or two later in a pseudepigraphical work called the Life of Adam and Eve. This book has Eve bringing sin and suffering into the world. For example, when she seeks to relieve Adam's suffering, she asks God "to transfer his pain to me, since it is I who sinned" and asks Adam to "give me a portion of your pain, for this guilt has come to you from me" (*L.A.E.* 35:2-3). In another version of this work Eve proclaims: "I have sinned, O God; I have sinned, O Father of all; I have sinned against you....I have sinned before you, and all sin in creation has come about through me" (*Apoc. Mos.* 32:2).[6] Although some early Jewish sources are kinder to Eve,[7] most contain negative views.

Early Christian sources also express negative views, beginning with the New Testament: "For Adam was formed first, then Eve; and Adam was not deceived, but the woman was deceived and became a transgressor" (1 Tim 2:13-14). Not only is Eve associated with sin; her creation is viewed as secondary and, by implication, of lesser importance. (This perception is problematic, as explained below.) Augustine, the early Christian thinker most responsible for the doctrine of original sin and arguably the most influential figure in the development of Western Christianity, blamed both Adam and Eve for the transgression. However, he focuses the blame on Eve, asserting that she is inferior to man (*City of God* 14.13) and proclaiming: "it is still Eve (the temptress) that we must beware of in any woman" (*Letter* 245.10).[8] Augustine's ideas about female subordination, which became common in Christian religious literature, are rooted in ideas of gender hierarchy and male control assumed to have begun in Eden.[9]

The association of the first woman with sin, sexuality, and lust continues and grows in postbiblical texts. Some rabbinic texts connect Eve with temptation, sin, and death.[10] But, while most consider both Eve and Adam culpable, they focus on the Golden Calf incident as the exemplar of sinful behavior.[11] Christian sources in general are deeply interested in issues of sin and punishment. The serpent plays an increasingly satanic and phallic role. And the more Eve is identified as the source of sin and seduction, the more urgent becomes the need to control, subdue, and dominate her. Eve represents all women, and all women thus require sub-jugation by wiser and superior male figures. This powerful connection with Eve and sin is remarkable, given the absence of that word from the Eden tale. (More below about Eve and her putative sin.)

Subsequent Jewish and Christian interpretive traditions (discussed in the epilogue) show the same tendencies as the texts just cited, and many of the earliest interpretations have endured. The themes of female sin and inferiority, although not in the biblical text, have been prominent for two millennia. In addition to religious texts, Western literature and art are replete with retellings and depictions of the Eve story, endlessly expressing those themes.[12] Perhaps the most influential has been *Paradise Lost*, arguably the greatest English epic poem. Milton's recasting of the Eden tale became so influential that many of our present recollections of the biblical story—like assuming that the forbidden fruit is an apple—are based more on Milton's poem than on the biblical narrative itself. Some recent feminist critics see positive aspects of Milton's Eve.[13] But ultimately "[Milton's] hierarchical world view led him to assume that every crea-ture had its proper place in an elaborately descending order from God who is pure spirit, to angels, men, women, plants, and finally non-living creatures."[14] Milton saw both political rulers and husbands as God's depu-ties, controlling the state and the family, respectively. Adam and Eve were both created in God's image, but Eve less so: Adam's "perfection far excell'd Hers in all real dignity" (*Paradise Lost* 10:150-151).

Eve indeed has "fallen"—fallen to a negative perception in the inter-pretive tradition. The term Fall does not occur in Genesis 2–3 or any-where in the Hebrew Bible; it entered the interpretive world through Greek thought. Plato describes heavenly perfections losing their wings and *falling* to the earth to be implanted in humans (*Phaedr.* 246c-d, 248c-d). The idea of *falling* from (divine) grace (Gal 5:4; cf. Rom 3:23) became a specifically Christian theological interpretation. The extensive postbiblical use of Fall is a good example of how an interpretive concept became so familiar that its absence from the Genesis story itself goes unnoticed. The term is anachronistic and thus inappropriate for discussing the Eden story in its Hebraic context. Its use at the beginning of this paragraph merely highlights how enduring are derogatory perceptions of Eve or the Eden story.

Another example is the notion that Eve tempted Adam. This notion is not in the text of Genesis but first appears in early postbiblical sources.[15]

In an early third-century CE work, Eve "persuaded" Adam to eat the forbidden fruit (Tertullian, *Or.* 8.8). By the next century, she beguiles him.
And it gets worse, as the words "wicked," "temptress," "deception," and
other pejorative terms enter theological discourse, appearing over and over
again into the medieval and modern periods. A classic twentieth-century
commentary on Genesis proclaims that "The one [Eve] who has been led
astray [by the serpent] now becomes a temptress."[16] Neither temptation
nor seduction is in the biblical text, but these words and others like them
appear all too frequently in interpretations. Most Muslim commentaries
also blame Eve, although she is never mentioned by name in the Qur'an,
for the beginnings of sin.[17]

The interpretive traditions loom so large, and many of them are so
well known and even authoritative, that they occlude our vision of the
Eve of Genesis. Another and perhaps more insidious kind of interference
with our ability to see her is the problem of translations, for most of us
read about Eve in languages other than the original Hebrew. Translations
are by their very nature interpretations, for no language can be rendered
exactly word-for-word into another one. Judgments about nuance are
always necessary, especially when a word has more than one meaning or
when the syntax of the two languages differs. To be sure, good translations usually provide accurate renderings; but they can also—sometimes
unconsciously—subtly change and distort the meaning of the original,
especially when the culture of the translators is far removed from that of
the original text.[18] The process of translating the Hebrew Bible into other
languages began in the same centuries that the interpretive literature of
early Judaism and Christianity was forming, and the ancient translations
exhibit similar bias and distortion.

Perhaps the best example is the Latin translation of the Bible, the
influential Vulgate. Commissioned by Pope Damasus in 382 CE, it became
the authoritative scripture of the Catholic Church. The translator was St.
Jerome, a highly competent Hebrew scholar, but a man whose writings
show hostility toward, and fear of, women. His misogynist views subtly
influenced his renderings of passages about women; they were "such a powerful and all-pervasive influence upon him that the accuracy of his Vulgate
translation itself has been affected."[19] The Vulgate has been an exceptionally
important translation: it became the standard Roman Catholic Bible; and it
also influenced many subsequent translations, especially ones in Romance
languages. It has thus affected much of the Judeo-Christian world. The
smallest and most subtle examples of antifemale bias in St. Jerome's

translation can have far-reaching consequences. The matter of translation bias will figure in this chapter and the next.

Many of the negative perceptions of Eve mentioned here were noted by Phyllis Trible, a pioneering and influential second-wave feminist biblical scholar. She lists nearly a dozen "consensus" claims about Eve—all misogynist views that are either debatable readings or are absent from the text altogether.[20] And she observes that, ironically, the power of traditional interpretations has led the opponents of an androcentric order no less than its advocates to misunderstand the tale.[21] Both feminists who write off Genesis 2–3 as hopelessly misogynist and conservatives who invoke it accept gender-related dogmas they assume the text contains. Some misreadings have achieved a canonicity of their own and interfere with the ability to read Genesis 2–3 on its own, in its Israelite context, apart from later influential expositions. These obstacles are considerable but not insurmountable. By acknowledging that biblical texts were both responsive to and reflective of their own world, and by considering the conditions in that world, we can rediscover the Eve that existed before she was linked with sin and suffering. We can come closer to recovering the Israelite Eve of the Hebrew Bible before the overlay of later traditions began to form.

Genre and Setting

The enormous interest in the Eden narrative throughout the ages has not escaped feminist biblical scholars. They have rightly been concerned about the powerful and usually detrimental impact of the interpretive tradition. First-wave feminist scholars were painfully aware that biblical texts like the Eden story were barriers to securing the vote for women; second-wave feminist scholars realized that their goals of gender equality were impeded by values thought to be embedded in this tale; and third-wave feminists have highlighted its exploitative potential. For almost two centuries feminist scholars have contributed to the extensive body of scholarship on Genesis 2–3.

This deceptively simple tale clearly operates on many levels and conveys profound messages about human existence. No wonder it has attracted so much scholarly attention over the ages. A survey of all the feminist expositions, let alone of all that other scholars have written, is inconceivable.[22] In joining that wide array of scholarship on this influential biblical episode, it would be presumptuous to claim that my (or any) analysis is the only possible approach. Rather, my aim is to consider the narrative in relation to the problems and concerns of the Israelites, the people closest in time to its emergence among the cultural productions of the Iron Age (see chapter 1, p. 15, for an explanation of Iron Age), and to suggest its meaning for them. This can be termed a "culturally cued" reading in that it connects a literary production with its context—the "realm of concrete and particular social, economic, and cultural realities."[23] It is not a systematic study of the entire episode. Rather it begins in this chapter by looking closely at several features or passages that relate to gender roles and relationships as established in Eden. And in the next chapter it focuses on a single troubling verse (3:16) in which God sets forth the conditions of Eve's life out of Eden. In both, traditional androcentric or misogynist interpretations are contested.

Genre

Contextualizing a biblical text properly begins with a consideration of its genre, for the nature of the genre is relevant to how it is understood. What kind of literature do we have in Genesis 2–3? Several different terms are used for these chapters, and examining them helps us understand their literary character and their function in Israelite culture.

Except for the poetic verses near the end of chapter 3, the Eden tale is a narrative. Broadly speaking, it is a marvelous example of folk literature, or folklore, a term designating a culture's traditional narrations of various kinds. Genesis 3 in particular—if we can get beyond the church fathers and Milton and the array of writers who appropriated the story for their own purposes—is a story with a situation, a plot, and a resolution.[24] More specifically, it is a creation story or "myth." The latter word does not mean either that these two chapters of Genesis are false or that they are recounting some quaint and antiquated story. Rather, it suggests that Genesis 2–3 is a traditional, metaphoric tale about something that was deeply important to the Israelite community in which it arose and was transmitted.

Like all peoples, the Israelites sought to understand the nature and meaning of their existence. Their interest in creation was not a scientific one but rather an existential one. Where do humans fit in the overall scheme of the created realm?

The Hebrew Bible begins with two literary units, each addressing that question but with different focuses. The first comes in Genesis 1–2:4a, a unit formed by an *inclusio* (a literary device in which similar or identical opening and closing words or phrases frame a section). Genesis 1:1 mentions "the heavens and the earth," and Genesis 2:4a contains the same words; together they mark the beginning and end of a literary unit. That unit is a cosmogony, describing how the world/cosmos as the Israelites observed it came into existence. It is usually attributed to priestly authors, who shaped it in the mid-first millennium BCE. Like their counterparts in Babylonia, Egypt, Greece, and Rome, they crafted tales about people and god(s) that would help them understand their place in the cosmos.²⁵ The Genesis cosmogony is a true *mythos*, a story relating humans to divine action and situating them within the cosmos as it appeared to Israelite observers before the rise of modern science.

Ancient creation tales typically have a strong etiological character. Derived from the Greek word *aitia* ("cause"), an etiology (or aetiology) is an "explanation" of how things got to be the way they are. It provides the cause of a phenomenon in the natural or human world. Etiologies begin when the storytellers observe something, often but not necessarily something puzzling or problematic, in their own world and then proceed to account for it. Etiologies help prescientific people answer the perennial questions about how they fit into the natural and social worlds. Etiologies are fundamentally ahistorical and unscientific. But that doesn't mean they are untrue. They originate in the stirrings of the human imagination, not in the reasoned hypotheses of the scientist. Their truth lies in the realm of beliefs, not facts. Also, in linking causality to divine action, mythic etiologies function as sanctions for the present order, thereby enabling people to accept the conditions of their present. This last point is particularly relevant to understanding Eve (and Adam) out of Eden.

The next unit of Genesis, which focuses on the creation of humans rather than the cosmos, is also mythic and even more etiological. This unit (Gen 2:4b–3:24, but usually referred to as Gen 2–3) too is delineated by an *inclusio*—"to till the ground" appears in 2:5 and 3:23. Usually attributed to "J" (a writer who uses *Yahweh*—Jahwe in German, hence the J—for God's name) and perhaps predating Genesis 1 by several centuries or more, it accounts for the nature of human existence as the Israelites knew it. In many cultures, including ancient Israel, narratives about "first" humans tell how conditions in the narrator's present originated in primordial time.

For the Israelites, these mythic "events" provided an "explanation" for important aspects of their reality: mortality, male and female roles, female-male pair-bonding, and more. They accounted for the essential qualities, including the difficulties, of human existence.²⁶ The Eden story is exceptionally rich in accounting for reality; it has thus been called "a catena of nestled, densely packed etiologies, each conforming to the style and goal of genres deployed in other Near Eastern (creation) narratives."²⁷ Indeed, the sheer number of etiological features about humans and the lack of attention to the creation of the natural world—no mention of cosmic features (light and dark; sun, moon, and stars)—make the Eden tale more of an "extended etiological narrative" than a creation story.²⁸ To be sure, animals and trees as well as humans are created in the story; but they serve the story line rather than showcase the cosmos as God's created realm. Etiological functions dominate in Genesis 2–3 as they do throughout Genesis 1–11, which focuses on primordial times.

In accounting for fundamental aspects of human existence, the Eden tale also has both archetypal and prototypal meaning. Found in folklore the world over, archetypes are the "original" version of something; their features represent features of all subsequent versions of the same thing. Qualities of all females and males, in other words, are revealed in the qualities of the first female and male according to the Israelite storyteller. Eve as mother, for example, prefigures and models the maternal role of all women (Everywoman Eve). At the same time, Eve and Adam are proto-types, presenting the roles of a specific group: Israelite women and men in their Iron Age environment. Prototypal qualities are not necessarily universal—after all, the kind of farming described in the preceding chapter and prescribed in the text is hardly a universal economic system.

The first two humans appear in a mythic account at the beginning of a longer narrative that eventually takes us into real time. Although the Eden tale is couched in temporal language because it presents human life, its characters did not exist in real time but rather, as first humans, myth-ically represent all humans.

Setting

Just as the characters do not exist in real time, their Edenic locale is not the Iron Age reality described in chapter 3. Life in the real Israelite world, outside the garden, comes only at the tale's end. The narrative itself unfolds in an imagined place, a garden that would have seemed powerfully attractive to agrarians living in the unforgiving highlands of Palestine. The "garden" of Genesis 2–3 and elsewhere in the Hebrew Bible is not what the word conjures up for most of us: vegetable gardens with plants and herbs in neat rows; or an array of ornamental trees and flowers with a profusion of flowers and scents. The biblical imagery associated with gardens fits neither of these images.

What then is the setting of Eden? What does "garden" connote? The Hebrew noun is *gan*. It appears forty-one times in the Hebrew Bible, and its feminine form (*gannah*) appears another sixteen times. Many of these occurrences, as we might expect, are in Genesis 2 and 3. But the word appears often enough elsewhere so that looking at other contexts reveals the salient features of gardens for the Israelites.[29] The fundamental quality of gardens is revealed by the root from which *gan* and *gannah* are derived—a verb appearing eight times and meaning "to protect, surround." Gardens are safe, protected places, surrounded by walls or fences (e.g., 2 Kgs 20:6; Isa 31:5), quite different from the open fields of Israelite peasants.

Other features of gardens in biblical texts contrast sharply with agrarian reality:

- Water in gardens comes from a variety of sources, such as fountains, wells, or streams. Supplies are plentiful and permanent—not like the unpredictable and often insufficient highland rains. In fact, abundant water was the sine qua non of gardens. Life in the eschatological future, as one prophet imagines, will be "like a saturated garden, like a spring of water, whose waters never fail" (Isa 58:11). Eden has four rivers, providing an unending and copious water supply, but rain in Eden is never mentioned.
- Vegetation in gardens consists of trees, none of which are the olive trees or other species important for the Israelite subsistence economy.
- A garden's trees are ornamental and grow in thickly forested groves. Sometimes they are fruitful, but their fruits are luxury fruits and not dietary staples (e.g., Num 24:6; Ezek 31:8).
- Gardens are the domains of the elite, with only the privileged—royalty or, mythically, God—having access to them (e.g., Gen 13:10; Esth 1:5; 7:8; Ezek 28:13).
- Perhaps their most important feature in relation to the Eden story is that gardens are planted (e.g., Jer 29:5), as is the Eden garden (Gen 2:8), or "made" (e.g., Amos 9:14)—but never worked. Gardens are low-maintenance spaces, sustaining growth with little or no human involvement. They resemble the contemporary concept of "permaculture," a term for

systems that are self-sustaining, or nearly so, because they follow internal mechanisms for productivity in relation to their natural habitats.[30] The Edenic garden similarly requires minimal human intervention, although this is not clear from English translations. God instructs the primeval person "to till it and keep it" (Gen 2:15), and "till" implies agricultural activity: digging into or plowing the soil. However, the two Hebrew verbs (ʿbd; šmr) in that phrase do not denote independent actions but function together in what is called a hendiadys. In adjective-poor Hebrew, this figure of speech allows for two words joined by "and" to form a single idea—in this case, the minimal work required to maintain self-sustaining growth. Like the keepers of the royal forest in Nehemiah 2:8, the first couple watches over the Eden garden; they are keepers not cultivators. Their function is a world apart from the vicissitudes of agrarian life in the Mediterranean basin (described in chapter 3), just as Eden is of a different order than the often dry and rocky fields and pasturage of the Palestinian highlands.

In short, the Eden garden is diametrically opposite to Israelite reality. Like the royal parks of Mesopotamian culture, it is a place of pleasure for the elite, not the site of arduous peasant agriculture.[31] Keeping this in mind, along with the nature of Genesis 2–3 as a mythic and etiological tale accounting for the harsh reality of life in the agrarian highlands, we can turn to some specific features of its language and message, especially as they relate to the first woman.

Creation of the Woman

Any consideration of female and male in the Hebrew Bible, whether deity or human, must take into account that Hebrew is a gendered language. All nouns are either feminine or masculine; and there is no neuter, as there is in German, for example. Thus some grammatically masculine or feminine Hebrew words can refer to items we would consider neutral, like grass (m.) or shoe (f.). Other terms of either gender, in referring to people, can have an inclusive or general meaning. Masculine forms are particularly problematic in Bible translations because they are sometimes rendered as masculine when the context indicates they have a collective, common-gender sense. Modern translators do not always recognize or acknowledge its neutrality or inclusiveness. But ancient audiences, hearing a masculine noun, would have known not to take it at face value.[32]

Take, for example, the passage in the Genesis 1 creation story where God creates *'adam* in the divine image (vv. 26 and 27). Older translations use "man" for this grammatically masculine word. The NRSV and other newer versions realize that God is creating all people, both female and male; and they render *'adam* as "humankind," "human beings," "humans," or "people." Using inclusive language here is not a matter of being politically correct but rather of acknowledging that the term signifies generic humankind and not a (male) individual. It collectively designates human beings, differentiated from God and animals.

But what about the Eden episode, where God creates a living being from a clod of dirt, as deities do in other ancient Near Eastern creation stories? God forms an *'adam* (Gen 2:7), here virtually always rendered "man" because the narrative then describes how a woman is formed from part of the *'adam*. That first being would have to have been male, so the reasoning goes, if the second is female. But is that necessarily so? This is an important question because assuming male priority is so often used to privilege males—if men were created first, they must be more important. We need to look further at *'adam*, first by noting a literary feature and then by addressing the issue of whether it connotes a man or a generic human.

The translation "man" ignores a striking and significant wordplay between *'adam* and the substance used to form *'adam*, namely *'adamah*, "[arable] land," a term designating cultivable land. The creation of *'adam* from *'adamah* signals the integral connection between the first human's bodily substance and the cultivated ground that provides subsistence.[33] The *'adam* is not created in Eden but is placed there only after the garden is created (Gen 2:8). The *'adam* of 2:7 anticipates conditions outside Eden, which are hinted at in Genesis 2:5 (cf. 3:17-19, 23), a verse discussed in chapter 5. It signifies humanity as cultivators of the arable land outside of Eden: agrarians were to be of the same material essence as the soil of their fields. This agricultural connection is intensified because the human is created not just from the "ground" but rather from the "dust of the ground." "Dust" (*'apar* in Hebrew) is a misleading translation; the word here means loose dirt. Dense sun-baked soil had to be broken into clumps or clods (by plowing or hoeing, as noted in chapter 3) before crops could be grown. In the agricultural imagery of the Eden story those clumps of loose soil, not powdery dust, are the substance from which God forms humanity. "Clods" would better represent the Hebrew.[34]

Virtually all English translations of Genesis 2:7 fail to capture the literary connection between 'adam and 'adamah. Using earth/earthling or human/humus would better capture the Hebrew wordplay. (English "human" is not the combination of hu with man; derived from Latin humanus, it is probably related to both homo, "man," and humus, "earth"). The translation might be:

> Then God Yahweh formed the *earthling* [or *human*] from clods of the *earth* [or *humus*] and breathed into its nostril the breath of life; and the *earthling* [or *human*] became a living being.

These two words, 'adam and 'adamah, are not simply a pun; they are organically connected. And they are not mere labels; they are also signifiers of the very essence of what they designate. The use of 'adam indicates that the essence of human life is not its eventual classification into gendered categories but rather its organic connection to the arable earth, the 'adamah, that reddish-brown substance that can be cultivated to support life. Human life is inextricably related to that which makes life possible, arable land. Agricultural imagery shapes the details of the Eden account of human beginnings, as befits an agricultural people.

As an earth creature the 'adam is not inherently gendered. The word 'adam is a common, grammatically masculine biblical noun, appearing some 530 times beyond the opening chapters of Genesis. But it is not socially masculine; in none of those instances does it refer to a specific (male) individual but rather has an indefinite, generic sense, denoting a human being.[35] English translations routinely use "he" or "him" in sentences referring to an 'adam, but only for grammatical agreement and not because the noun denotes a male. But what about when a male character is named Adam? As already noted, that name does not appear in the Eden episode but rather comes in Genesis 4:25 (or 5:1), which itself may be a redactional addition.[36] Moreover, the name Adam (like Eve and many other biblical names) is more of a symbolic label than an authentic designation of an individual. In other words, the 'adam created by God in Genesis 2:6 likely represents a sexually undifferentiated first human. More specifically, given that the surgical procedure of Genesis 2:21-22 produces two gendered beings (Woman and Man), the prior 'adam is androgynous.

The concept of an androgynous first person resonates with its ancient Near Eastern context. In the dominant Mesopotamian conception, humanity originates from a single androgynous body made from clay that is the matrix for the two sexes.[37] A similar idea, albeit with different imagery, appears in ancient rabbinic literature.[38] An androgyne is a body with the nature or characteristics of male and female combined. But androgynes can be basically male and completed by the female, or basically female and completed by the male. Historically the former has dominated.[39] The Eden story belongs to that dominant tradition: the first human of Genesis 2:7 is androgynous and sexually undifferentiated but basically male and then becomes the male human of Genesis 2:23. At that point a Hebrew gender pair—*'iš* ("man") and *'iššah* ("woman")—designates the two people produced by God's surgery. This is similar to the Mesopotamian concept of humanity originating with one androgynous being (*amilu*), thus putting the "initial emphasis on *human* in contrast to deities and animals."[40] The essential distinctions at creation are those separating the human from the divine and from other living creatures.

The Eden account has a similar concern with those distinctions. After creating the single human (Gen 2:7), God places the human in the garden, with its magnificent trees and abundant water (Gen 2:8-15). God then instructs the person about what can and cannot be eaten (a term discussed below); with both female and male contained in this androgynous being, both are recipients of God's directives. But the creation of humanity is not yet complete. This etiological tale must account for the fact that humanity consists of female and male, alike yet not exactly the same.

Humanity, composed of two separate sexes/genders, is about to be launched; and the terminology establishes the relationship between the two. God wants the first person to have an *'ezer kenegdo*. A look at the two Hebrew words in this phrase—a noun (*'ezer*) and a prepositional phrase (*kenegdo*)—is revealing. The noun's root *'zr* means "to help." God is typically its subject, as when Jacob refers to the "God of your father, who will help you" (Gen 49:25), although it can also denote assistance (e.g., 2 Chr 32:3). The same is true for the noun. Which is it in the Eden story? The second word in the phrase solves the problem, for *kenegdo* means "corresponding to" or "on a par with." The two people will be neither superior nor subordinate to each other; the phrase connotes a nonhierarchical relationship. NRSV's "helper as a partner" and the New American Bible's "suitable partner" capture the sense of the Hebrew, especially because "partner" suggests that the two were once *part* of each other. "Counterpart" would be similarly apt in designating the second person as of the same essence as the first; the two complement each other. However, the phrase probably does not imply legal or social parity.

The same can be said for Genesis 1:26-27, where God creates humanity, both female and male, in the divine image. This passage has often been heralded in support of gender equality. Already in the nineteenth century first-wave feminists cited it as affirming "the eternity and equality of sex.... [with the] masculine and feminine elements, exactly equal and balancing each other."[41] However, like "counterpart," it probably concerns sexual and gender dimorphism as a feature of humanity but does not establish social equality of gendered humans.[42]

Back to 'ezer kenegdo. Yet another translation is possible, one that would retain the counterpart idea and also take into account that 'ezer can be derived from a Hebrew root meaning "to be strong, powerful" rather than the one meaning "to help."[43] The phrase would then be translated "powerful counterpart." Because women had considerable power in agrarian Israelite households in the Iron Age (see chapter 9), this reading is compelling.

Reading 'ezer kenegdo as counterpart or partner is also indicated by noting that God's first attempt at creating a second person fails (Gen 2:18-20). God first creates animals and birds, which are earth creatures created from the 'adamah but not counterparts. The God-human hierarchy established when God creates 'adam is now extended: God > human > animals/birds. Humanity has been differentiated from and stands between the creator and the creatures. And God goes back to the drawing board. To assure that the second would be a counterpart of the first, God makes one from the other (Gen 2:21).

Looking at the Hebrew terms for God's surgical procedure is instructive. But first, the translations. In virtually every rendering, God removes a "rib" from the human to make another one. The Hebrew word is ṣela' ("rib" or "side") and occurs some forty times in the Hebrew Bible, mostly in architectural contexts: the tabernacle texts of Exodus, and the 1 Kings and Ezekiel temple texts. In none of those other passages is the translation "rib" justified. Yet, like many of the technical architectural terms, it is used in several different ways and its meaning is unclear.[44] One usage (1 Kgs 6:34), apparently describing the two leaves of a double door, is intriguing. Used for large entryways, a double door consists of two doors, each about half the width of the door frame, each hinged to the door frame on its outer edge. The doors are identical, except that their hinges are on opposite sides. Together they form a wide door; alone they occupy only half the entryway and have no value. One by itself is only a door side, not a whole door. The imagery is remarkably apt for Eve and Adam. They are virtually the same, and their combination produces humanity; but a male or a female "side" without the other could never produce the whole.

Postbiblical sources are generally not helpful for studying Genesis 2–3, for, as already noted, their comments are often distortions or misreadings of the Hebrew text. Yet one early Jewish reading is worth noting in relation to *sela'*. The first-century CE philosopher Philo (discussed again in the epilogue), in his treatises on creation, generally views the first man more favorably than the first woman. However, in discussing Genesis 2:21-22, he makes a remarkable statement:

> What is the side [*pleura*] which He took from the earth-born man, and why did he mould the side into a woman? The literal sense is clear. For by a certain symbolical use of "part," it is called a half of the whole, as both man and woman, being sections of Nature, become equal in one harmony of genus, which is called man....woman is a half man's body. (*Questions and Answers on Genesis* 1.25)[45]

Aside from his contestable view that the first human was male, the idea of side, half of a whole, has survived in Philo's writings. His comment about equality refers to the physical body and the function of male and female in procreation, in accord with the dualistic thinking of his day (see the epilogue); but it nonetheless suggests an understanding of *sela'* as side rather than rib.

The very next verse likewise suggests that the first human's side, and not just one skeletal piece, became the second human: "bone of my bones, flesh of my flesh." In the Iron Age sense of anatomy, bones and flesh were a human's constituent pieces. The two persons produced by divine surgery are of common substances. And now that there are two humans, gender—or possibly sex—comes into view. The first androgynous being (Gen 2:7), more male than female, is now fully male; and he immediately proclaims that his counterpart is fully female: "this one shall be called Woman, for out of Man this one was taken" (2:23). He uses the words *'iš* and *'iššah* for Man and Woman.[46] Like *'adam*, the former is grammatically masculine but with maleness not intrinsic to its meaning. Appearing more than 2,000 times in the Hebrew Bible, its primary sense is to denote an individual who is representative of a group. Its male gender comes from the social context of its biblical uses, hence the typical translation "man." It is paired in this verse with the grammatically feminine *'iššah*, which is not actually the female form of *'iš* but functions that way, with woman as the counterpart to man. The assonance of the two words helps make that connection.

These terms mark social gender. But in this case they seem to represent physical sex too because of the etiology in the following verse (Gen 2:24): men leave their parents and cling to their wives and become "one flesh." This verse is often interpreted as referring to an original matriarchy or to the practice of matrilocal marriage (when a man joins his wife's family). However, it more likely provides closure to the creation of humanity, which began with the creation of the first human in 2:7. Now there are two humans, female and male; they are similar—one made of the other—yet different. They are now sexually differentiated so that they can (eventually, out of Eden) procreate. In sexual union they will become one flesh, echoing their original unity and sameness. The hierarchical relationship between parents and child is to be superseded by the union of a set of complementary individuals. Powerful Israelite patrilineality (see chapters 2, p. 21; 6, p. 108; and 10, p. 200) is trumped here by the procreative imperative of sexuality. This verse perhaps also functions as an etiology for pair-bonding (or marriage), with the impulse for sexual union situated in the primordial unity of the first human.[47] But the first reported sexual union does not take place in the garden. Life in Eden must first play out in a way that takes the first couple to the reality that includes procreation.

Life in the Garden

The deed that results in the banishment from Eden has been labeled "sin" since antiquity, although that word is absent from Genesis 2–3, as already noted. It first appears in the next episode, the account of Cain and Abel in Genesis 4. The Eve-Adam and Abel-Cain tales are part of a longer etiological narrative, ending in Gen 11:26.[48] Although these two tales are typically viewed as separate episodes, they can also be viewed together as the opening section of Genesis 2–11. Together they tell the story of the first family, offspring included. And together they account for the two subsistence modes known to the Israelites: agriculture, with its small but important animal husbandry component; and pastoral nomadism (which probably had a small agrarian component and thus was not pure pastoral nomadism).⁴⁹

The agrarian mode, despite its unrelenting difficulties (described in chapter 3), is accepted as normative throughout the Hebrew Bible. But not pastoralism. Pastoralists were often perceived negatively by settled peoples of the ancient world—for good reason. Living on marginal lands, they often depended in part, and often in unwanted ways, on nearby agrarians. They sometimes competed with farmers for pasturage or stole their animals.⁵⁰ Raids by Bedouin have plagued village farmers well into the twentieth century.⁵¹ Because pastoralists were a menace to peasant farmers, they were often considered adversaries. Pastoral groups on the desert fringes of ancient Palestine (e.g., Amalekites, Kedarites, and Midianites) are characteristically portrayed as enemies in the Hebrew Bible (e.g., Judg 6:3-6; Jer 49:28-32) and in other ancient Near Eastern literature. They appear as dangerous and inferior barbarians in classical literature.⁵² It is no wonder that prophetic texts contrast the wilderness habitat ("wasteland") of pastoralists with the Eden (e.g., Isa 51:3; Joel 2:3). The subsistence mode of semi-migratory peoples is the polar opposite of Eden, with its abundant water and lush growth. Cain the wanderer (Gen 4:14) is the archetypal pastoralist.

The narratives of Genesis 2–3 and of Genesis 4 are complementary episodes that together provide etiologies for the agrarian and pastoralist subsistence modes. Neither is Edenic. The difficult life of both is etiologically portrayed as the result of human misdeeds. However, from the agrarian perspective of the Israelites, pastoralism is far less desirable. The misdeed causing the agrarian reality, disobedience, is thus less reprehensible than the truly heinous act of murder, which leads to the endless wandering of transhumants. Fratricide deserves the label "sin." Sin comes knocking (literally "couching," i.e., "lurking," in Gen 4:7) at the door; Cain fails to resist its pull and is condemned to a migratory existence. Noting the absence of the word sin from Genesis 2–3 would be an argument from silence. However, because Genesis 2–3 and Genesis 4 can be considered together as the story of the first family, the first son emerges as the one to commit the first sinful deed. Later exegetes may have considered the disobedience of the first couple—especially Eve—a sin; but the biblical narrator of the primeval tales does not, nor do authors of other Hebrew Bible texts.

If sin is absent from its vocabulary, can a key term of the Eden episode be identified? Does its language reflect a theme of great significance for the Israelites but overlooked because of the dominant focus on human sinfulness?

One way to identify a theme is to note the recurrence of a word or phrase. Repetition is one of the rhetorical ploys of ancient Hebrew narratives for drawing attention to something important. A word used repeatedly for thematic purposes is called a "key-word" or "word-motif" (*Leitwört*).[53] This device differs greatly from English style, which emphasizes variation in vocabulary: "Whereas English prose composition eschews repetition...ancient Hebrew prose enjoys it."[54] Thus we don't always appreciate biblical repetition—if it is visible in English translations. But often it is not, for Hebrew roots can appear as both nouns and verbs, used together to form a repetitive pattern. A case in point is the oft-repeated term *'kl* ("to eat") in Genesis 2–3. This is the root of the Hebrew words for both "eat" and "food," two words that would not constitute repetition in English.

The root *'kl* appears more frequently than any other word in Genesis 2–3 except *'adam*—twenty-one times in relation to human consumption. This strikingly frequent recurrence makes eat/food a word-motif. The significance of its repetition is intensified because twenty-one is a multiple of seven, a sacred number in the ancient Semitic world. These features rhetorically signal an important theme: the Israelite concern about food. Anxieties about sufficient food supplies (see chapter 3, pp. 54–55) are given concrete form and dramatic emphasis in the frequent repetition of *'kl*, which would have had a powerful effect on its audience, as noted by the Jewish philosopher Martin Buber. In working on a translation of the Hebrew Bible into German in the 1920s, he attempted to preserve recurring terms because he recognized their dynamic quality: "The measured repetition that matches the inner rhythm of the text, or rather, that wells up from it, is one of the most powerful means for conveying meaning."[55]

This food/eat word-motif signals a major existential issue. The importance of food is also highlighted because the very first words a human hears are about eating (Gen 2:16-17). Note too that in the Genesis 1 creation account, as soon as humans are created, their food sources are announced as part of God's blessing (Gen 1:28-29). This role of eat/food in the opening chapters of the Bible has been overlooked because of translation issues as well as the focus on other themes. Moreover, contemporary readers are generally unaware of the food anxieties of biblical antiquity. Food is a concern for us in the developed world—but because we have too much, not too little. This impedes our ability to grasp that the Israelites could not contemplate the beginning of human existence apart from concerns about food. Food and humanity are intertwined—in the Eden story as well as in biological reality.

The food/eating theme in the Eden story also advances the narrative plot, serving as a vehicle for introducing the fateful act of disobedience. In signaling the integral relationship between sustenance and survival, it prepares us for the denouement, at the end of Genesis 3, when the first humans leave Eden and enter the real world. Their roles in that world are set forth in the etiological mandate of 3:16-19. Yet women's tasks in food production (see chapter 7, pp. 128-132) are anticipated in Eden. Both humans eat the forbidden fruit. The woman, however, is the one to hand it to the man—just as Israelite women provided edible foodstuffs to the members of their households.

What led the woman to take the fruit for herself and then the man? Her interaction with another character in the tale, the serpent, sets the stage for this disobedient act. The serpent of Eden is *not* the satanic being that it becomes in traditional interpretations, especially in Christianity and Islam (e.g., Rev 12:9).[56] (This later pejorative association is yet another of the misleading interpretive moves in traditions about the Eden tale.) The serpent character reflects the widespread human fear of snakes because of their danger to humans and animals and also because of the awe of this creature's mysterious ability to rejuvenate. The etiological outcome of the Eden story (in Gen 3:14-15) thus ends badly for the snake. God curses it and consigns it to its seemingly unnatural locomotion, slithering on the ground, and to its role as the enemy of humans.

Serpents are ambiguous creatures, with positive as well as negative elements as indicated by the term describing the serpent in the garden. It is called "more *'arum*" than the other animals. Like the serpent itself, the word *'arum* is ambiguous—it can have positive as well as negative connotations.[57] The typical translations "crafty" and "cunning" convey the negative aspects. Perhaps, because it has not yet received the negative qualities it receives in Genesis 3:15, the word for the serpent of Genesis 3:1 is better rendered "prudent" or "intelligent" as in Proverbs, where it typically appears as an antonym of someone foolish or simple (e.g., Prov 15:5). The perspicacious talking animal perceives the value of eating from the very tree declared off limits. It informs Eve that its fruit will make her "like God, knowing good and evil" (Gen 3:5) or, better, "knowing good and bad," meaning "knowing everything"—because "good and bad" is a *merism* (a figure of speech in which opposites denote everything in-between).[58]

Eating the fruit will give humans higher cognitive powers. Eve discerns
the tree's gastronomic potential and esthetic qualities, and the serpent
points out its possibilities for cognition.

The serpent speaks to Eve in this scene perhaps because of her intellect. Rather than a blot on her character, her dialogue with the reptile is a
function of her intellect. The biblical association of wisdom with the feminine, embodied in Woman Wisdom of Proverbs (see chapter 7, p. 138),
is foreshadowed.[59] The interaction between Eve and the serpent also gives
her the speaking part that, as already noted, exceeds Adam's. All told, the
woman in the serpent scene of Genesis 3:1-6 "both exhibits wisdom and
seeks greater wisdom."[60] Yet in eating the appealing fruit the first couple
makes a decidedly unwise move. They disobey God. The consequence is
not only mortality but also the reality of agrarian life anticipated at the
beginning of the Eden episode and prescribed in its closing section.

5

Eve out of Eden: Genesis 3:16

PERHAPS NO SINGLE verse of the Hebrew Bible is more troubling for issues of gender relations and women's roles than Genesis 3:16. Ever since the earliest translations of the Bible, this verse has been rendered in a way that reflects two persistent beliefs about women's lives outside the garden: first, women must suffer pain in childbirth; second, women must be subordinate to men. But would a contextual reading of 3:16 substantiate the traditional interpretations? This chapter begins by considering the information in Genesis 2–3 about the environment outside Eden and about the nature of the humans who will inhabit that real world. Then it turns to 3:16, first by looking at the translation traditions and then by examining the verse line by line. Finally, an aspect of the ancient context, which informs the reading of the last line of 3:16, is presented.

Outside of Eden: The Environment and the Humans

The first couple departs the garden of Eden to begin life in the real world familiar to the narrator and to the audience of the story. As an etiological tale, Genesis 2–3 (especially 3:16-19) accounts for the difficulties that Israelite agrarians face. The *inclusio* that frames the tale reveals that farming life awaits the first humans: the phrase "to till the ground" appears in 2:5 and 3:23. But 2:5 does more than indicate the agricultural mode of subsistence; by listing what God had *not* yet created, it anticipates its features:

1. GRAZING LAND: "no pasturage (*śiaḥ haśśadeh*) was yet on the earth (*'ereṣ*)"
2. AGRICULTURAL LAND: "nor had any field crops (*'eśeb haśśadeh*) yet sprouted"

3. RAIN: "For God Yahweh had not sent rain upon the earth (*'ereṣ*)"
4. HUMANS: "nor was there a human (*'adam*) to work the arable land (*'adamah*)"[1]

These four elements are essential for the highland agricultural system (described in chapter 3) that was the context for life outside Eden.

The first two elements are the two kinds of vegetation that supported ancient Israel's mixed agrarian economy. The first element (*śiaḥ haśśadeh*) is commonly rendered "plant of the field" (KJV; NRSV) or "shrub of the field" (NJPS). The word *śiaḥ* denotes the small bushes and shrubs that grow in semiarid or arid areas with too little rain for growing crops (see Gen 21:15). Those areas typically provide grazing land—pasturage—for animals, especially the goats and sheep forming the pastoral component of the Israelite agrarian economy. Thus "pasturage," which indicates the specific kind of field growth, is a preferred translation. The second element (*'eśeb haśśadeh*) refers to a different kind of vegetation: "field crops" (NRSV "herb of the field"), mainly the grains that were the major foodstuffs. This phrase recurs in God's words to the man in 3:18, which proclaims that these field crops (NRSV "plants of the field") are food for humans.

The third element is rain. The Israelite dry-farming system relied on rainfall; water from springs, ponds, or rivers is thus excluded from the anticipated reality. Rain will make both pasturage and field crops possible. But the latter depends also on human labor, necessitating a fourth element: a "human" (*'adam*) to work the arable land (*'adamah*). In designating cultivatable land, *'adamah* is a more specific term than the one used for the first element: *'ereṣ*, "earth," which often denotes earth as the antithesis of heaven (as in Gen 1:1; 2:4).[2] Also, the play on words (*'adam* and *'adamah*) in 2:5 anticipates the wordplay in the account of the creation of the first person from clods of dirt (*'adamah*) in 2:7.

The narrative proceeds to indicate that water covers the whole earth (Gen 2:6). God then creates the fourth element of Israelite life (Gen 2:7): *'adam*, the single, sexually undifferentiated human (divided into a woman and a man in Gen 2:21-23; see chapter 4, pp. 72–76). Next God plants the garden with wonderful trees (Gen 2:8-9); and a river that divides into the four rivers of Eden simply "flows" (Gen 2:10).

The creation of the first three elements is not specifically mentioned but is assumed in 3:17, when God proclaims that the arable land (*'adamah*) is "cursed" (Gen 3:17), meaning that farming it will be difficult. Also, in mandating the man's unending toil, God mentions the field crops (*'eseb haśśadeh*; in 3:18) to be grown on that problematic soil. Finally, in the closing words (3:23) of the *inclusio* demarcating the Eden tale, the man is sent out "to work the arable land from which he was taken" (my translation), words that echo the fourth element of 2:5. Life outside Eden is agrarian.

The narrative then provides more information about humans. The act of disobedience causing the first couple to be expelled from the garden gives them two attributes of full humanity. First, when they eat the forbidden fruit, their eyes "were opened" (in 3:7). According to the serpent's interpretation of the prohibition, verified by God (in 3:22), having one's eyes opened means gaining the ability to know everything (see chapter 4, pp. 79–80). They now have enhanced consciousness or higher cognitive powers; they become "wise" (cf. 3:6), which makes them like divine beings—as God says (3:22), they would become "like one of us." Second, in 3:7 the humans make clothes from fig leaves. Clothing is perhaps the most quintessential mark of human as opposed to animal life. Few societies lack some kind of body covering, no matter how minimal, whereas animals have only the outer layers of their own bodies. To modify the adage "clothes make the man," the Eden tale understands that clothes make us human. (The tale will have more to say about clothes.)

The humans are thus somewhat like God but differ from animals. Yet they share a feature of animal life that differentiates them from divine beings: their misdeed brings them mortality, as anticipated by the words *mot tamut*. The translation of those words—"you shall die" (2:17; 3:4)—is misleading. The Hebrew words are a double verbal form of the verb "to die," with the repeated verbal root indicating intensification. Thus the double verb probably does not mean that the disobedient couple will drop dead on the spot—otherwise God would have lied to them.[3] Rather, mortality for humans will be initiated. Like all other creatures, individual humans will not live forever; life outside Eden means loss of access to the life tree that might grant them immortality (3:22, 24). Yet their species will survive through procreation.

Procreation becomes explicit immediately after God's words to the couple in Genesis 3:16-19 but before the departure from Eden. In 3:20 the woman is named *ḥawwah*, "Eve." Based on the root "to live," her name means "life-giver"; as the first woman, Eve thus signifies the maternal potential of all women. The etymological explanation of the text calls her the "mother of all living," making her the "vehicle for human permanence and eternity."⁴ That the man names her is often considered an act of domination, but the story line requires it.⁵ Humans, not God, give names in this story (also 2:18); and the man is the only other human. The man realizes (now that his eyes are open!) that life will continue through pro-creation and gives her an etymologically appropriate name.

The next verse (3:21) indicates the place of humans in the created realm. God makes proper "garments" for the first couple and "clothed them." Clothing is not simply a protection from the elements; it can also indicate status. Judging from its use elsewhere in the Hebrew Bible, the word (*ketonet*) used here for garment denotes an article of clothing sig-nifying a special position. And the causative form of the verb "clothe" (*lavaš*) is typically used when someone is being invested to a role with status.⁶ For the first couple, fig leaves won't do.

The Eden tale thus establishes the special status of humans—having wisdom like divine beings but being mortal like animals. It also makes it clear that women will have children. Yet these features don't tell the whole story of Eve's life out of Eden. What will agrarian life be like for Everywoman Eve? Genesis 3:16 provides the answer; it specifies the dif-ficult life of Israelite women that, along with the challenges facing men, likely prompted the etiological tale. A look at some of the translations of that verse indicates the issues surrounding its interpretation.

Genesis 3:16 in Translation

The Bible is the most translated book in existence. People have been translating the Bible for over two millennia, and there is no end in sight. Some of the translation energy stems from the desire to make the Bible available in every possible language. New translations are also necessary because of changes over time in the vocabulary and style of the lan-guages into which the Bible is being translated. The "thee" and "thou" of the King James Version (KJV), for example, are archaic; and some of its words are obsolete. In addition, new data about ancient Hebrew frequently become available, making more accurate translations possible. And archaeology, which continually expands our knowledge about the biblical world, helps determine the accuracy of words chosen to represent Hebrew terms.

Thus there is no such thing as a final, fully accurate translation of the Hebrew Bible. Translations themselves are interpretations, for words do not always have an exact equivalent in another language. Similar issues arise with differences in syntax and style, as for the use of repetition noted in the preceding chapter. Experts are constantly trying to find better and more precise ways to render the Hebrew text. Thus it is always incumbent on exegetes to reexamine texts, especially those fraught with meaning, in their original language. Genesis 3:16 is one such text. Examining it anew may reveal readings that fit the Hebrew text and context better than do existing translations. But first, some examples of ancient and more recent versions.

The oldest translation, from Hebrew to Greek, was begun in the late third century BCE and is known as the Septuagint. For Genesis 3:16 it reads:

> I will greatly increase your pains and your sighing. In pain shall you bring forth children. And your turning shall be to your husband, and he shall rule over you.[7]

The Vulgate (Latin) translation of the fourth century CE (see chapter 4, pp. 64–65) gives this reading:

> I will multiply your toils and your conceptions; in grief you will bear children. And you will be under the power of your husband, and he will rule over you.[8]

Both translations take the two nouns in the first clause as two objects of the verb ("multiply"), a construction considered below. Moreover, the Vulgate's translation of these two words is unique among all the translations I examined in not assigning childbirth pain to Eve; this may be the best way to understand the Hebrew, as will become clear. However, in his commentary on Genesis, the translator of the Vulgate (Jerome) argues that this verse denotes a woman's "pain"[9]; and this commentary had an enormous influence on subsequent exegetical and homiletic traditions.[10] Moreover, the presence of the phrase "under the power of your husband" (Latin *sub viri potestate*) gives a hierarchical cast to the Vulgate. The translation of an unusual Hebrew word with "power," like the Septuagint rendering ("turning") of the same word, is puzzling; both are discussed further below.

These early translations feature women's pain and subordination. Fast forward to English translations, which are similar. These examples include Jewish, Catholic, and Protestant translations.

A perennial and still influential best seller is the classic King James Version (KJV), which celebrated its 400th anniversary in 2011. Like the Septuagint and Vulgate, it retains the Hebrew syntax of the first line of 3:16 better than other translations:

> I will greatly multiply thy sorrow and thy conception; in sorrow thou shalt bring forth children; and thy desire shall be to thy husband and he shall rule over thee.

The Jerusalem Bible, a Roman Catholic translation that appeared in French in 1956 and in English ten years later, gives a particularly harsh twist to the last line:

> *I will multiply your pain in childbearing,*
> *You shall give birth to your children in pain.*
> *Your yearning shall be for your husband,*
> *yet he will lord it over you [emphasis mine].*

A more recent Roman Catholic translation, the New American Bible, softens the last line but retains the language of pain and domination:

> *I will intensify the pangs of your childbearing;*
> *in pain shall you bring forth children.*
> *Yet your urge shall be for your husband,*
> *and he shall be your master.*

So too does the New Jewish Publication Society translation (NJPS), completed in 1962:

> *I will make most severe*
> *Your pangs in childbearing;*
> *In pain shall you bear children.*
> *Yet your urge shall be for your husband*
> *And he shall rule over you.*

A translation widely used in college and university courses and by most mainline Protestant denominations, the New Revised Standard Version (NRSV) was released in 1989 and is used in this book (unless otherwise specified). The NRSV reads:

> *I will greatly increase your pangs in childbearing;*
> *in pain you shall bring forth children,*
> *yet your desire shall be for your husband,*
> *and he shall rule over you.*

The best-selling English translation (according to units sold in 2010)[11] is the New International Version, completed in 1978 and revised in 1984. It provides:

> *I will greatly increase your pains in childbearing;*
> *with pain you will give birth to children.*
> *Your desire will be for your husband,*
> *and he will rule over you.*

Finally, the widely used New Living Translation (second edition, 2004) aims to use contemporary language. Atypically among modern English versions, it reads "pregnancy" for the second noun in the first clause (as do the Vulgate and KJV); and it gives alternative readings for the second half of the verse:

> I will sharpen the pain of your pregnancy, and in pain you will give birth. And you will desire to control your husband, but he will rule over you.
> (Or: And though you will have desire for your husband, he will rule over you.)

These translations have somewhat different vocabulary and syntax, but they consistently have God assign childbirth pain and subordination to Eve and thus to all women. The translations of this verse exhibit the self-perpetuating quality often characterizing Bible translations, with previous translations influencing later ones. Translators may strive to provide "new" or "fresh" renderings but virtually always consult existing ancient and modern versions. Especially when passages are very familiar, new translations tend to be very similar to previous ones. This relative consistency over time does not necessarily mean that traditional renderings are the most accurate ones. A fresh look at Genesis 3:16, which prescribes the reality of life for Everywoman Eve, is warranted.

God's Words to the Woman: Genesis 3:16

The grammar of this verse presents no special problems. However, because both its syntax (the way the words of a clause relate to each other) and the meanings of some of its words entail interpretive choices that can be contested, more appropriate renderings may be possible. The options of syntax depend to a certain extent on the meaning of the words, and thus sensitivity to the lexical possibilities is especially important. Looking at how certain words are used in analogous contexts elsewhere in the Hebrew Bible will help identify the translation nuance best suited for this verse.

God's words to the woman in Genesis 3:16 are situated between God's words to the serpent and to the man. All three are poetic, and each begins with a brief prose introduction identifying the intended recipient. However, there are some differences.[12] One is that God's address to the woman is shorter, but assigning any significance to the relative brevity would be speculative. Another difference is that God tells both the serpent and the man—but not the woman—that they will be assigned hardships because of something they did (Gen 3:14, 17). One can conjecture about this too, wondering whether the woman's confession to God in verse 13 preempts the necessity for God to assign blame. One more difference is that only the serpent (and the ground, in 3:17)—but neither the woman nor man—is cursed. This perhaps implies that God is not making humans intrinsically subject to evil or misfortune.

As a poetic unit (following the narrator's introduction: "To the woman he said"), Genesis 3:16 can be subdivided in various ways. Here it is divided into four lines as in most English translations. These poetic lines exhibit the parallelism—correspondence between elements and thus ideas of successive poetic lines—that is a fundamental feature of Hebrew poetry.[13] Because parallel elements are rarely if ever exactly equivalent, the meaning of the first of parallel elements is amplified by successive ones. Parallel lines develop a thought, and sets of parallel lines typically present related concepts. Understanding these features of parallelism is important for appreciating the dynamics of the successive lines of this verse.

A Close Reading of Lines 1 and 2

The first line (NRSV, "I will greatly increase your pangs in childbearing") has four words in Hebrew. The first two are verbal forms of the root *rbh* ("to be great, big, numerous"); together they serve to empha-size or strengthen the action represented by the verb. Because English has no syntactic equivalent to this verbal doubling, some translations add an adverb for emphasis (e.g., "I will greatly increase") whereas others use a single word (e.g., "I will multiply"). Although the addition of the adverb helps convey the presence of two words in the Hebrew, the use of "increase" or "multiply" is problematic because it assumes an existing state that is being intensified. How can something that doesn't already exist be augmented? Thus "I will make very great" is perhaps a better rendering, especially considering the nature of the two other words in this line.

The other two words are both nouns and are joined by the common conjunction *waw* ("and") prefixed to the second one. They are commonly translated with "pangs" (or "pain") followed by "in childbearing" (or "in childbirth"). These familiar renderings are rarely examined; after all, giv-ing birth is accompanied by painful uterine contractions. But does the Hebrew of this line really mandate pain? There are several problems with the usual translations.

The first is an issue of English grammar. Both nouns have the pro-nominal suffix "your"; and both are objects of the double verb. But they are not both translated as direct objects because sometimes two words joined by the connector "and" express what in English would be a noun and a modifier. A classic example of this device, called hendiadys, is "unformed and void" meaning "formless void" (Gen 1:2). Many trans-lations of Genesis 3:16 take the two nouns to be a hendiadys, meaning "painful childbirth." However, because "multiply your painful childbirth" or "increase your painful childbirth" would not be good English, transla-tions commonly use a noun plus a prepositional phrase: "your pain(s)/ pangs in childbirth/childbearing."

Hendiadys in this verse is possible—but it's not necessary. The Septuagint, quoted above, uses a compound direct object ("thy pains and thy sighing"); so do the Vulgate ("your toils and your conceptions") and the KJV ("thy sorrow and thy conception"). None uses "childbirth" for the second noun in this line. Does that second noun really mean childbirth? Probably not. For one thing, the Hebrew Bible has a fairly nuanced vocabulary for the stages of procreation, with separate terms for conception, pregnancy, labor, and delivery. The second noun (*heron*) means pregnancy, not birth.[14] Often used with the term for sexual inter-course, it signifies the beginning of pregnancy, as when Abraham has sex with Hagar and she becomes pregnant (Gen 16:4). Another reason to reject "childbirth" as a translation relates to the parallelism of the first two lines. The second line does refer to childbirth. Because exact synonyms are rarely used in parallel lines, the second line develops the first, augmenting it in some way but not repeating it. The mention of bearing children in the second line thus precludes a reference to childbirth in the first. Again, "pregnancy" is a better translation of *heron*: God is proclaiming that women will have numerous pregnancies.

But what about the first noun (*iṣṣabon*)? If it means "pain," as most translations indicate, the first line would be proclaiming painful pregnancy. Yet normal pregnancies involve discomfort but are not particularly painful, and no biblical passage mentioning pregnancy associates it with pain. If "pregnancy" is the better translation of the second noun, the first one cannot be "pain." In fact, *iṣṣabon* never means childbirth pain in other biblical texts. The biblical vocabulary for that kind of pain offers three other words (*ḥbel*; *ḥyl*; *ṣir*); these words appear often in childbirth imagery (e.g., in Ps 48:6 [Heb. 48:7]; Jer 6:24; 22:23; 50:43; Isa 13:8; 21:3; 66:7) but *iṣṣabon* does not.[15] Just as the second noun does not indicate childbirth, the first noun does not denote pain.

Then what does it mean? Its verbal form (*ṣb*) appears fifteen times in the Hebrew Bible and refers to *emotional* or *mental distress*, not physical pain.[16] For example, an abandoned woman is "grieved in spirit" (Isa 54:6). One text does involve physical pain (Eccl 10:9), but it refers to lacerations rather than the accompanying pain and is probably from a different root.[17]

As for nouns, five noun forms in addition to *iṣṣabon* occur in the Hebrew Bible:

• Like the verb, one (*aṣṣebeh*), denotes *mental anguish* or suffering (e.g., Prov 10:1; Job 9:28).
• The second (*oṣeb*) similarly indicates a troubling state, or *suffering* (e.g., Ps 139:24). In one passage it is part of a wordplay on the name Jabez, a man who wants to avoid suffering even though his mother had suffered at his birth (1 Chr 4:9-10).
• The third (*ma'aṣebah*) refers to a place of *suffering* or torment (Isa 50:11).
• The fourth (*aṣeb*), used only once (Isa 58:3), denotes *laborers*.
• The fifth (*eṣeb*) once means *mental anguish* (Prov 15:1) and three times refers to physical *labor* (e.g., Ps 127:2, which perhaps alludes to Gen 3:17 in depicting the difficult *labor* required to produce food [literally,

"bread"]). It also appears in the second line of Genesis 3:16, considered below.

Four of these nouns represent either *mental anguish* (as does the verb) or *physical toil*, but not both. The fifth apparently can denote either. None, with the dubious exception of the suffering of Jabez's mother, refers specifically to physical pain. The two concepts—anguish and toil—perhaps come from different roots.[18] Or they may be semantically connected because onerous physical toil of the kind necessitated by ancient Israel's environment (see chapter 3) all too often caused frustration and anxiety, that is, mental anguish. Moreover, the Septuagint renders both *'iṣṣabon* of the first line of 3:16 and *'eṣeb* of the second line with *lype*, a Greek word that can refer to mental anguish as well as bodily distress, rather than with one of the two Greek terms associated specifically with childbirth pain.[19] The usual English translation ("pain") of both the Septuagint and the Hebrew is misleading.

Now, back to *'iṣṣabon*, the sixth noun from the root *ʿṣb*. It appears only twice in the Hebrew Bible besides 3:16. In the next verse, 3:17, God tells the man that growing crops will involve *'iṣṣabon*, "toil." That this refers to exhausting physical labor and not simply "difficulty" seems certain in light of its third usage, Genesis 5:29, which refers obliquely to the Eden story. Noah's name is linked to "comfort," for Noah will offer comfort to people who, because of the cursed arable land, are burdened with "work and the toil (*'iṣṣabon*) of our hands." The word "toil" breaks up a common biblical phrase, "work of the hands," with "work" meaning agrarian labor (e.g., Exod 23:16; Judg 19:16; Hag 2:17). "Work" and "toil" together convey the great difficulty of agrarian labor.

Because *'iṣṣabon* means "toil"—not "pain" and not simply "work"—in the other two passages in which it appears, the *'iṣṣabon* proclaimed for the woman in the first line of 3:16 similarly denotes *exhausting* physical labor. Thus the first line consists of the double verbal form "I will make great," followed by two direct objects: "toil" and "pregnancy." Women out of Eden will work hard and also have many pregnancies. God is mandating women's role in production and reproduction. Note that the Vulgate understood it this way: "I will multiply your toils and your conceptions." Jerome, good Hebraist that he was and despite his misogyny (see chapter 4, pp. 64–65), understood labor rather than pain, pregnancies rather than childbirth. (However, as already noted, his influential commentary on Genesis mentions "pain.")

Now what about the second line of the verse (NRSV, "in pain you shall bring forth children")? It consists of three words in Hebrew: a prepositional phrase (one word) followed by a verb and its object. Because it is parallel to the first line, its subject matter is similar. The pregnancies of the first line are paired with having children in the second line. The verb is *yld*, often translated "to bear," which generally means having rather than bearing children. Men too become parents. In biblical genealogies, male ancestors "beget" offspring (e.g., Gen 5:6; NRSV "became the father of... " doesn't do justice to the Hebrew). When *yld* does refer to a mother giving birth, it is usually used intransitively; for example, Rachel asks her handmaid to "bear" (i.e., "give birth") on her knees (Gen 30:3). When followed by a direct object as in 3:16, where it precedes "children," it means becoming a parent.

The noun at the beginning of the second line is prefixed by the preposition "with" and is typically translated "pain." However, that noun is *'eṣeb* and, like the related word *'iṣṣabon* ("toil") in line 1, denotes either mental anguish or work, not pain. Which might it mean here? Because words in parallel poetic lines are usually not synonymous, it likely signifies mental anguish rather than toil: the stress or exhaustion accompanying parenthood. The Vulgate's rendering, "in grief you will bear children," seems to have this meaning; Jerome understood mental anguish rather than physical pain. Yet, because the semantic range includes toil, it may simultaneously express that notion too. Perhaps "hardship" would convey that both anguish and work accompany parenthood.

The parental stress of ancient Israelite agrarians was not like today's child-rearing anxieties, as parents face the challenge of raising competent children with good values, although those goals are arguably always part of parenting. Rather, as explained below in discussing infant mortality, the mental suffering of parenting was likely produced by the difficulty of keeping newborns alive. Because of high infant mortality rates in the ancient world, anxiety about the viability of one's offspring would have been considerable.

One final comment about the semantic range of these words for mental anguish and hard work. Pain may hover in the background. Physical distress inevitably accompanied the arduous toil of both women and men. An ethnographic description of Greek peasantry reports that "the lot of man is toil and sweat and exhaustion—torments (βάσανα) as the villagers put it."[20] Some of women's household tasks involved muscle and joint trauma that today is labeled repetitive stress syndrome (see chapter 7, pp. 129–130, and epilogue,

p. 208). Like God's words to the man in 3:17-19, the first two lines of 3:16 reflect the difficulties facing agrarian Israelites. Emotional anguish and physical pain are not entirely separate experiences or concepts. Perhaps "hardship" also captures both kinds of distress as well as toil.

A Close Reading of Lines 3 and 4

Appropriate translation is also an issue for lines 3 and 4 of Genesis 3:16. They are syntactically connected to line 2 and to each other. Both are introduced by the conjunction *waw*, usually rendered "and" (but sometimes omitted). Its presence indicates that lines 3 and 4 are related to the first two lines and also connected to each other. Thus God's words to the woman all relate to household work and generational continuity.

Line 3 (NRSV, "yet your desire shall be for your husband") has three words in Hebrew. The first is the preposition "to" (or "toward"), prefixed by *waw* (translated "yet" in the NRSV), and the second is a noun with the suffix "your." The noun is the common biblical word *'iš*, which, as explained in chapter 4, usually is a generic term for a person as a representative of a group but in some contexts denotes a male person, as here, where it means "man" as part of a gender/sex pair.[21] In Genesis 2:23-24 *'iš* is used with *'iššah* for the joining of male and female for reproduction (see chapter 4, p. 73). Thus *'iš* (rather than *'adam*) is used in this verse—for it is connected to sexuality and thus reproduction, which is one of the themes of the first two lines of 3:16 and arguably the whole verse. Translating *'iš* as "husband" rather than "man" is common in English translations; similarly, *'iššah* (which means both "woman" and "wife") is usually rendered "wife" (e.g., in Gen 3:17). These translations seem anachronistic for Genesis 2–3, for the social processes shaping marriage do not yet exist; "man" and "woman" are preferable. Either way, the "your" attached to those nouns in Genesis 3 is not an indication of legal ownership or possession. Rather, "your" denotes the pair-bonding of the primal couple—one is part of the other, a sexually dimorphic pair originating from a single human.

What about the third word in line 3? What is directed "to your husband/man"? First, note that the line lacks a verb and thus expresses a stative, already existing condition that the woman directs to her partner. The third word is *tešuqah*, a rare biblical word consistently translated "desire" in this verse. Virtually all modern commentators take it to mean sexual desire, chiefly on the basis of its use in one of the two other passages in which it occurs. The Cain-Abel episode uses it (Gen 4:7) for the strong attraction or "desire" that sin has for Cain. And in the Song of Solomon, the woman asserts that her lover's passionate "desire" is for her (7:11). In all three texts *tešuqah* seems to indicate intense feelings, and they are erotic in Genesis 3:16 and the Song. Sexual desire, the precursor of the pregnancies and childbirth of lines 1 and 2, is what the woman directs to the man: "To your man is your desire."

But wait—some ancient versions and interpretations understand it differently. The Septuagint has "your turning [or, returning] shall be to your husband." Why such a different reading? Perhaps the Septuagint translator had a different Hebrew text, one that has *tešubah*, which is similar to *tešuqah* and means "turning/returning." Another possibility is that the translator simply did not know the rare Hebrew word and assumed it was the word for turning/returning.[22] Either way, the woman would be (re)turning to the man, thereby restoring the primeval condition of bodily unity, which existed before God divided the first person into female and male and is subsequently restored by the pair-bonding (sexual) unity of female and male, "bone of my bones and flesh of my flesh" (Gen 2:23).

As for the Vulgate, Jerome is a minority of one; his misogyny apparently comes into play in his translation: "you will be under the power of your husband." However, in his commentary on Genesis, Jerome reveals his understanding of the Hebrew as "turning."[23] And virtually all other ancient translations, like the Septuagint, and also early Christian and Jewish exegetical traditions understand the text to say turning or returning.[24] Rather than focus on sexual desire, they have the woman (re)turning to the man. They apparently understood the rare *tešuqah* to have a semantic range overlapping with *tešubah*, with the woman being drawn (as by desire?) to the one to whom she is turning/returning.[25] Thus to understand the third word of line 3 as unbridled sexual passion, as modern commentaries typically do, seems unjustified.[26] These commentaries have probably been influenced by later translation traditions, beginning with the earliest English versions (the sixteenth-century Tyndale and Geneva Bibles and seventeenth-century KJV), which have "lust" or "desire." (It is not clear when or why the shift from "turning/returning" to "desire" took place.)

Understanding *tešuqah* as turning/returning provides another connection between God's words to the woman and God's words to the man. Just as there is a lexical link between "toil" in this verse and in verse 17, so too does the woman's "returning" in this verse resonate with the man's mortality—his "return" to the ground, or its clods, which appears twice in verse 19. The words there for return (*šub* and *tašub*) are from the same root as *tešubah*, the word that apparently overlaps semantically with the *tešuqah* of verse 16. Together, the idea of returning for both the woman and the man creates a fascinating echo—even a reversal—of the creation of humans. Life outside of the garden will mean that: (1) the female is rejoined with the male, temporarily undoing the separation of 2:22-24 and thus allowing for procreation; and (2) the man will rejoin the soil (i.e., die), reversing the creation of humanity *from* the soil in 2:7. Procreation is accounted for, and individual human mortality is the concomitant.

This brings us to the fourth line, consistently rendered from antiquity to the present as "and he shall rule over you" (NRSV), or something similar. Perhaps more than any other text in the Hebrew Bible, this line has been used to justify gender hierarchy: divinely ordained female subservience and male dominance in all aspects of life. Its influence on sexual politics has been profound and persistent for over two millennia. What God tells the man in the next few verses about onerous physical toil has not always been taken literally and absolutized; but what God tells the woman has too often been treated as a dictum for all time. That is, commentators frequently contextualize God's words to the man, rightly seeing them as etiological statements accounting for the difficult lives of ancient Israelite agrarians in the context of a challenging environment. Yet God's words to the woman are virtually never contextualized. The classic treatment of von Rad, for example, mentions the Palestinian environment in relation to Genesis 3:17-19 but not for 3:16. He merely notes the woman's "severe afflictions and terrible contradictions" and her life of "humiliating domination."[27] Another commentator refers to this line as the cheerful acquiescence of the narrator (God) to the social order of female inferiority as the chattel of their husbands.[28] Modern exegetes and ancient expositors alike see the fourth line of 3:16 as a statement of divinely ordained patriarchal control of women in society. Feminist scholars follow suit.[29]

But is this long-standing understanding the only possible one? The line must be examined anew and then contextualized.

Like the preceding two lines, this one is short, just three Hebrew words. The first is the masculine singular pronoun "he" with the prefixed connector *waw* ("and"). This separate pronoun is not grammatically necessary, for subject pronouns are part of the verb in Hebrew. Perhaps it is used here simply to balance out the poetic line by adding another syllable. But it may also serve as a pronoun of emphasis.[30] The separate "he" would be calling attention to the subject of the verb—the man to whom the woman is turning.

The third word is the feminine pronoun "you," with an attached preposition: "(over) you." The crux is the second word, a verb from the root *mšl* ("to rule"). Occurring nearly eighty times in the Hebrew Bible, it indicates domination exercised by a wide range of people or places. They form a continuum from God as ruler of the world at one end (e.g., Ps 22:28 [Heb. 22:29]) and a person's self-control at the other (e.g., Prov 16:32).

An important issue in this verse is whether male control is to be absolute. Does someone who rules over another exercise that control in all circumstances? A negative answer is implied by the use of *mšl* in Exodus 21:8, where a man with authority over a female servant is not thereby entitled to sell her; his control has limits. Also, Israelite monarchic rule is, theoretically, subject to limitations (Deut 17:14-20). In Genesis 3:16 the limited scope of male rule is implied by the fact that the last two lines of this verse are grammatically and thus thematically connected to the first two. That is, the third line alludes to the sexual relations required for the pregnancies-and-birth theme of the first two lines; this last line develops that theme further, giving the man and henceforth all men mastery in marital sex—but not dominance in all aspects of life.

This reading has support in the interpretive tradition. As already noted, virtually all postbiblical translations and interpretations consider line 4 a divine mandate for general male domination and even male superiority. However, several modern scholars reject that idea and instead see the dominance in the context of the sexuality of the preceding lines. For example:

> No such expression of "male chauvinism" is, however, called for in the present context which deals exclusively with woman's sexual predicament. The passage has thus been consistently misunderstood as an assertion of woman's general subservience to man, whereas in reality the two parts [lines 3 and 4] of the second hemistich hang closely together....Medieval Jewish commentators had no doubt about the correct interpretation of the verse.[31]

Those illustrious medieval scholars—the eleventh-century commentator Rashi and the twelfth-century writer Ibn Ezra—did not see line 4 as a proclamation of general male domination.

Like the rest of Genesis 3:16-19, line 4 has an etiological function. It implies resistance on the part of women to sexual relations and so mandates that men overcome female reluctance. Why must men dominate sexually? The answer lies in the ancient context, specifically the infant and maternal mortality rates in Iron Age Palestine, considered in the next section. For now, the point is that to assume that this line establishes divinely sanctioned male supremacy in all aspects of life is to wrench it from its literary and life setting. Rather, it is part of a four-line sequence focusing on procreation. Moreover, to assume it means general male domination is to ignore Israelite household dynamics in which women exercised managerial power, making their relationship to their spouses complementary, not subordinate (see chapter 10). The typical translation of line 4—"and he shall rule over you"—may be lexically correct but does not convey the parameters of male rule: male control of female sexuality. Contextual issues as well as literary ones inform that meaning.

God's Words in Context

The discussion of the environment outside of Eden in the second section of this chapter drew on the description in chapter 3 of the difficulties facing Israelite agrarians. Those difficulties etiologically originate in God's punitive proclamation that men face arduous agricultural labor on land with compromised fertility (Gen 3:17-19). Genesis 3:16 similarly mandates labor for women—but they must also bear many children. In traditional societies everywhere peasant women are both workers and mothers. The Eden narrative sees both these female roles as onerous; and disobedience in the garden is the etiological cause.

It does not require much imagination, given the importance of leisure time and activities in our own lives, to understand why Israelite peasants of both genders would find unending days of toil unwelcome. But women generally have positive feelings about producing offspring. What makes the second of these roles, procreation, so problematic? Actually, procreation itself is not the problem in 3:16. Rather having many pregnancies and experiencing anguish in childbearing are given the negative spin because of the problems of procreation among Iron Age agrarians.

As for most agrarians, children were important for several reasons. They were an essential part of the household work force, especially because of the labor-intensive periods of Israelite cropping patterns (see chapter 3, pp. 50–52). Agrarians facing significant environmental constraints usually attempt to increase crop yields by cultivating more fields, thus securing additional resources for lean years; their labor needs would then increase, pushing households toward a larger number of offspring. Children were also needed because as adults they cared for parents who survived into old age; there were no senior centers for the elderly. Finally, inheritance (discussed in the next chapter) was also a significant issue. Households were defined by their cross-generational continuity, which requires an heir. Although eldercare and inheritance require only one child, preferably male, the labor needs essential for survival were best served by having several viable offspring.

Notice the word viable. Infant mortality rates factor into this discussion, for the number of times a woman was pregnant was related, at the least, to optimal family size. How many pregnancies were needed to produce the two to four children of the average nuclear family in ancient Israel (family size is considered in the next chapter), given the significant infant mortality rates?

Precise determination of mortality rates for both infants and adults in antiquity is problematic. For one thing, examining skeletal remains provides a skewed sample, for most come from the well-built tomb-caves of elites, who had better nutrition and lighter workloads than peasants and thus longer lives and healthier newborns. The simple shallow or pit graves of ordinary people have rarely been identified.[32] Another problem is that archaeologists in earlier generations were more interested in grave goods than bones, and their publications often lack meaningful presentation of osteological remains. Finally, the antiquities law in Israel since the late 1970s has made the excavation of tombs that might contain the bones of Jews or Israelites illegal. Despite these problems, reasonable estimates are possible using data from: (1) the few tomb groups from Palestine for which skeletal remains have been analyzed; (2) other ancient societies in the Mediterranean basin; and (3) ethnographic or archival records of premodern societies from the medieval period to the present.

Inadequate nutrition and the presence of endemic and epidemic disease (see chapter 3, pp. 53–58) to which children are especially susceptible a priori suggest that infant mortality was high. The data bear this out. Today, in the remote Wakhan Corridor in northeastern Afghanistan, infant mortality hovers around 60 percent.[33] Ancient Greece probably had an infant mortality rate of 50 to 70 percent, figures similar to the 50 to 60 percent mortality rate in medieval Italy.[34] Other mortality tables, without including the affects of endemic disease, suggest about 50 percent for the first five years of life.³⁵ A severe epidemic could make the rate even higher. The greatest risk is in the first year of life, but children remain vulnerable to disease and to problems resulting from inadequate nutrition for several more years. As high as these figures are, they do not take into account lost fetuses resulting from miscarriages (which today can terminate as many as 30 percent of pregnancies), preterm stillborns, and other complications of pregnancy.³⁶

Consequently, with a survival rate of about 50 percent, having three children survive beyond the age of five would have entailed as many as six pregnancies—or more if preterm losses are included. Estimates for ancient Greece suggest that simply replacing the population would have required every fertile woman to bear six children.³⁷

The more pregnancies a woman had, the greater her own risk of dying. Adult life spans in ancient Israel are suggested by estimates from around the Mediterranean basin. Bronze Age skeletal remains from a site near Jerusalem suggest a life span of 30 to 40 years for men and 20 to 30 years for women, with Iron Age life spans even shorter.³⁸ Data from a number of Palestinian sites suggest that life expectancies were shortest in the Iron Age.³⁹ A tomb group from the western Mediterranean, with the data for women and men combined, shows an expectancy of 23 years.⁴⁰ Estimates for ancient Egypt suggest 33 years for men and 29 for women. Combined male and female life spans are put as low as 20 years for ancient Greek peasantry; and in ancient Rome life spans were 25 years for men, somewhat less for women.⁴¹ These low estimates are not unreasonable, given the life expectancy in many third-world countries today—under forty in some African countries.⁴²

These shockingly low life expectancies are the result of including the deaths of infants and children. People who survived childhood would live beyond the averages. Still, life spans were relatively short compared to those in today's developed world; and, unlike today, men generally outlived women probably because the risks accompanying pregnancy, childbirth, and lactation meant greater female mortality rates. Ancient populations had virtually no way to deal with the complications of labor and delivery. Consider the grim situation in early modern Europe:

> A whole variety of conditions, such as haemorrhage, pelvic deformity, disproportion between the sizes of a child's head and the pelvis, severe abnormal presentations such as transverse lies, eclampsia and uterine inertia in labour, are likely to have posed problems

which were beyond the capacities of those attending the birth to
alleviate.[43]

Ancient Greek women were subject to these common complications,[44]
which would have affected Israelite women too. Even if delivery pro-
ceeded smoothly, mothers and their newborns were particularly susceptible to infections that were often fatal, for the ancients had no concept of
pathogens and the need for sanitation. In addition, inadequate nutrition
in pregnant and lactating women increased their vulnerability to infection
and disease.[45]

One more factor was the mother's age. Young mothers are at greater
risk for childbirth difficulties and death than are older ones, even today.
A recent UN publication reports that complications of pregnancy and
childbirth are a leading cause of teen deaths—in Latin America, for example, pregnant girls under sixteen are three to four times more likely to die
in childbirth than women in their twenties.[46] Although there is no direct
evidence about the average age of marriage in ancient Israel, information
from later periods and from elsewhere in the ancient world suggests that
girls married in their mid- or even early teens.[47] Even if young teenage
mothers survive childbirth, their offspring often have low birth weight
and other problems causing illness and sometimes death.

For all these reasons, the fate of the matriarch Rachel, who dies giving
birth to her second son (Gen 35:16-18), and of Bathsheba, whose first son
dies soon after birth (2 Sam 12:15, 19), would have been all too familiar
to Israelite women. Similarly, the eschatological hope that "No more shall
there be…an infant that lives but a few days" (Isa 65:20) would have
resonated with many women. Awareness of frequent infant and maternal deaths meant a general apprehension of losing one's newborn or succumbing to the risks of childbirth. An unwillingness to conceive—sexual
aversion, or pregnancy reluctance—is a common response to these issues.
The mandate in line 4 of Genesis 3:16 for men to control female sexuality
can be understood as a cultural measure to encourage or sanction multiple pregnancies. (Male control of female sexuality is further contextualized in chapter 10.)

An analogy from more recent times shows the reality of pregnancy
reluctance and society's response. In nineteenth-century France many
young women, aware of the suffering of motherhood, were reluctant to
marry or, when married, to have multiple offspring. Concerned about the
falling birthrate, French leaders believed that population increase was in

the national interest and thus provided government incentives for women to marry and have children.⁴⁸ In the Hebrew Bible, God's words proclaiming male control of female sexuality can be understood as a way to overcome pregnancy reluctance so that agrarian households would have essential offspring. In both cases the goal was motherhood in the service of a greater social interest.

Mandating motherhood in the service of society can be situated in anthropological perspective. Societies characteristically develop reproductive strategies appropriate to their demographic needs. Some encourage population growth if the reproductive rate does not meet the minimum levels for sustaining the population; others discourage it when overpopulation is disruptive or taxes the available resources. Increasing, decreasing, or maintaining the population often requires institutional or cultural sanction. In today's world we are familiar with institutional policies aimed to curb increase. In antiquity, it was not unusual for groups to develop myths or beliefs to support reproductive practices, usually ones encouraging reproduction, that benefit the group. "Customary beliefs and practices promoting fertility...are fundamental to the adaptive strategies by which agrarian parents maintain family food supply and obtain both current support and long-term personal security."⁴⁹ Cultural values encouraging childbirth to maintain or even increase population are embedded in Genesis 3:16.

The Hebrew Bible is not the only ancient document to reflect a demographic issue. A Mesopotamian text deals with the opposite problem, overpopulation, by promoting a decrease in human fertility. The early second-millennium BCE Atrahasis Epic has the gods instituting miscarriages, infant (and adult) mortality, and celibate vocations for women. These measures are in response to the "great noise of mankind," in other words, uncontrolled demographic increase and the ensuing social and economic problems. This text apparently was a response to recurring eras of overpopulation that strained the resources of the land.⁵⁰

Genesis 3:17-19 mandates exhausting labor for men, and 3:16 orders women to work hard and have multiple pregnancies. Together these passages reflect the Israelite environmental and demographic context. They explain and validate the hardships of agrarian life in Iron Age Israel.⁵¹ These etiologies exemplify the function of religious ideology in archaic societies: religious beliefs serve to legitimate and stabilize existing conditions or structures, especially ones that are difficult to establish or accept without the compelling and authoritative force of religion.⁵² Religious beliefs as ideology can have a generally benign function. They can also have a more pernicious function—explaining or condoning inequalities that supposedly contribute to a greater good. For example, they can support the exploitative power of religious and political elites by depicting their roles as divinely ordained.

It is beyond the scope of this discussion to explore where the Genesis 3 etiologies, or any biblical texts for that matter, would fit into this continuum between the benign and the exploitative (but see chapter 9 and the epilogue). To do so would mean considering the interpretive tradition too. For example, the ideology of the fourth line of verse 16 gives religious sanction to the sexual dominance of men to ensure adequate procreation; this is arguably a benign function in its ancient context. But it has produced an interpretive ideology of the general subordination of women. Neither the ancient function nor the interpretive development is attractive to most contemporary readers. But having the ideology of the text placed in a historically contingent context, in which it would have benefited the household and community, contests the validity of the interpretive ideology and highlights its positive function.

THIS DISCUSSION OF the four lines of Genesis 3:16 provides the basis for suggesting a translation, with accommodations to English syntax,[53] that may capture the meaning of the Hebrew:

> I will make great your toil and many your pregnancies;
> with hardship shall you have children.
> Your turning is to your man/husband,
> and he shall rule/control you [sexually].

The context of this verse is peasant life in the Iron Age, when female labor and fecundity were essential for the subsistence farming practiced by most Israelites. As explained in the last chapter, the first female and male are archetypes, signaling some essential qualities of all human beings: mortality and the ability to become wise. They are also prototypes of Israelite agrarians, modeling the separate but complementary roles of women and men in their Iron Age context. Eve initiates the productivity and procreativity of Everywoman Eve. The activities that comprise both these roles, which are explored in chapters 7 and 8, take place in the household—described in the next chapter—in which she lived.

6

Eve's World: The Household

WHERE DID EVERYWOMAN Eve live and work? The spatial and social contours of her life were the context for her everyday activities and inter-actions and for special occasions marking the rhythm of her life. The household was the social and material setting for her economic, social, and yes, even political and religious roles.

The monarchies of the Iron II period have garnered the lion's share of academic attention. Scholars tend to focus on institutional structures, their change over time, and their relation to other structures. They take a top-down view of the sociopolitical pyramid, giving less attention to lower levels: the tribes that compose the "state," the clans that compose the tribes, and only lastly if at all, the individual households that compose the clans. But the pyramid is widest at the bottom, for the household was the most numerous unit of society. Relatively few people had regular or even any contact with the processes of structures further up the pyra-mid. This is not to suggest that the overarching social and political insti-tutions had no impact on household life; rather, the day-to-day dynamics of household life were focused on subsistence activities, not on the poli-cies and practices of the other levels of society. As a quasi-independent unit, the household should not be considered functionally subordinate to clan, tribe, or monarchy. (Those larger units are considered in the second section of this chapter.)

The Israelite household was the immediate and determinative social context for everyone, sustaining and shaping daily existence for its mem-bers. As the basic unit of both production and consumption, it was the single most important economic and social unit; it was also an integral part of Israelite political and religious structures.[1] The household is the most salient feature of biblical antiquity for reconstructing and under-standing women's lives. Examining it provides a glimpse of their lives that otherwise would be impossible. Several decades ago, few social scientists and even fewer biblical scholars ventured to analyze households and their material and social dynamics (see chapter 2). But now, using archaeological discoveries, biblical texts, and ethnographic analogies, the household existence of most Israelite agrarians—women, men, and children—can be reconstructed.

There is a caveat, however. Looking at the household means avoiding the dangers of presentism, or present-mindedness, in which present-day experiences and assumptions color attitudes to the past. Life patterns in today's high-tech industrialized world differ significantly from those of ancient Israelite agrarians. Thus we must refrain from anachronistically applying current ideas or perspectives in considering women's lives in the biblical past. The third part of this chapter draws attention to presentist issues.

The Household

The context of the agrarian life of ancient Israelites was the "household." This word is not exactly synonymous with "family," although it is sometimes used to designate the people who constitute a living group. Nor is it the same as "house," the space in which people lived. The former takes into account the human component but not the material one; and the latter stresses the material component but not the human one. From an anthropological perspective, neither of those meanings alone or even together is sufficient.

A broader understanding of the term *household* begins by recognizing that it encompasses both humans and their "hardware," the physical aspects of daily life. But there's more—a critical aspect of a household was the set of functions or activities that made life possible. The household thus has three main components:[2]

- A material one: the dwelling in which people lived, all its installations and artifacts, its lands, and its animals. Its lands might be contiguous to the dwelling, but some fields and also structures, such as huts and burial places, might be at a remove from it.
- A human one: the kin group living in the domicile and using its material elements. The basic kin group was sometimes (usually in well-to-do households) augmented by outsiders—servants, slaves, or sojourners. However, the human component of the "typical" household

of this study would rarely have included people unrelated by birth or marriage.

- A performative one: activities performed by the household's women, men, and children (and occasionally others). These activities were the myriad processes required for the subsistence economy (see chapters 3 and 7). Household activities focused on economic ones: producing food, textiles, and many of the tools and installations necessary for household activities. In this respect, the Israelite household is similar to the *oikos*, a term used to designate the household as the basic *economic* unit of ancient Greek society. Processes relating to social, religious, and political life also were part of household life and did not necessarily operate independently of other activities. Social relations, for example, might be embedded in household economic activities.[3] Identifying and describing women's subsistence tasks are thus important steps in envisioning and evaluating other aspects of their household existence.

The first two components—the material and human ones—are discussed in the next two sections of this chapter; the installations and artifacts used or made by women are also discussed in chapters 7 and 8, which focus on the third component, women's household activities.

The Material Component: The Domicile and Other Features

The Hebrew Bible contains an incredibly detailed description of the abodes of God—the wilderness tabernacle and the Jerusalem temple— and of the king. But it tells us very little about the domiciles in which most people lived. Fortunately, archaeological excavations provide ample information about the architectural features of the typical Israelite dwelling, and ethnographic data enable researchers to determine the function of its various spatial areas.

The typical dwelling is often called the "four-room house" because many Iron Age domiciles associated with the Israelites have four rooms on the ground floor. This structure was an intentional architectural concept, but the examples are not all cookie-cutter versions. Adaptations were made to accommodate fluctuating family size, functional needs, and terrain: some have only two or three rooms; the subdivision of existing rooms or the addition of rooms means that some have five or more rooms; and many likely had a second story and thus additional rooms. There are so many variations of the four-room house that another designation is preferable:

"pillared house," because a row of pillars separates two or three of its rooms in many examples.

Awareness of the general features of the pillared house is helpful for understanding women's workspaces and also the general flow of activities that brought women into contact with others. The description here is of an average four-room type, for its basic plan is found in the variations too.[4] Scholars disagree about some of its features; thus several possibilities, or sometimes the likeliest possibility, are presented.

The pillared house was built of stone, although in areas with access to good clays, sun-dried mud bricks sometimes formed part of the superstructure. Roof beams and the main door were wooden. Its ground plan features three parallel rectangular rooms (longrooms), entered through a doorway to the middle one, with a fourth rectangular room (broadroom) running across the rear of the other three. The central longroom, which is usually larger than the others, has a beaten earth floor. It may have been partially unroofed, forming an interior courtyard; or an exterior courtyard may have been located in the space outside its main entryway. One of the side longrooms is sometimes paved with cobbles or flagstones. The other longroom and the broadroom—both often subdivided—have beaten earth floors. Because the transverse room or rooms at the rear are furthest from the entrance, they may correspond to the "innermost parts of the house" mentioned in biblical texts (e.g., Amos 6:10). Sometimes traces of plaster have been preserved, suggesting that the walls were plastered, both inside and out.

Other features have not survived and are suggested by ethnography or ancient depictions. Although small windows were probably placed in the upper part of exterior walls, the interior would have been poorly lit except in the partially roofed courtyard or near the open door. The wooden roof beams were covered with brush and a mud and straw plaster, packed firmly to form a waterproof covering. The roof's flat surface provided additional workspace and also served as a place for sleeping in the hot summer months. An average pillared house was about 30–35 feet long and 35–40 feet wide; it would seem small to us moderns, with so many of us accustomed to spacious homes or apartments.

Because this house plan is quite rare before the Iron Age and east of the Jordan River, it is often considered an indigenous Israelite architectural development.[5] Some of its features seem especially suitable for people engaged in subsistence farming that included some animal husbandry. Specifically, the cobbled or paved room was probably used for stabling a small number of livestock in the winter months, with the body heat of the animals producing welcome warmth rising to the sleeping rooms above. This arrangement was still practiced in early twentieth-century Palestinian villages.[6] Also, the back transverse room—the one furthest from the entrance—was suitable for keeping the large jars in which grain and other commodities were stored from one harvest season to the next; if subdivided, part was also used for household activities. This house type persisted for nearly 600 years, coinciding with Israelite presence in the land (ca. twelfth to sixth centuries BCE).

Other household structures were the small huts or shelters some-times built on distant fields; people working long hours in those fields, especially during harvest seasons, used them when there was no time to travel to the main dwelling for food or rest. Another kind of structure on household land, although perhaps not for all households, was the family tomb or burial place.

A household's landholdings—on level areas in nearby valleys, on ter-raced hillsides of the settlement, or both—were its chief economic resource. Fields, olive trees, and vineyards were situated on household lands; and small subsidiary gardens were interspersed with field crops, trees, or vines or were planted close to the dwelling. Because of irregularities of the ter-rain and perhaps also because of the inevitable fragmentation that results when lands are subdivided for heirs, a household's landholdings were not always contiguous. Rather, they consisted of small plots interspersed with those of other households and perhaps marked with boundary stones (see Deut 19:14).[7] Pasture lands were located beyond the cultivated lands in areas too marginal for crops, and they shifted as animals consumed the shrubs and undergrowth on which they grazed. Animals were household property, but pasturage probably was not held by individual households but was part of a settlement's collective territory (see below). In the case of larger walled settlements, pasturage for part of the year was apparently the area immediately outside the fortification walls (see chapter 3, p. 42).

A household's physicality included the installations and the many items needed for producing food, textiles, and other commodities. Altogether they were still relatively few compared to the myriad objects people accu-mulate today. Moreover, not all households had every kind of installa-tion needed for the processing of foodstuffs. Some installations were too large and costly to be obtained by each peasant household, and commu-nal installations have been identified in many rural communities. Olive presses, for example, have been discovered in special production "zones" at some sites, and communal storage facilities for oil and wine have also been recovered.[8] In addition—and this is an important part of the discussion of women's activities—installations like ovens and olive presses are sometimes found between dwellings and apparently served several households. The kinds of equipment that women used in carrying out their household activities are described in the next two chapters.

Some or all of a household's physical components constituted what is called the *nahalah* in the Hebrew Bible. Usually translated "inheritance," it can refer to immovable property (lands and buildings) and also to animals and, presumably, other movable property.[9] Still, the land on which crops were grown was of primary importance; land after all was food. Without arable fields and terraces, economic survival was not possible. The powerful attachment of household members to their immovable property is reflected in the strong biblical measures to prevent its alienation, that is, its transfer to an outsider (e.g., Lev 25:25-28). The national Israelite narrative understood that a household's land would be transferred across generations patrilineally (through the male line) and would belong to a householder's descendants "forever" (e.g., Exod 32:13). The narrative of Naboth's vineyard shows that a small householder could refuse to relinquish his "ancestral inheritance" (*nahalah*) even to the king (1 Kgs 21:1-3). Israelite patrilineality could be set aside if a man had only daughters, as in the case of Zelophehad's daughters (Num 27:1-8; Josh 17:3-4); the importance of keeping lands within a descent group trumps the strong patrilineal principle. Eventually estates did begin to form—but not until the very end of the Iron Age—for the buying and selling of land is "not primordial" in societies where land provides the basic support for most households.[10]

Some biblical texts situate this territorial inalienability within the concept of all land belonging to Yahweh, who transfers it to Israelites as tenants (e.g., Lev 25:23; 1 Sam 26:19). Whether this concept was widely held throughout Israelite history is not known. It is also possible that land was not "owned" by households but was held by the communities, with individual tracts assigned to each household as its *nahalah*. Whether they technically "owned" their land or not, most people—like agrarians everywhere who depend on land for survival—probably subscribed to the idea that a household's land was its permanent possession to be transmitted from one generation to the next. Even tenant farmers would have identified with the land they worked; peasants who farm land as part of a tenancy relationship typically feel connected to those lands, which are their means of subsistence and their way of life.[11] Moreover, even with male off-spring as the preferred heirs, the entire family group that worked the land would have identified with it (see the last section of this chapter). With the hands of all—women, men, and children; young and old—immersed in the soil that was the source of their sustenance, the attachment of all to that soil was strong.

The Human Component: Family Members (and Others)

The people in a household were first and foremost a small group of kin. But the size and composition of this kinship group are matters of some discussion. Family groups, after all, are not natural configurations but rather social ones, affected by historical and environmental context.[12] How many wives did a man have? How many children were there? Was it simply a nuclear family with parents and their children, or was it a larger, complex family group?

The family in biblical antiquity is frequently imagined to have been a large one, with several wives and many children. The idea that polygyny (multiple wives) was common is probably based on the familiar ancestor narratives in Genesis: Abraham has three wives (one a slave-wife), and Jacob has four (two of them secondary). Also, many biblical kings are said to have numerous spouses and concubines (e.g., 1 Kgs 11:3; 2 Chr 11:21; but cf. Deut 17:17). However, the patriarchs—with their servants, vast flocks, and precious metals (e.g., Gen 13:2; 14:14-15)—are depicted as elites, as of course were the kings. Virtually no ordinary Israelite in the Hebrew Bible seems to have had more than one wife except Elhanan, whose two wives are necessary for the literary dynamic of the narrative (1 Sam 1). Also, one wife (Hannah) is barren; given the critical importance of offspring for a household's livelihood and continuity, having an infertile wife was likely grounds for even a peasant man to take a second one. Still, given that women's life spans were shorter than men's (see chapter 5, p. 99), it would have been a demographic impossibility for most men to have had multiple spouses. Thus the basis of the nuclear family in most households was the conjugal pair, as presented in Genesis 2:24.

As for children, the ancestor narratives and the passages about kings again provide unrepresentative information. The tradition that the patriarch Jacob had twelve sons suggests that large families were the norm. But note that it took four women to produce Jacob's sons for an average of three per woman, which is probably the average number of children

in an Israelite nuclear family. Similarly, the large brood of some mon-
archs, like their many wives and concubines, signifies their high status.
For example, the Judean king Abijah (or Abijam) has fourteen wives who
bear twenty-two sons and sixteen daughters (2 Chr 13:21), fewer than
three children per wife.

The biblical information suggesting three children per woman means
that a two-parent nuclear family had about three surviving children.
Estimates based on ethnography and the size of Israelite dwellings fit
remarkably well with the biblical data. Sophisticated analytical methods
indicate a nuclear family of between four to six people, meaning two to
four children.[13] The likelihood (mentioned in the last chapter) that women
had to have multiple pregnancies, as many as eight, to reach optimal family size is based on this estimate.

The number of children is usually related to social and economic factors, with families typically having enough offspring to reproduce themselves and to meet labor needs but not too many to overburden their
resources. Premodern peoples, perhaps without being fully aware they are
doing so, usually (but not always) manage to regulate reproduction in
beneficial ways. For the Israelites, the delicate balance of enough children
for labor but not too many to feed was threatened when too few children
were born or when, all too often, insufficient crop yields meant hunger
and malnutrition (see chapter 3, pp. 53–58).

The basic nuclear family unit, then, was smaller than we might have
imagined. But does a single nuclear family constitute the full human component of the household? Probably not. Ethnographic evidence indicates
that when the labor of women is an important part of household life and
when there are labor intensive periods in the annual agricultural cycle—
both conditions of Israelite life (see chapter 3, pp. 50–51)—*complex* families are usually formed. Households with more than two adults provided
more labor and also enabled the pooling of child-care resources so that
women could carry out their tasks.[14]

Complex families, which are living groups larger than nuclear families,
can take several different forms. They can be *extended* families, in which
several kin in addition to the nuclear family share a dwelling area; many
possibilities for this, such as the addition of aunts or uncles or cous-
ins or elderly parents, can be imagined. However, clues in the Hebrew
Bible suggest that Israelite complex families were *joint* families (a term
sometimes used interchangeably or synonymously with extended families). Joint families are those with more than two generations—usually

not more than three in ancient Israel because of the relatively short life spans—living together. In both large and small settlements, the household would include a senior couple, unmarried children, and married sons with their wives and their offspring.[15] (Households were generally *patrilocal*, meaning that sons brought wives into the household, whereas daughters moved out to the households of their spouses. Thus marriage was when a man "took" a woman—took her from her family's household to his [e.g., Gen 24:67].)

Of course, the configurations of a complex family were hardly stable, for its composition shifted over relatively short periods of time according to deaths and births of its members. No single pattern of family organization can characterize all households at a given time or any individual one over time.[16] Moreover, the core family group was probably augmented in other ways from time to time. Family members from related kin groups might join a household if they were orphaned or otherwise isolated, producing a combined joint and extended kinship group. Wealthier households had servants. And displaced itinerants or fugitives were "sojourners" or "resident aliens" (Hebrew *gerim*; e.g., Exod 23:12) in Israelite households, although perhaps only in elite households.

Just as the configuration of household members varied according to circumstances, so too did the occupancy pattern of pillared buildings vary, specifically, in relation to the location and perhaps also to the prosperity of the group. In isolated farmsteads or tiny settlements, a single, large pillared building may have housed a complex family group.[17] More often, as archaeological evidence suggests, small pillared houses, each housing a nuclear family, were grouped together in a compound.[18] Another scenario has a complex family occupying a single pillared building with a second story and thus more living space.[19] In all these cases, the complex household would have had about fifteen members, sometimes more and sometimes less. This figure corresponds well with social science estimates and with ethnographic data from Ottoman-period Palestine, both indicating that the average maximum number of inhabitants in a multigenerational household was sixteen.[20] In the few large "urban" settlements (see chapter 3, pp. 40–41), non-elites might be wage earners or work in nonagricultural trades; in these cases, domiciles might house a single nuclear family.[21] But most settlements were agricultural villages and towns with households consisting of complex family groups, the dominant form everywhere for land-owning peasants.[22]

Most scholars find a biblical correlate for the household in the deceptively simple phrase *bet 'ab*, which literally means "house of the father."
The Hebrew word for "house" can mean simply a domicile, or it can refer
to a dynasty ("as the house of David," e.g., 1 Kgs 13:2). The phrase "house
of the father" or, better, "father's house/household," is not used uniformly
in the Hebrew Bible. But it generally denotes a group of humans, usually
a complex family but sometimes a nuclear family, that constitute a living
group and sometimes includes the domicile and landholdings too. That
is, it incorporates the material features—especially the land—that were
essential for the survival of the living group in its present and also its
continuity over generations.

So important was this smallest unit of Israelite society that the term
bet 'ab is used for other levels of society in the Hebrew Bible, metaphorically indicating the close-knit aspect of real or putative kin groups. It
can elliptically refer to all Israel: Israelites—sometimes called "house
of Israel" (e.g., 1 Sam 7:2-3; cf. 2 Sam 12:8)—are all descendants of the
"house" of the father Jacob (Gen 46:27; see also Num 26:4-62; 1 Chr
1-9); and genealogies form a pseudo-kinship structure linking all parts of
society.[23] Similarly, "father's house/household" is used metaphorically for
the other two levels of society beside the national one, namely the clan
and the tribe (described in the next section). Despite some fluidity in its
usage, the basic configuration was likely stable throughout the Iron Age.
Moreover, except in truly urban settings in which goods could be obtained
in a market and in which subsistence could be procured by means other
than agriculture, people could survive only by being part of a household.
That is, there was virtually no such thing as individual existence, a feature
of ancient society very different from our own and discussed further in
the last section of this chapter.

This discussion of the *bet 'ab* would not be complete without drawing
attention to the phrase *bet 'em*, literally "house of the mother" but better rendered "household of the mother" or "mother's household." A small
but significant set of biblical texts use this phrase.[24] It first appears in the
endearing story (Gen 24) of how the matriarch Rebekah gets a husband.
Her future father-in-law Abraham sends a servant to Mesopotamia, where
she lives with her family, to find a suitable wife for his heir Isaac. After
meeting the servant, Rebekah hurries home to tell "her mother's household" about the encounter (24:28). The phrase also appears in Ruth 1:8
when Naomi encourages her two widowed daughters-in-law to leave her
and return to their "mother's household." The female lover in the Song of

Solomon twice expresses her strong feelings for her beloved by saying she wishes to bring him to "her mother's household" (3:4 and 8:2). In addition, several verses in Proverbs depict a woman building or maintaining her household with wisdom (9:1; 14:1; 31:21, 27). Also, the narrative of the Shunammite woman (see chapter 9) refers to "her household" (2 Kgs 8:1).

What is striking about all these instances of "mother's household" is that they appear in passages focusing on women. Rebekah is the major, and dynamic, character of Genesis 24, which is sometimes called the "Courtship of Rebekah" because of her centrality in the story. The entire book of Ruth is about two women, Ruth and Naomi, and their courage in reclaiming Naomi's ancestral lands, that is, her late husband's patrimony. The woman in the Song of Solomon, a book in which female figures outnumber male ones, is more prominent and perhaps more dominant than her male counterpart. The Proverbs verses mentioning a woman's household are in passages featuring female Wisdom, a wise woman, and female household management. And the Shunammite woman is central to the narratives in which she appears (see chapter 10, pp. 190–191).

Taken as an aggregate, these instances of "woman's household" suggest that when texts have a female focus, the prominence of women in the myriad household tasks (see chapters 7 and 8) meant the identification of the household with the senior female. Moreover, the social reality of practical female wisdom in household life may underlie the propensity to view wisdom, a grammatically feminine word in both Hebrew (*hokmah*) and Greek (*sophia*), as female.[25] At the same time, the dominance of "father's household" in the Hebrew Bible indicates that the household was identified with the senior male with respect to its patrilineal concerns and the place of the household in the larger network of sociopolitical groups, to which we now turn.

The Larger Context: People/Nation/Monarchy, Tribe, and Clan

Unlike more primitive cultivators, who may be isolated from larger social and political structures, the peasant farmers of the Iron Age were the foundational part of a complex society.[26] A series of sociopolitical units formed the people "Israel," a term that probably represents a group of loosely aligned chiefdoms in the Iron I period and then the Israelite and Judean monarchies in the Iron II period (perhaps with a brief period of a single monarchy at the beginning of that period). A full examination of those units, or levels of society, is beyond the scope of this book. However, each is briefly described, for their social and especially economic interconnections likely had an impact on peasant households. Information about Israelite clans and tribes comes largely from the Hebrew Bible, which is hardly a monolithic document and certainly not a sociological treatise. Yet it surely reflects social reality, albeit a reality that changed over the many centuries of Israelite existence. Categories of organization established by social scientists have enabled scholars to make sense of biblical data.

Israelite society apparently consisted of several levels of organization: households were part of clans, clans part of tribes, tribes part of the people/nation/monarchy. This appears clearly in the narrative of a fellow named Achan, who disobeys an order from God. The narrator identifies him by naming his household, clan, and tribe (Josh 7:16-18). Many other texts refer to a person's clan and tribe; and important biblical figures are often identified by their tribe of origin. For example, when Saul first appears in the Bible, his father, grandfather, and great-grandfather are mentioned—and so is his tribe (1 Sam 9:1-2).

The English word "tribe" is used for two different Hebrew words (šebeṭ and maṭṭeh), which are virtually synonymous in most cases. Each of the twelve tribes of Israel bears the eponymous name of one of the twelve sons of Jacob.[27] Although typically grouped in the Bible as commensurate units, they varied in size and population and had different histories of formation and survival. Despite the picture presented in the book of Joshua, they probably were not a united group in the Iron I period. Yet archaeological evidence correlated with biblical details indicates that at least some of these tribal groups occupied highland areas in that period; some were chiefdoms while others had more diffuse leadership.[28] In other words, even in the premonarchic Iron I period, some peasant farmers may have been channeling resources (taxes) to chiefs or sub-chiefs who controlled several highland areas.

Under the monarchies taxation was almost certainly a feature of Israelite life. The increase in monumental architecture (e.g., fortifications, palaces) characterizing the larger settlements of the Iron II period and corresponding to references in the Hebrew Bible (e.g., 1 Kgs 9:15) entailed tapping the resources of the peasantry.[29] The words of the prophet Samuel, when asked to help establish a kingdom, are telling. He warns people that a king not only will conscript their offspring for service to the realm, as soldiers and as workers in the palace and on royal lands, but will also tax them: "He will take the best of your fields [i.e., grain] and vineyards and olive orchards...and the best of your cattle and donkeys...[and] one-tenth of your flocks" (1 Sam 8:14-17; cf. 1 Kgs 4:7). Similarly, the extensive sacrificial offerings mandated in priestly texts served to enrich the religious establishment.

To be sure, not all kings had the same policies for funding the state apparatus; some may have been powerful enough to exact tribute from weaker neighboring kingdoms, while others were pushed to expand their taxation policies when the dominant superpowers exacted tribute from them (more on this below).[30] Yet throughout the Iron II period some of the agricultural yield of most households often went to "sustain a privileged way of life for the crown and the bureaucracy" in both Jerusalem and Samaria.[31] Royal systems of collecting agricultural products are perhaps evident in archaeological finds, notably the handles of large jars bearing the inscription "to/for the king." Scholars debate the function of these stamped jars, which begin to appear in the late eighth century BCE, perhaps because of the economic pressure of Assyrian imperial control (mentioned below); one possibility is that they held taxes paid in kind or even tithes.[32]

The clan, the level of Israelite society between the tribe and the household, is more difficult to describe. The biblical terminology involves two distinct terms. The more common one is *mišpaḥah*, which usually denotes a group of related households located near each other; but, as noted, it sometimes overlaps in meaning with *bet 'ab*. Often rendered "family" in Bible translations, it thereby conjures up inaccurate notions of a nuclear or extended family. Thus the NRSV, NJPS, and other versions more sensitive to historical context now use the more accurate rendering "clan" (or "kindred"). The other term (*'elep*) appears less frequently and seems to be used in military contexts to designate clans as subunits—sometimes as many as fifty—of a tribe.[33]

Whatever their designation, clans varied in size and strength as indicated by Gideon's protest when he is summoned to leadership: "How can I deliver Israel? My clan [*'elep*] is the weakest in [the tribe of] Manasseh?" (Judg 6:15). The distribution of clans probably took several forms: a single settlement might consist of one clan; several small settlements together might constitute a clan; a large clan might be spread out over several settlements; or a large settlement might hold several clans. Clan lineages did not always represent true biological connections, but they were conceptually part of ancient Israel's "family tree"—genealogies using kinship imagery to emphasize group bonds.

The clan's function is exceedingly difficult to ascertain. Economically, it may have been the mechanism through which tribute or taxes were channeled to tribal elders, chieftains, or kings.[34] Yet it probably also provided assistance to individual households that composed the clan. (Women's roles in allocating assistance are presented in chapter 7.) In addition, archaeological and ethnographic data suggest that the clan was the facilitating mechanism for the communal food-processing activities of the smaller settlements (see above). The work at a settlement's oil press, for example, was probably organized by clan elders. Settlements with two oil presses were likely occupied by two clans, and some larger settlements with as many as five presses would have been home to five clans.[35] This pattern of sharing large installations too costly for most individual households to own and maintain was observed in Palestinian peasant villages studied early in the twentieth century. These villages were typically inhabited by several descent groups or lineages (equivalent to the Israelite clan), each with its constituent households grouped together in its own sector of the settlement. After the olive harvest, most of the olives picked by a household were taken to the oil press that served its lineage (clan).[36] The clans perhaps also held certain lands collectively—pasturage and a settlement's communal areas.

THE CONNECTION OF peasant households to the other levels of society varied. In the premonarchic Iron I period households were probably taxed by the tribe (or chieftaincy). In the Iron II period households paid taxes (in kind) to the monarchies, which seem to have been intent on amassing oil, grain, and wine for trade. Still, it is unlikely that taxes were always collected systematically, given the fractured terrain and the remoteness of many settlements.[37]

Otherwise, households retained the products of their labors. The large estates that gradually formed in both northern and southern kingdoms may have engaged in commercial transactions, namely marketing grain and other commodities to their own urban centers or those of neighboring polities.[38] However, most landowning peasant households produced only for their own consumption beyond what was exacted from them as taxes. The combined zooarchaeological, ethnographic, and anthropological evidence shows that there was no market economy in Iron Age Israel.[39] As already suggested, because of the specter of shortfalls, peasants retained surpluses rather than marketing them.

Peasant economies thus continued throughout the Iron Age and were not greatly affected by national events and policies until the onset of imperial control of Palestine from the late eighth to the late seventh century BCE by the Assyrians, who apparently imposed exorbitant tribute (e.g., 2 Kgs 15:19-21), which had devastating consequences for peasant farmers living on marginal lands.[40] Assyrian domination exacerbated peasant hardship, putting "pressure on the fragile ecosystem and its ability to sustain peasant life."[41] It is no wonder that the voices of biblical prophets, often championing the poor, emerge at this time. And it is probably at this time that wealth becomes a factor in the different sizes of pillared dwellings.[42]

Aside from taxes and tribute, however, local communities continued independently of the central government throughout the Iron Age.[43] Recognizing the local autonomy of most settlements is important in assessing the situation of women. Some scholars suggest that women's lives became more circumscribed under the monarchies, with centralized bureaucracies intentionally trying to undermine complex families.[44] That view is based on the analysis of Deuteronomic regulations and fails to see that these biblical texts are more relevant for understanding elites, many of them urbanites in post-eighth-century Jerusalem, rather than for assessing the lives of the peasant majority.

Overall, the connections of ordinary households to the monarchy were distant and sporadic, whereas interactions with local lineages (probably clans or subclans, depending on the size of the settlement) were probably frequent and important. Local affairs, such as the organization of communal food-processing installations, were managed independently of centralized government.[45] And the various services we expect today from government, whether local, state, or national—at least the ones relevant to premodern times—were provided informally at the local level by both women and men. The role of women in the social and political mechanisms of their settlements is presented in the next chapter.

Problems of Presentism

Reconstructing the experiences and roles of women in their households is hindered not only by our distance in time and space from ancient Israel, which I have tried to overcome with the information provided in this chapter and chapter 3, but also by more subtle impediments. Perceptions of the past are too often distorted by "presentism," in which the ideas and perspectives familiar to us in today's world affect our interpretation of past events or conditions. That is, we tend to anachronistically read the present into the past and in so doing misunderstand and misrepresent the past. Although we have much in common with our fellow humans everywhere and throughout history, there are also fundamental divergences.

One of the most influential articles associated with the emergence of gender archaeology was an essay on "Archaeology and the Study of Gender," published in a leading anthropological annual in 1984. It gave credibility and respectability to research that examined and evaluated the lives of women in past societies. Its authors stressed the importance of resisting the temptation to project what we know about our own world onto the past, and they insisted that researchers recognize "the intellectual obstacles involved in reconstructing the characteristics of social life in the past."[46] Nearly three decades later, the need to be aware that the organization and meaning of past behaviors are not necessarily the same as in the present is no less compelling.

When it comes to the world of the Bible, it is especially difficult to conceive of its otherness in many aspects. Because the Bible remains a part of the present for people who consider it sacred and authoritative, the biblical past is brought into a kind of equivalency with the present. Yet, for all the continuity, there are significant differences. Because this book explicitly seeks to understand Israelite women in their ancient setting, a final step in examining the family household as the context of women's lives is recognizing several characteristics of ancient life that are fundamentally different from what we experience today, for the latter may interfere with our ability to evaluate Everywoman Eve's experience.

Collective vs. Individual Identity

The reader may have noticed that the discussion of different levels of society did not include the individual as a discrete unit. To be sure, a single person is the smallest component of any social group; and we are accustomed to thinking about people as autonomous beings, separate in important ways from their familial and social contexts. However, as best we can tell, the concept of the individual as a fully separate and independent entity was not part of the ancient Hebraic mindset. (Postmodern views would also question whether the individual is a fully separate entity.) Like most premodern agrarians, Israelites were embedded in their immediate material and human context. They were so interdependent in a variety of economic, social, and religious ways that they were rarely viable as individuals, as already noted. They would not have understood the intense individualism of many modern societies. Rather, people were "deeply embedded, or engaged," in their social context and "enmeshed in obligations of kinship."[47] The relationship between individuals and their kin was fundamentally different from the one prevailing in most Western societies: "In the ancient world, a person was not an individual in the modern sense of the word. Individuals were first and foremost members of groups."[48] To put it another way, Israelite society was an "an aggregate of groups rather than a collection of individuals."[49]

The identity of Israelites was thus relational, in contrast to the individuation and separation that typically characterize human development in much of the industrialized world. With group existence as the fundamental grounding of life, a person's sense of herself or himself as independent of the group upon which she or he depended for survival would have been very different from our own sense of self, with our independent goals and life trajectories. This aspect of Israelite identity was recognized almost a century ago by Johannes Pedersen, a Danish biblical scholar committed to the idea that social context was important for understanding biblical texts. His study of Semitic culture indicated that the individual was thought of as a totality, with unity of body and soul. This led him to conclude that because people are greatly endangered if cut off from their social matrix, they are inexorably and inextricably linked to that context:

> Life is not something individual, to be shaped according to the needs of each individual. Man [= person] is only what he is as a link in the family...we always see a community rising behind it [a person]. What it is, it is by virtue of others. It has sprung up from a family which has filled it with its contents, and from which it can never grow away. The family forms the narrowest community in which it lives. But wherever it works, it must live in community....[50]

The intimate and important connection of a household to its landholdings was thus mirrored by the interrelated destinies of its members. A person's sense of individual agency was derived from her or his contribution to household life rather than from individual accomplishment. Household members did not act on their own wants or desires; rather they worked with the others in their household to benefit the group and its holdings.[51] The merging of self with the household and its members did not obliterate a sense of self but did produce a collectivist, group-oriented mindset—the well-being of the individual was inseparable from that of the group.

Anthropologists have observed this in Greek mountain villages, where individual fulfillment means achieving household goals, and the very idea of personal accomplishment is "alien to the women" (and men) of the community.[52] Individuality still exists, but the "solidarity of the family group restricts the expression of purely individual feelings, opinions, and personality."[53] In peasant societies in general, people "are much more closely interdependent in behavior and ideology than citizens of modern Western states," for their identities are "not primarily as individuals but as members of a group, a lineage, or a family."[54] This collective mentality is not limited to ancient agrarians and remote Greek villagers; it has also been recognized in rural families in the United States in the twentieth century before the modernization of agriculture. The household provided the overarching life context, and the "self merged with the family and farm."[55] Women who married into a farm family identified fairly quickly with their marital household while not losing contact with their natal families (a feature, discussed in chapter 7, of Israelite *patrilocality*). Amazingly, even late in the twentieth century, and despite the strong pull toward individualism and the flood of media content urging young people to indulge themselves and to make life choices of their own, small independent farm families maintained an ethos valuing the whole—the family farm—more than its constituent members.[56]

This strong identification of agrarians with their collective unit contrasts strongly with what has developed since the industrial revolution, namely, the place of work removed from the place of residence. The modern separation of the living quarters of the family from the economic basis of life entails a person-centered ethos, fosters the notion of individual choice, freedoms, and interests, and necessitates the interaction of individuals with a wide range of non-kin others. (The impact of industrialization is manifest in the other presentism issues considered here and in the very concept of patriarchy, discussed in chapter 10.)

Because of the intrinsic collectivism of Israelites as smallholders, individualistic elements of human existence were subordinated to group interests. Rather than being an autonomous entity, a woman was someone's daughter, mother, wife, and so forth. These relationships were integral to the life-creating and life-sustaining activities situated in the household.

Israelite women lived in a world utterly lacking the focus on achievement and self-fulfillment that characterizes individual development in much of today's world. Thus they must not be judged by the same criteria we would apply today; they cannot be considered the victims of sexism or gender bias because they (like their spouses) could neither choose their own life paths nor even conceive of choosing them.

Assessment of Women's Work

The next two chapters present the array of women's activities in agrarian Israelite households. Most would fall under the rubric of housework in today's middle-class culture: the routine, unpaid chores—cooking and cleaning and minding young children—needed to keep a home running smoothly. As such these tasks are consistently considered supportive and secondary, and they are consequently marginalized and trivialized.

These negative evaluations of women's unpaid housework are rooted in the identification of women with the home in Western ideologies since the end of the eighteenth century.[57] With the industrial revolution came the removal of significant economic processes from the household: wage-earning labor (mainly by men) took place in a workplace separate from the home and became more important than unpaid labor (mainly by women) in the home. Women's housework became seen as simply housekeeping chores with little economic value. Familiarity with these work patterns led to assumptions that women's work in premodern contexts was not valued and earned no social power or prestige; the critical economic importance of women's household work in premodern agrarian societies was not perceived.

It is now clear that this low esteem for women's work is a relatively recent phenomenon and that contemporary notions about household work, whether done by women or by men (as is becoming somewhat more common today) must not be the basis for understanding the meaning or value of women's household activities in a premodern society.[58] The traditional concept of men as breadwinners and women as homemakers must be set aside; otherwise, the role and meaning of women's economic and other roles in ancient Israel will be obscured.

The reality is that women's activities in traditional societies have significant economic value.[59] The gender (or feminist) archaeology described in chapter 2 has produced studies showing that women's household roles, in both subsistence tasks and craft production, functioned in traditional societies in ways that challenge our often unexamined yet persistent notions of women's work as unimportant. They have shown that the low esteem in which domestic labor is often held is not a "diachronic and cross-cultural phenomenon, but largely a recent one, linked to the development of a 'modern' society with values oriented towards productivity, efficiency, and economic rationality."[60] Assigning low status to female labor across cultures highlights the way traditional androcentric and ethnocentric perspectives lead to distorted and inaccurate evaluations of premodern cultures.[61] As research in a Sardinian village has shown, women and men perform different tasks but their contributions to the household economy are valued equally.[62] The substantial contributions of women and men to the household economy in peasant cultures mean positive regard for both of them.

A related issue in assessing women's work is the assumption that tasks performed by men are innately more valuable than those performed by women. Tasks in the modern world tend to be evaluated by their economic return and the power that accrues to those holding highly remunerative positions. Today some women contest this notion, resisting the use of economic measures as the chief criteria of worth and decrying the idea that unpaid labor and child-rearing have less value than the production of income. In an ancient society with little or no wage labor, these kinds of valuation were irrelevant.

Another consideration is that gender is not fully independent of class and age in forming attitudes about people's value. Also, the fact that the identity of individuals was subsumed into the household and lineage may have precluded the attachment of strong differential values to gendered tasks. And even if some tasks were more highly valued than others, status accruing to people because they perform a particular activity does not necessarily correlate with high status in all areas of life.[63]

Private/Public Dichotomy

A pioneering book, the first to address issues of women's status from an anthropological perspective, was published in 1974: *Women, Culture, and Society*.[64] Among its many influential articles is Michelle Rosaldo's "Women, Culture, and Society: A Theoretical Overview."[65] Like several others in the anthology, this essay differentiates between prestigious public life, consisting of political and economic institutions and activities associated with men, and private or domestic (family) life associated with

women. Her analysis was based on the postindustrial revolution, capitalist divide between work and family, which were perceived as separate,
gender-identified spheres. Many early feminist anthropologists accepted
this division and used women's association with the restricted domestic
sphere as an explanation of their subordination, which they assumed was
universal.

But not for long. It soon became clear that the public/private binary
may exist in certain industrial, capitalist contexts but that it could not be
superimposed on all cultures everywhere. Even Rosaldo recanted.[66] And
Conkey and Spector weighed in: "The structural opposition inherent in
the public-private notion and the gender linkages associated with it may be
appropriate in describing western, industrial, suburban societies but it dis-
torts the structure and character of gender relations in many other groups."[67]
The Western ideology contrasting family life with public affairs is simply
incompatible with what we now know about many other societies. The
binary opposition between public and private and the linked gender asym-
metry have been strongly critiqued as "reductionist, ahistorical, and static
representations" that project "a 'Western folk model' onto the rest of the
world."[68] Anthropological and historical research indicates that in premodern societies the "public" and the "private" are really overlapping domains.
Household activities have significance for *both* realms—the domestic *is* political and the private *is* public, and thus the two are not distinct realms.[69]

Because the Israelite household *was* the workplace, that is, the fundamental economic unit, and because its activities entailed social relations beyond the household (as noted above and as described in the
next chapter), interactions with the larger community on matters of
social and political import were part of the lived experience of both
women and men.[70] Even with respect to Israelite religious life, often
thought to be centered in extra-household personnel and organizations,
the continuity between household religious practice and community
cultic institutions is now recognized.[71] The household was organically
connected to the larger kinship group(s) and other community structures around it.

CLEARLY IT IS a challenge to consider the life experiences of Israelite
women apart from current assumptions. But overcoming presentist stereotypes is essential as we turn to examine women's roles and responsibilities in the Israelite household, the locus of economic activities, social and
political interactions, and religious behavior.

Note that the term "household" is used in the following chapters somewhat loosely in reference to the domain of an adult woman with children. Its human components may sometimes be a complex family or sometimes the nuclear family within the larger complex group. Because the exact living patterns were so varied, consistency in this regard is not possible.

7

Women and Household Maintenance, Part I: Economic, Reproductive, and Sociopolitical Activities

MANY PEOPLE HAVE the impression that women in biblical antiquity were "only wives and mothers." This somewhat condescending phrase is a typical response to a question about Israelite women's lives that I pose to undergraduates, many of them familiar with the Hebrew Bible, in the first class of a course on women in the Bible and the biblical world. These students have not yet been warned about presentism and thus have super-imposed current ideas about female domesticity on an ancient setting. But soon they learn about the varied and essential tasks of women in Israelite agrarian households. They quickly understand that the self-sufficient agrar-ian household was the locus of a full range of productive activities as well as the setting for biological reproduction, and they realize that it was the arena for nearly all activities of both women and men.

Everywoman Eve's context was the household, the central institution for most economic, social, educative, political, and religious aspects of life throughout the Iron Age. The phrase "only a wife and mother" would have been incomprehensible to Israelite agrarians. For them "wife" (*'iššah*) was as much a job description as an indication of marital status. It is a term that encodes a series of productive and managerial tasks that, along with childbearing and child-rearing, were part of daily life. And it signi-fies other related responsibilities in the realms of social interaction, polit-ical process, and religious practice.

Women's household responsibilities and activities are best characterized by a single umbrella concept: *maintenance activities*. This term gained cur-rency in gender archaeology in the late 1990s when archaeologists working in the west Mediterranean became dissatisfied with traditional analyses of household activities. Those analyses often viewed households in terms of their economic and biological functions, seeing households as units of production and reproduction, and also considering more abstract but nonetheless significant social, political, and religious aspects of household life.[1]

These features—economic, biological, social, political, and religious— certainly have a legitimate place in the discussion, for they present familiar concepts and are useful descriptors. However, all of them emerge from Western intellectual discourse and give the impression that each is a discrete set of activities, as is generally the case in the modern world. When used for traditional societies, these terms fail to capture the complexity and significance of women's activities. The idea of a discrete economic role, for example, makes sense when remunerative work takes place outside the home and when work done within the home (except for paid work done in a home office) is not considered economic. Yet to consider men's work in food production in premodern societies as an economic role while not so designating women's work in food preparation obliterates a significant economic aspect of female labor. Traditional analytical categories are all too often characterized by an "appalling absence of concepts that tap women's experiences."[2]

In response to these dilemmas of reporting and conceptualizing women's activities, gender archaeologists began calling them maintenance activities. This concept "encompasses a set of practices and experiences concerning the sustenance, welfare and long-term reproduction of the members of a social group."[3] Reproduction refers to generational replacement (childbearing) and also to cultural continuity, and the group includes the household and its community context. Maintenance activities are the "basic tasks of daily life that regulate and stabilize" the life of the household and its community.[4] Household maintenance means more than meeting the physical needs of its members through the provision of food and clothing; it also involves care of the young and the ailing, the socialization and education of children, the organization of household space, the fostering of linkages with kin and neighbors, and the performance of household rituals. And this list is not necessarily exhaustive—other tasks may be embedded in these or escape specific categorization. Group survival depends on all these activities. Using the term *maintenance activities* draws attention to and valorizes women's contributions to household life. Instead of being marginalized as secondary behaviors or epiphenomena that are somehow less important than what men do, women's activities are thus recognized for their essential role in sustaining their households and communities.[5]

Despite the conceptual limitations of traditional categories, this examination of women's maintenance activities uses those categories as a convenient way to organize the various facets of women's experience. The widely recognized economic dimension of household life, for example, must be considered; but its interrelationship with other dimensions will be emphasized. However, the word "function" to designate a set of household activities is avoided. This term carries a "heavy burden of causative and teleological connotations," as Wilk and Netting presciently noted, also suggesting that it is preferable to indicate what people do and not how groups function: "We do not in fact see people or groups function: we see them act."[6] Although we cannot observe directly what women did in Israelite households, a likely scenario of their activities is possible using the resources described in chapter 2. Archaeological remains are especially useful for the household processes that used material objects, and ethnographic reports are invaluable for reconstructing the interactions inherent in the performance of maintenance activities.

Both these resources, along with biblical texts, contribute to the gender attribution of household tasks. As noted in chapters 2 and 3, the division of labor by gender in traditional societies is rarely absolute: women sometimes perform men's tasks and vice versa. At the same time gender is a prominent feature in the performance of subsistence tasks in even the simplest societies—most activities are typically the responsibility of one gender and not the other.[7] For reasons of efficiency, and because group life is strengthened through cooperation and interdependence, not everyone performs all the same maintenance tasks. However, not all activities are universally performed by the same gender. One cannot assume, for example, that women are *always* the cooks. Thus care must be taken to establish the likelihood that specific activities in Israelite households were largely in the female domain.[8] Biblical and other ancient texts that mention women in relation to productive tasks are especially useful, given that the artifacts used in those tasks are not, as already indicated, gender noisy. Ethnographic data and ancient iconographic representations are also important resources.

Women at Work (Economic Activities)

Economic features are an integral part of household life in traditional agrarian societies. The basic term for household in the Hebrew Bible, as noted in chapter 6, is similar to the Greek word *oikos* in designating a unit of production. For some ancient Greek writers this word designated the material basis of household life, and *oikonomia* (economy) meant household management. The Greeks, like the Sumerians, Babylonians, and Israelites, were well aware of the economic aspects of the household.[9]

A full list of women's contributions to the household economy is certainly not presented in the Hebrew Bible or any other ancient text, the "job description" of a woman in an elite household in Proverbs 31:10-31 notwithstanding. This is not surprising, for women's tasks are virtually invisible in the official records and laws of more recent premodern eras, whereas informal records and ethnographic observations make it clear that women performed myriad tasks.[10] Thus a priori it seems certain that women had chief responsibility for many household processes and also shared responsibility for some others. In examining their tasks, an important consideration will be the spatial location of their activities, for maintenance activities in premodern societies are integrally related to social interactions and relations. Grain-processing is given the most attention because it is the one most visible in the archaeological record and because cereals were the largest component of the Israelite diet.

Food-processing

Food-processing in most cultures is largely women's work according to ethnographic data.[11] And biblical texts, such as Samuel's famous warning about the liabilities of monarchic rule, link women to cooking and baking (1 Sam 8:13). Because few of the crops produced by Israelites could be consumed without some kind of preparation, numerous food-processing activities were necessary. Those that took place in or near the domicile and that left the clearest traces in the archaeological record are the tasks considered here, for they provide information not only about women's activities but also about where they took place. Fortunately, archaeological data (grinding stones and ovens) are plentiful for the most important foodstuff of the Israelite diet.

The grains of cereal crops were the mainstay of the Israelite diet for most people throughout the Iron Age (see chapter 3, pp. 47–48). Biblical texts (e.g., 1 Sam 8:12; 1 Kgs 19:19) and ethnographic data together indicate that the plowing, sowing, reaping, threshing, and winnowing needed to produce grains and release their kernels were largely (though not entirely) male tasks;[12] and they were seasonal. But these steps were just part of the process. Only the grains of cereals, and not their outer husks, are edible; and their nutritional starch cannot be digested in raw form. Transforming grain into edible form—porridge or gruel but more commonly bread—involves a complex series of procedures: parching or soaking, grinding, kneading, and heating and/or leavening. These tasks were performed nearly every day, year-round; and they were largely women's tasks as the evidence overwhelmingly indicates.[13] For example:

- Ethnographic data from Palestine and elsewhere in the Middle East uniformly show women carrying out all the steps for transforming grain to edible form.
- Biblical texts (e.g., Lev 26:26; Jer 7:18) associate women with grinding and baking; and the woman of Thebes rescues her people by killing the enemy using a tool she has at hand, a grinding stone (Judg 9:53-54; 2 Sam 11:21).
- Small terracotta figurines from the East Mediterranean depict women grinding or kneading, as do Egyptian terracotta models and wall-paintings.

Identifying women as bread-producers leads to some important questions, namely: What were the technologies involved? How much time did the process take? Where was it done? What were its social concomitants? These questions can be answered for grinding and baking, the two steps in the grain-processing sequence for which archaeological data are available.

Grinding

Converting grains to flour involved crushing them by placing them on a large, concave stone, tray or basin, variously called a grinding slab, slab, quern, saddle quern, or grindstone (the term used here). Usually made of basalt, grindstones have a concave work surface, a flat bottom, and are generally twice as long as they are wide (approximately 2 feet long and a foot wide, although some are larger or smaller). Grains are scattered on these stones and then ground into flour by rubbing them, in a backwards and forwards motion, with a smaller convex stone (about 6 by 10 inches, with some larger and others smaller). The smaller stone is held with two hands and is called a grinder or handstone (the term used here). These sets of upper and lower grinding stones are probably equivalent to the term *reḥayim* (NRSV, "hand-mill"), a Hebrew dual form appearing in several biblical texts.[14] The importance of grinding is evident in Jeremiah 25:10, where the sound of grinding stones indicates happy family life, probably because it meant there was sufficient grain for food.

This laborious process was probably the most time-consuming part of a woman's workload. It has been calculated that it took about an hour to prepare one and three-quarters of a pound of flour. Daily per capita consumption of flour has been estimated at slightly more than one pound per adult.[15] (The average adult in a mid-twentieth-century Palestinian village consumed up to two pounds of bread daily, and bread was sometimes the entire meal.[16]) Two adults and four children would require about four pounds of flour, and thus it would have taken two or more hours a day to prepare sufficient flour.

Archaeological data are fairly consistent in suggesting that each household, or perhaps each nuclear group within a complex household group, produced its own flour and that, just as important, women performed this task in the company of others. The occurrence of several sets of grinding stones in a single Iron Age dwelling unit is not atypical,[17] and it indicates that several women were grinding at the same time. Iconographic evidence from the ancient Near East provides similar evidence: several terracotta figurines depict pairs of women at what may be a grinding basin or a kneading trough.[18] And a New Testament passage—in which Jesus speaks of two women grinding together (Matt 24:41)—likely indicates a practice going back many millennia. Several women working side by side at the same task at the same time is an example of what anthropologists call "simple task simultaneity,"[19] which is a common way of organizing the kind of time-consuming and tedious labor that characterized grain-processing in the biblical period. It is not difficult to understand why Iron Age women, lacking the diversion of television or music, would want the company of others performing the same "daily grind." This regular interaction, which likely involved women from nearby households as well as the several women of a complex household during the course of a day, has indispensable social and political value, as discussed below.

The location of these grindstones with their accompanying handstones in individual dwellings is also significant. Flour production apparently was an indoor activity whatever the season, for they are rarely found in outdoor space. However, the variation in room size and in floor treatments of pillared dwellings has not produced a consistent pattern for the location of food preparation objects. Therefore, archaeologists have not been able to identify specific spaces of pillared dwellings as "kitchens." The relatively small size of the dwellings meant that most rooms or parts of rooms were multi-use spaces, with activity areas shifting during the course of a day or according to the season. Still, more often than not, the artifacts of flour production are recovered from the large central long-room.[20] Less frequently they appear in one of the side longrooms, and rarely are they found in the rear broadrooms. This pattern indicates that women were either within the area of traffic flow in and out of the domicile or that they were in one of the side longrooms with ready access to the movement of others. This feature also has implications for the social and political dynamics of the community, considered in the last part of this chapter.

Baking

Once sufficient flour was produced and the dough was prepared, the bread had to be baked. Sometimes this was done simply by placing the dough on a heated stone or on a griddle placed over a fire. But bread was generally baked in dome-shaped clay ovens, up to 3 feet in diameter and probably (because none have been found intact) over a foot high. They were heated by burning wood or sometimes dried dung. Unlike grinding tools, which were replaced by more efficient machines (milling tools; see the discussion in the epilogue) in the Hellenistic and Roman periods (ca. 330 BCE–350 CE), the manner of construction and use of these ovens continued virtually unchanged in villages until well into the twentieth century.[21]

The number of these installations and their location in a settlement reveal a pattern of shared use. Sometimes they are found in interior spaces of a dwelling, usually near the entrance, where ventilation would be good and where there was easy access to people coming from outside. Ovens found within the dwelling are usually small and were probably used only in the most inclement weather. Ovens are also found in outdoor spaces: in courtyards, in open areas between dwellings, or in open areas between groups of dwellings.[22] The spatial location of ovens suggests that they were often shared by households, a usage pattern that makes sense in an environment lacking an abundance of suitable fuel. One oven serving a number of households is not only fuel efficient but also pools the labor involved in collecting fuel and laying the fire. One biblical text reflects the practice of shared ovens. According to Leviticus 26:26, a single oven would be used by ten women when flour for bread is scarce; presumably it would serve fewer than ten (but more than one) in normal times, as indicated by a postbiblical Jewish source mentioning that three women prepare dough together but use only one oven (*m. Pesaḥ. 3:4;* see also *y. Pesaḥ.* 3, 30b).

Although ethnographic evidence for women grinding together does not exist in the Middle East because the technology has changed radically since antiquity, the pattern of shared bread baking has abundant witnesses. In traditional Greek villages, as many as five or six families shared an oven, which served as a gathering place for women.[23] Early twentieth-century observations in a Jordanian village indicate that seven to ten women shared an oven, and the use of ovens by several women in Palestinian villages is also attested.[24] In southeastern Turkish villages seven or eight women usually shared an oven.[25] In fact, communal ovens have been reported in the Mediterranean area in the late twentieth century in France and the early twenty-first century in Spain.[26]

Other Food-processing Activities

Many other food-processing activities, for which archaeological evidence is unclear or lacking, were surely women's responsibilities. Drink production in general, for example, is often a female task in premodern societies.[27] The strong cultural association today between men and beer notwithstanding, women were the brewers in the ancient Near East. The technology of beer brewing in the ancient world differed from modern methods; because malt cakes baked by women were used in beer brewing, women produced beer.[28] Although not as common as wine in ancient Israel, beer produced by women should not be overlooked as a liquid source of nutrition in the Israelite diet. (Wine, as suggested in chapter 6, was often—but not always—produced in village installations organized by men, as was olive oil.)

Ethnographic data provide strong evidence associating women with other food-processing activities. One example would be the preparation of dried foods. Women set fresh fruits out to dry, following distinct procedures for each type of fruit, and then packed them in suitable storage containers.[29] Legumes—lentils and chickpeas—also required drying and storage. Another example would be the collection and drying of herbs; once dried, they were perhaps pulverized with pestles (in the small basalt mortars often found near the grindstones used by women in Israelite dwellings) and used to season food and also for health-care purposes (described in the next chapter). The list could go on, with women preparing many components of the Israelite diet.

Textile Production

Like the conversion of grain to bread, the transformation of fibers (wool or flax) to garments and household fabrics (floor coverings, bags, and other items) required a sequence of activities. Several are represented by archaeological remains: spindle whorls used for spinning, loom weights for weaving, and needles for sewing. The fibers were mainly produced by men (e.g., Gen 38:13; 1 Sam 25:4), although both female and male youth tended flocks (e.g., Exod 2:16; 1 Sam 16:19). But textile work is strongly associated with women, often working together.[30] For example:

- Ethnographic data attest to weaving as women's shared work.[31]
- Biblical texts mention women as spinners (Exod 35:25-26) and weavers (2 Kgs 23:7), Rahab dries flax (Josh 2:6), and the woman of Proverbs 31 is engaged in textile work (vv. 13, 19, 22, 24).
- Wall paintings and tomb models from pharaonic Egypt and ceramic and metal depictions from the classical world show women working together at a loom and carrying out other textile-producing tasks.[32]

Several sets of the weights used to hold yarn taut on looms are sometimes discovered in Iron Age dwellings, indicating the presence of several looms and pointing to weaving as a joint female activity. Also, like grinding tools, weaving tools are typically found in the main activity areas of pillared dwellings; or like ovens they are sometimes found in outdoor space, suggesting that weaving took place outside in the summer months.[33]

Textile tasks were inordinately time-consuming. Experimental archaeology (in which researchers perform tasks using replicas of ancient tools), for example, has shown that it takes about 100 hours of spinning wool to produce enough yarn for a single garment. Many hours were first invested in cleaning the wool; many more were then required for setting the loom, weaving fabric, and sewing a garment.[34] Ethnographic information indicates that it took two or three women a week to produce a simple flat-weave rug.[35] It is no wonder that, like grinding and baking, textile work was done in the company of others. But it wasn't only a matter of camaraderie: setting and manipulating threads on a loom required the cooperation of two or three people, making shared labor not only desirable but necessary.

Making Implements and Installations

Traditional analyses of ancient societies assumed that men were tool-makers and builders, perhaps because of male prominence in those fields today. Gender archaeology has challenged those assumptions, for ethnography has provided compelling evidence that implements (including containers) and installations are typically made by those who use them. After all, the users of a product understand its function and seek technological refinements that provide the most useful item.[36] Metal objects—probably produced by specialists and not in individual households—were likely produced by men. But what sort of objects might women have produced?

Ironically, the most ubiquitous items recovered from Palestinian sites dominate archaeological publications but are rarely discussed in terms of who created them. Those items are the ceramic vessels used for cooking, storing, and serving food. Because food-preparation activities were female-specific, women likely created appropriate vessels for those tasks.[37] Male specialists probably produced quantities of certain types of pottery for markets, for (as noted in chapter 2) a biblical text set in the urban context of late Iron II Jerusalem refers to a (male) potter (Jer 18:3). However, that does not preclude the production of simple household wares by women, as attested by the presence of female village potters in twentieth-century Cyprus and Turkey.[38] In traditional communities in twentieth-century Palestine, virtually all handmade vessels for domestic use were produced by women.[39] Like many other women's tasks, producing ceramics involved several stages—digging the clay and levigating it (i.e., mixing it with water and letting it stand so that coarse particles and impurities will separate from the finer-textured clay needed to make vessels), forming and firing the vessels. These processes are typically performed by an experienced potter assisted by younger women learning the process. In fact, making larger forms would have been impossible without the cooperation of several women. Pottery-making is a "network" activity, with neighboring women working together.[40]

Baskets made from plant fibers (e.g., rushes or twigs) were part of the highland repertoire of household objects used as containers for food, although examples have survived only at sites in the dry Jordan valley. Several different Hebrew terms are used (e.g., Exod 2:5; Deut 28:5; Judg 6:19; Jer 24:1; Zech 5:6), probably indicating a variety of types. Ethnographic evidence suggests that women made the baskets.[41] Older women transmitted the techniques for procuring fibers and weaving containers to younger ones.

Stone tools for household use, especially grinding, were perhaps also fashioned by women. Because the technology in the Middle East has changed since antiquity, ethnographic evidence showing women as their producers is lacking. However, in some parts of the world where grains are still processed as they were in Iron Age Israel, women make stone tools for household use.[42] Thus it is quite possible that Israelite women made their grinding equipment, with the technological expertise of older women passed down to younger women assisting them.

Construction of certain household installations can also be attributed to women. Ethnography indicates that the bread ovens described above were constructed by the women who used them. Women had exclusive control of the sophisticated technology involved, and oven construction was a collaborative effort, with a senior woman supervising the work of daughter(s), daughter(s)-in-law, and children.[43] And women probably worked with men to build or remodel their domiciles, according to ethnographic evidence from Palestine, and worked alone to construct field huts according to ethnographic evidence from Greece.[44] A biblical text mentions that "Shallum…and his daughters" (Neh 3:12) helped reconstruct Jerusalem's walls after the return from exile. (Biblical scholars, unfamiliar with ethnographic reports, are sometimes incredulous about this verse and suggest changing the text to Shallum's "sons" instead of "daughters.")[45] The Nehemiah passage postdates the Iron Age but likely reflects a long-standing practice of women doing construction.

SEVERAL IMPORTANT FACTORS emerge from this examination of many of women's economic activities:

- All involved processes essential for the survival of the household.
- Women's tasks were often complementary to those of men (see the discussion in chapter 9), as when they transformed raw products produced mainly by men into edible or wearable form; they also assisted men in some activities (mentioned in chapter 3).
- Many of women's time-consuming and physically demanding tasks were technologically sophisticated, with the requisite knowledge passed from senior experts to younger women according to ethnographic reports.
- Many if not all of women's tasks were done together with other women, a feature frequently observed in traditional Mediterranean cultures.
- Women performed most of these tasks in the main activity areas of pillared dwellings.

Women and Children (Reproductive Activities)

However they may depict its characteristics, studies of the household uniformly include women's role in biological reproduction as part of household life. But they rarely include the role of women in the reproduction of social identities. Yet women not only bear children but also bear the major responsibility, at least when their offspring are young, for teaching them how to behave and what to value. In addition, they instruct their children, mainly daughters, in the technologies of the economic activities described in the preceding section. Thus reproduction refers to both having children and teaching them life skills. These are largely interdependent processes whereby the "wider social and cultural norms, rules, and ideals, as well as the more particular 'way of the household' are internalized, mediated, and experienced."[46] Reproduction is an important maintenance activity because it creates children and also socializes them as "future full members of the group."[47]

Childbirth has already been discussed in several chapters, and thus the focus here is on women as educators and socializers of the young. However, it should be emphasized that, unlike in the developed world today, bearing and raising children were not understood as discrete aspects of a woman's life. Nor did women choose, as many do today, whether to work, have a family, or both. With life spans being relatively short (see chapter 5), as much as half of an Israelite woman's life would have been taken up with motherhood. How different that is from the situation in the developed world today, in which women choosing to have children might devote only about one-eighth of an 80-year life span to fulltime motherhood! For Israelite women, adulthood and motherhood were virtually coterminous. Yet maintenance tasks dominated daily life. Thus in subsistence societies in which offspring are critical for household survival and continuity, child-rearing is integrated into daily maintenance routines and does not stand out as a central or separate responsibility.[48] The socialization of children, also essential for household continuity, was likewise integrated into daily activities.

The range of household maintenance activities in today's developed world is significantly smaller than in biblical antiquity, and public education is generally required. Yet the socialization of the young is still an important part of family life. All the more so in the Iron Age, where the household was the only arena in which children could learn basic social and technical skills as well as the cultural patterns of their household and community. The information imparted by mothers to the next generation was all-encompassing in terms of the life skills needed in agrarian households.

A child acquired most technical expertise simply by experience. Children in traditional societies are an integral part of the household labor force. Toddlers perform a few simple tasks and have some regular assignments by the age of six, and children older than ten are often like adults in their contributions to household work.⁴⁹ Biblical texts mention the labor of children: for example, helping with harvest (Prov 10:5) and gathering firewood (Jer 7:18). Younger children of both genders tend to stay with their mothers and gain a rudimentary knowledge of her tasks, and older children accompany and work with the same-gender parent. And as they work, they learn. Children's labor provides welcome assistance and is also the mechanism for imparting knowledge about the task itself. How else would children learn how to grind flour or set a loom or construct an oven? Moreover, women tend to have the primary role in managing the pool of child labor, assigning tasks to both girls and boys even when the latter are dispatched to work with their fathers.⁵⁰

Women also impart social and historical knowledge. Older women, who are less able to perform the full range of maintenance chores, help care for small children, presumably their grandchildren. In traditional societies like ancient Israel that lack schools and general literacy, the oldest living generation—grandparents, especially grandmothers—often take charge of "the narrative activities of the group," transmitting family and community lore to the youngest members of the household.⁵¹ Note that the ancient Greeks called traditional stories *geroia*, "old woman's stories" (cf. Latin *fabulae aniles*, "tales of old women"). These terms later became the pejorative "old wives' tales," but they originate in the role of senior women transmitting cultural traditions. Old women are often among the most gifted storytellers in traditional societies.⁵² Perhaps some women's stories found their way into biblical narratives identified as folk tales.

The book of Proverbs contains admonitions about behavior that likely originated in the instructions of both parents.⁵³ What children learn from their mothers includes, among many things, the practical wisdom of how to negotiate relations with others in the interests of social stability and continuity. More generally, as the nineteenth-century American preacher Hosea Ballou famously proclaimed, "Education commences at the mother's knee, and every word spoken within hearsay of little children tends toward the formation of character."⁵⁴ All proverbs come from real-life situations and serve utilitarian purposes, including encouraging, rebuking, or giving advice to children. Everyday speech becomes family lore transmitted orally and sometimes elaborated into pithy metaphoric sayings grouped together for pedagogical purposes. Ultimately such groups found their way into the fragmented set of sayings in the central section of Proverbs (10:1–22:16), which is apparently older than the other sections and comes from a family/folk setting rather than the educated royal or urban context of the other sections.[55] Many proverbs in the central section reflect the experiential world of agrarians; they emphasize the interpersonal relationships that would be important for households interacting closely with each other, as the next section explains.

Proverbs as a "wisdom" book exhibits a strong connection between wisdom and women, perhaps echoing the woman's affinity for wisdom in the Eden tale (see chapter 4, p. 80). Consider the Hebrew word for wisdom, ḥokmah, which is grammatically feminine (as is Greek sophia). It has a wide set of meanings, more than the English word used to translate it: it can refer to technical expertise and pragmatic life skills as well as more abstract qualities of sagacity. It also designates a quasi-divine figure known as Woman Wisdom (especially in Proverbs 1–9). As suggested in chapter 6, this female personification of wisdom is probably rooted in the roles of women as teachers of both life skills and technical skills. Woman wisdom is a cultural expression of the primary role of women in socializing the young and managing the household.[56]

Proverbs is also noteworthy in its several references to both mother and father as educators whose wise words should be heeded. Examples are "Hear, my child, your father's instruction, / and do not reject your mother's teaching" (Prov 1:8), and "My child, keep your father's commandment, / and do not forsake your mother's teaching" (Prov 6:20). "Mother" and "father" form a poetic pair, together denoting the complementary role of parents in educating their children in a society that probably lacked schools, except perhaps for some elites.[57] The parental roles were complementary, but they were not the same. Women were the primary caregivers for both female and male children for the first few years of their lives, played a dominant role in instructing girls until they were married, and likely continued to be authoritative figures for boys as they progressed toward adulthood.

By example and word, children learned the technical skills and behavioral patterns essential for the continuity of household life from both parents, with women perhaps having the dominant role in this aspect of household reproduction. Woman's parenting responsibilities were far more comprehensive than we can easily fathom, accustomed as we are (unless we home-school our children) to handing our children at ever-earlier ages over to others to care for them and teach them. The instructional wisdom of women was an integral factor in the daily life of Israelite agrarians. Mothers taught their children the dynamics of household life and how to perform its myriad activities; and they also modeled modes of interacting with others.

Women's Interactions (Sociopolitical Activities)

A striking feature of many of the economic activities of Israelite women described above is that they were carried out in the company of other women. This is typical of peasant women in traditional Mediterranean societies: women share both daily and seasonal tasks with other women. Embedded in the production of food, textiles, and other household necessities were regular social interactions. These interactions in turn produced relationships that were neither a hypothetical web of casual acquaintances nor a frivolous or unimportant feature of women's lives.[58] Rather, women's informal associations were essential for the maintenance of the household and the community in the challenging highland environment described in chapter 3. They formed the core of a rich cultural world with vital social and political functions, for women's interactions had ramifications for the sociopolitical dynamics of their communities.

The ways in which the connections among women benefited their households and communities are usually overlooked.[59] Researchers commonly focus on the more formal and visible forms of community organization and leadership, such as male village officials or lineage councils. Biblical examples are the frequently mentioned "elders," "chiefs," "heads," and "leaders" (e.g., Num 11:16; Josh 22:14; 1 Kgs 8:1; Ps 105:22). Equivalent female designations are lacking. Does that mean that women had no community roles? Gender-sensitive research into traditional societies has corrected the androcentric bias in examining sociopolitical life by recognizing the importance of informal women's alliances, called "women's networks," in maintaining community life. These networks operate differently than do men's formal structures and visible leaders; but they are no less important. Informal as they are, and as invisible as they may be to an outside observer, women's networks actually function as institutions providing critical social linkages. The tendency to equate "formal" with "important"

and "informal" with "unimportant" does not do justice to the dynamics
of women's informal alliances; and it occludes the way women's networks
perform essential functions.[60]

Two biblical texts reflect the existence of women's informal networks
in ancient Israel.[61] One is the well-known story of Ruth and her beloved
mother-in-law Naomi. Women's groups frame Ruth's experience in
Naomi's hometown, Bethlehem. At the beginning of the tale, the "whole
town" knows when Ruth and Naomi arrive; but "the women" are the
ones who greet them (Ruth 1:19). And at the end, the "women of the
neighborhood" (*šekenot*) attend the birth of Ruth's son Obed, destined
to be King David's grandfather (Ruth 4:17; cf. 1 Sam 4:20, where women
attend Ichabod's mother when she goes into labor). This group of women
names the infant. Although women outnumber men as name-givers in
the Hebrew Bible (by nearly two to one), this is the only instance of
a group of women naming a child.[62] In so doing, they signify solidarity
with the new mother.

The second is the passage about Israelite women seeking resources
for their journey out of Egypt from their female Egyptian neighbors
(*šekenot*). This text (Exod 3:22) suggests that residential proximity was an
important factor in the relationships that constituted the social world of
Israelite women. Moreover, the close relationship between Israelite women
and their Egyptian counterparts trumps the narrative theme portraying the Egyptians as the enemies. After all, the Israelite women request,
rather than steal, valuables to take with them (despite the biblical label
"plunder").

These biblical glimpses of women interacting with their cohorts evoke
questions: How did these groups function? What were their specific
activities, other than the ones revealed in these two texts? Ethnographic
data are invaluable in attempting to answer such questions, for informal
women's networks have been observed in many traditional Mediterranean
societies.[63] Their importance is greatest in societies, like Iron Age Israel,
existing at the subsistence level.[64] And their presence has both social and
political implications.

At the most basic level, this web of connections meant companionship and emotional support for women in the face of the drudgery of
their tasks and the inevitable difficulties they encountered. Women in
rural Crete, for example, spoke of the transformative quality of work
shared with another, changing mundane tasks into ones "of pleasure and
intimacy"; and the camaraderie of women working together in a Greek

mountain community helped them face their common challenges and gave them a sense of solidarity.[65] Women's relationships also mean cooperation in negotiating access to and supplying fuel for shared ovens. Or they mean providing help with technologically complicated or physically demanding tasks when additional expertise or another pair of hands eases the difficulty.

Working together forges a bond entailing the obligation of women to help each other, knowing that help will be reciprocal. The assistance may be as basic as lending a tool or utensil, as noted for peasant women in Greek farming villages.[66] But often the problems were much greater. Households in a premodern society, without access to the kind of social services we have come to expect from government or not-for-profit organizations, depended on mutual aid. Because their resources were limited and variable, individual households could not have survived without the assistance of others. The mutual aid characteristic of traditional communities was no less than a "third-order defense against food shortages, death, and famine."[67] Women's ties with each other were instrumental in facilitating help for households having difficulties. In fact, women are better positioned to do this because of their daily and direct interactions than are men whose agrarian tasks tend to be done alone or with sons.

Here's how it works. Because they spend many hours together, women have intimate knowledge of each other and their households. Their gatherings are opportunities to share not only tasks but also information. Women exchanged news at a neighborhood oven in early twentieth-century Palestinian villages while their bread baked; and when several women were weaving together, others gathered around them to exchange news while also helping to relieve the monotony of the weavers' work.[68] In rural Greece, most time-consuming female jobs took place in "sociable" space or courtyards and were essential for sharing information.[69] Sharing ovens in Turkish villages is a valued opportunity for socializing and the accompanying transmission of ideas and information; even women with their own ovens thus prefer to use communal ones.[70] The dynamics of women's interactions in a Sardinian village are telling: "Women are the typical channels of social communication. While they prepare the dough and bake the bread, they make an X-ray of the town."[71] They know, for example, if someone is about to give birth or has just done so, or if someone is ill or injured, or if a household has especially severe food shortages. Because of their solidarity, they rally to deploy assistance—by dispatching one or more of their number to assist in a birth (as in the book of

Ruth), sending an older son to help in the fields if a man is ill, or pooling resources to provide food for a desperate family.

Crises in one household in a traditional society could be ameliorated only by the assistance of people from other households. Indeed, even in today's world, with government agencies providing goods and services to those in need, volunteer organizations and the helping hands of neighbors still play a role. In biblical antiquity women's relationships facilitated the assistance all too often needed in the face of chronic food shortages and inevitable injuries and illnesses. Women's networks were the mechanisms for the mutual aid essential for survival. To the extent that kin groups in traditional societies tend to occupy small settlements or sections of larger ones, women's networks coincided with kin relationships—proba-bly the clan (*mišpaḥah*) described in chapter 6—intensifying even further the obligations to provide mutual aid. In anthropological terms, the clan functions as a "protective association" of households.[72]

Another aspect of women's informal networks is related to the kinship dynamics obligating related households to help each other. As already noted, Israelite marriage was *patrilocal*, meaning that a woman left her natal household to join her husband's. She was thus connected to two lin-eages—her husband's by marriage and her father's by birth. Because most settlements were small, it would have been common to obtain brides from a nearby village or town. This had the pragmatic function of creating alli-ances among neighboring settlements and contributing to the web of kin-ship in which households were situated. These inter-settlement alliances, coinciding in ancient Israel with clans, typically help maintain peace among contiguous settlements and increase the likelihood that related households would help each other in difficult times.[73] Because women typically retain their natal affiliations, they are positioned to maintain connections with households and thus lineages in nearby settlements in ways described below.

Women's intercommunity connections based on kinship also facilitated the dissemination of advances in female-gendered technologies. Teaching and learning the intricacies of various maintenance tasks, especially the more complex ones, in some cases might transcend the mother-child dynamic and the local social network. Gendered knowledge would have extended to other villages via kinship connections, thus contributing to the cooperative relationships among a group of settlements.[74]

In sum, women's social relationships in traditional societies character-istically extend beyond their own households. Through their quotidian

maintenance activities Israelite women established a framework of interpersonal relationships connecting neighboring households. And through
their connections with their natal households they facilitated alliances
with lineages in nearby settlements, which in turn were the basis for the
cooperation and reciprocity essential for survival in their uncertain agrarian world. Women's household maintenance activities were simultaneously
community maintenance activities. The significance of this for women is
considered in chapter 10.

Women's networks and intra-settlement connections also have some
specifically political implications. Political participation in traditional societies means involvement, whether directly or indirectly, in decision-making
processes concerning issues such as water rights, allocation of resources,
military action, and leadership positions.[75] But these processes were not
the sole domain of men. Anthropological research has shown that wom-
en's household activities have political consequences—women's relationships within and beyond the household are inextricably connected with
political alliances.[76]

Political action is not simply what officials do or what elders decide;
it cannot take place without information and perspectives that feed into
the leadership structures. The communication channels formed by their
shared activities mean that women are privy to information that was
often invaluable for community decision-making. Women working with
each other, but separately from men, typically have more access to certain kinds of knowledge than do men. They acquire "practical and community knowledge," different from that acquired by men, that they could
use "in order to assert their own wills."[77] For precisely this reason, for
example, women in a small (population 363) west Mediterranean village in the mid-twentieth century played political roles of some importance precisely because of their communication networks. Women, the
researcher noted, "are often both more cognizant than men of the needs
of the village and more able to aid in the accomplishment of individual
and community-wide goals."[78] Even in Muslim North African communities with rather rigid gender divisions, women's relationships with each
other, as observed in the 1960s, were "instrumental" because they "carry
considerable weight" in both economic and political matters.[79]

Working together in the main rooms of a pillared dwelling, or in its
courtyard or nearby outdoor spaces, Israelite women were not sequestered
nor were they cut off from the comings and goings of male household
members and the issues that concerned them. In all likelihood women

and men shared most household space, depending on the season and time of day.[80] Indeed, even in elite households in ancient Greece, which were often assumed to have had separate women's quarters, women and men are now known to have used the same household space and to have encountered each other as they carried out their daily tasks.[81] Thus what women learned from each other was readily transmitted to their male relatives. For example, they would have known when olives and grapes were being harvested and how extensive the yields were. This information likely informed the way the communal food-processing activities mentioned in chapter 6 were organized. In other words, data collected by women would have facilitated the collective decisions of village or lineage elders in assigning the use of agricultural installations.

Women's access to knowledge likely contributed to other community decisions. Legal or jural issues—theft, bodily harm, property disputes, and the like—inevitably arose. Women surely discussed with each other and then with the male members of their households the problems being adjudicated or handled by male officials, and ethnographic data suggest that they might influence outcomes.[82] The cohort of women functioned in some ways like today's information-providing focus groups, and the shared information influenced community decisions.

Moreover, when Israelites deliberated about matters concerning an individual household or about issues relating to the community as a whole, those discussions did not take place in some remote city hall, as in today's world. Rather, in traditional societies political life was carried out in households by both women and men.[83] Moreover, political discussions and negotiations are typically accompanied by food prepared by women. Although this may seem trivial to us today, with the ready availability of catered or take-out foods, women in traditional settings could affect the success of the proceedings by preparing suitable repasts. Also, the appearance of women at extra-household meetings of community officials at communal gathering places—the gate area in walled settlements (see, e.g., Josh 20:4)—cannot be ruled out. Although biblical legal materials may have little relevance for examining daily life in agrarian settlements, as noted in chapter 2, they do mention several cases in which women appear before community elders (Deut 21:18-20; 22:15; 25:7; cf. Num 27:1-2).

Women's kinship connections were also important for political processes. Remember that the so-called private/public dichotomy that characterizes life in industrial societies does not apply to premodern ones (see chapter 6, pp. 122–123). Households were integrated into wider and overlapping social domains and political alliances, often determined by kinship structures.[84] Ethnographers have noted that in third-world countries, where the state does not always reach into rural peasant households, politics are still conducted through kin relationships and are often based on information and connections supplied by women.[85] Indeed, "where social relations and political alliances are one and the same, women's social activities are also political activities."[86] Kinship ties maintained by women typically help preserve or restore peace among contiguous settlements, especially when resources are limited and disagreements about land usage or water rights inevitably arise. The book of Judges perhaps reflects this, for women in that biblical book frequently mediate (or sometimes disrupt) the bonds of power between men.[87]

In addition, because of their access to information from their natal communities about potential marriage partners for their offspring, Israelite women would have had a pivotal role in the very formation of alliances that were necessary for stable relations among neighboring settlements and that were also instrumental in forging coalitions to deal with hostilities or attacks from outside groups.[88] Marriage in traditional societies is not a private matter. Our current idea of marriage as a love-based relationship between two individuals would not have been understood by Iron Age Israelites. Marital unions could certainly involve affection and love (e.g., Gen 24:67), but they were primarily relationships among households and clans and sometimes tribes, in addition, of course, to being the mechanism for producing offspring and continuity. Note that the biblical word translated "groom" is *ḥatan*, which denotes a "man with a father-in-law," thus signifying the concept of a marriage as a union of two households—a man's parents with his wife's parents—rather than of a man and a woman.

All told, Israelite households were arguably settings in which political life was carried out by both women and men. Sherry Ortner, an anthropologist well known for her theoretical contributions to the study of gender in traditional societies, notes that women "systematically participate in the larger social rankings of their natural and marital families, and so participate in important ways in macro-political and economic processes."[89] Female political activity is not always visible, especially because we are conditioned to look at formal leadership positions in considering political dynamics; but it is no less important. Women's political participation in ancient Israel would have affected the allocation of resources and access to communal facilities, helped create and maintain alliances, and facilitated the resolution of conflicts within and among households or settlements. Political interactions among men typically rely on information, often unavailable to them directly, gathered by women in their informal networks or through connections with their natal lineages. How would those inter-settlement connections be maintained, given that women's daily activities centered on their households and those of their immediate neighbors? The answer lies in the likelihood that household members at times traveled to other communities for the religious events, described in the next chapter, that were an integral part of the fabric of the lives of both women and men.

8

Women and Household Maintenance,
Part II: Religious Activities

WHAT WERE THE religious experiences of Everywoman Eve? The Hebrew Bible tells us little about women's lives in general and perhaps least about their religious experience, which is probably of greatest interest today. Rather, attention is focused on the sacrificial cult carried out by male priests at the central shrine, with large sections of the Pentateuch providing instructions for sacrifices. Household or family sacrifices at other locales, presented as occurring before the Jerusalem temple was built, are mentioned (e.g., Gen 31:54; Exod 20:24 [Heb. 20:21]; 1 Sam 1:3-4); otherwise sacrifices are condemned (e.g., 1 Kgs 22:43 [Heb. 22:44]; Ezek 20:27-28).

But was sacrifice the only form of religious activity? And if sacrifices were offered only in Jerusalem, did that mean that household religious life consisted only of journeys to the temple, a long trip for many people? The simple answer is that temple sacrifice was *not* the only form of religious activity. People everywhere experience religious life in their own households and communities, making it inconceivable that the religious life of Israelites would be limited to temple sacrifice. Indeed, because there were virtually no temples in Israel and Judah in the Iron Age other than the one in Jerusalem (as noted in chapter 2), household religion was surely central to the religious experience of most people. The central shrine may loom large in the Bible, but that doesn't mean it loomed large in the life of Everywoman Eve and her household. The paucity of biblical evidence about household practices is a function of the national orientation of the Hebrew Bible (see chapter 2, p. 21) and does not mean that household religion was nonexistent or unimportant. Indeed, because the central sanctuary was largely inaccessible to most people and because religion is such an essential element of people's lives, a wide range of religious events and behaviors was surely part of Israelite households.

Biblical scholars have studied religion apart from the temple cult, but their research has tended to consider household religion more in terms of piety than practice. For example, Rainer Albertz's monumental work on Israelite religion uses the term "family piety" in discussing household religion and endeavors to identify which deities were worshipped.[1] Similarly, in his popular but controversial book *Did God Have a Wife?*, William Dever deals with non-temple religion and even considers women's roles; but mainly he aims to identify Asherah as a deity that Israelites worshipped.[2]

Dever's work notwithstanding, scholarly attention to women's religious practices has usually been nonexistent or misinformed.[3] One nineteenth-century scholar amazingly asserted that "women participated in all essentials of the cult, both as worshipper and officiant."[4] But most took the opposite view. Wellhausen, mentioned in chapter 1 as a giant in biblical studies, asserted that women had no political rights and therefore no place in religion.[5] Subsequently, for much of the twentieth century, scholars of Israelite religion generally ignored women. That changed with the impact of feminism on biblical studies in the late twentieth century. At the least, more women scholars meant greater interest in women's religious experiences. However, their interest typically meant determining the nature of women's participation in the priestly cult. Even Phyllis Bird's pioneering article, "The Place of Women in the Israelite Cultus," gives only passing attention to other forms of women's religious experience.[6]

In contrast, women's role in household religion is the focus here. Religious activities were integrally related to the maintenance activities described in chapter 7 and thus an essential part of household life. Indeed, cultic items (see below) have been discovered in all parts of Israelite domiciles. Household practices were usually related to life-death concerns, for they were based on the belief that household welfare was related to the will of the god(s). Referring to god with a lower-case *g* and a possible plural is intentional, for the Yahweh-alone idea dominating the Hebrew Bible was not accepted by all Israelites until the end of the Iron Age or later.[7] Before then, most Israelites acknowledged the deities of their Canaanite ancestors: El, Baal, Astarte, Anat, and Asherah (e.g., Gen 35:7; Judg 2:13; 2 Kgs 21:7). Because the religious acts directed toward one or more of those deities, or to Yahweh, were likely similar, these acts can be examined apart from the god(s) involved.

Religion for the Israelites was not simply or even mainly a matter of belief in one or more gods. Rather, belief in divine powers was not distinct from activities directed toward them—religion meant both belief in transcendent being(s) and performance of certain practices or rituals, often meant to influence them in order to secure household well-being.[8] Were we to focus on beliefs as the chief characteristic of household religion we would be succumbing to another kind of presentism (in addition to those mentioned in chapter 6), in which faith and spirituality are considered the hallmarks of religious experience. Religion in America today tends to be equated with belief in God, prayer, and attendance at religious services.[9] This concept is inadequate for studying the Israelites.[10] We cannot assume that people in the biblical past thought about their god(s) in the same way many people think about God today. Religion in biblical antiquity was "essentially a program of action.... [it] was not primarily something that people thought but something that they did."[11] In a world apparently without atheism, belief was assumed and religion was a set of intensely meaningful behaviors.[12] Deities were approached through actions, not by faith.

Accordingly, religious practices themselves are increasingly the focus of the study of household religion.[13] Archaeological remains and biblical and other ancient texts provide relevant information. Practices noted by ethnographers are also invaluable in giving a new dimension of meaning to biblical texts or generally establishing the importance of households in the religious lives of traditional cultures. Traditional Greek household life may be an apt analogy: the household is the center of family and religious life.[14]

Recent archaeological analysis indicates that households were the primary location for ritual activities in Iron Age Israel.[15] Whether individual dwellings had their own shrines—areas with benches or niches sometimes called "cult corners"—is debatable, given that few have been discovered. Structural shrines were probably situated only in the households of village or clan leaders, where they were likely used by both senior women and men.[16] Yet religious activities took place in every household, even without a shrine. Ritual objects recovered from Israelite dwellings testify to household religious activities. To be sure, identifying ritual objects is problematic because many utilitarian objects were also used for rituals.[17] Some items, such as incense burners or amulets, are explicitly cultic. But others served both ordinary and cultic purposes; a juglet, for example, might hold liquids for preparing foods or for pouring out libations.

Because foodstuffs, as will become clear, were an important part of house-hold rituals, almost all items used in their preparation were, in a sense, cultic objects.

Virtually all the household religious activities of Israelite women inter-sected with their other maintenance activities. An important reason for this is that most religious acts involved food, and women performed most food-preparation tasks. Another reason is the responsibility of women for bearing and raising children, a process often fraught with problems (noted in chapters 3 and 5) and addressed by religious behaviors. This intercon-nectedness of religion with maintenance activities makes it difficult to organize a discussion of them. The sections that follow—on health care, reproduction, festivals and feasts, and foodways—are thus clearly overlap-ping; but they nonetheless provide a way to consider Everywoman Eve's religious experiences.

Before proceeding, it is important to note that two conceptual issues frequently impede consideration of women's religious activities. The first is the tendency to see household religious activities as oppositional to those of the national or state cult. The former are considered "popular" or folk practices as opposed to "official" ones; as such they are often viewed as heterodox, deviant, or otherwise illegitimate. This separation into two mutually exclusive groups is thus value laden and is especially problematic when elites are aligned with the official, and others, especially women, with the popular.[18] Recent research has problematized this dichotomy, noting that because these categories are neither straightforward nor easily defined, they are inappropriately applied to ancient Israel. Specific prac-tices must be analyzed on their own terms and without this polarizing and misleading paradigm.[19]

The second conceptual issue is that some household religious practices can be designated "magic," a term often contrasted with religion and thus viewed pejoratively. This negative perception is particularly detrimental in considering women's religious practices, for men become associated with "good" religion and women with "dangerous" magic. A more anthropo-logical perspective indicates that, in attempting to manipulate or influ-ence supernatural forces by prayer or offerings or maneuvers, religion and magic are overlapping phenomena.[20] Both are forms of communication with the divine and are used by both women and men to relate to super-natural powers in traditional societies.[21] As practices intended to influence supernatural powers, magical behaviors are better considered instances of ritual power.[22]

Health Care

Illness was all too common in Iron Age households (see chapter 3, p. 54). Although people today may turn to prayer when they or their loved ones are ill, health issues are largely the domain of medical professionals. That was not always the case. Problems now handled mainly through medicine were addressed in biblical antiquity by religious practices. Throughout the ancient world "health care systems" were integrally related with religion. Illness was understood to have been brought about by divine will, perhaps because of a person's misdeeds or simply because of the deity's unknowable plans (as for Job). Semidivine demons (e.g., *ketev* in Ps 91:6 and Deut 32:24; translated "pestilence" in the NRSV but actually referring to a demonic force causing disease) were also thought to cause illness. And some reproductive problems (discussed in the next section) were attributed to demonic forces. Because of the divine or semidivine causes of health problems, prayer or incantations almost certainly accompanied treatment. Medical care was a religious activity.[23]

The household was the primary place for caring for the ill in ancient societies, even in those with well-developed healthcare techniques and professionals (like Egypt and Mesopotamia). Home health care was the "preferred and most common option."[24] Household healing practices go back to prehistoric times, for people have always sought to alleviate symptoms and end suffering. Treatment generally involved the use of *materia medica*, substances ingested, inhaled, or applied to wounds. For example, there are several biblical references to balm (Jer 8:22; 46:11; 51:8); and oils are mentioned as dressings for wounds (Isa 1:6). Babylonian texts provide recipes for concocting pharmacological substances.[25] Nearly a hundred different plants that grow in Palestine, some mentioned in the Bible, were used in folk medicine until recently.[26] (By folk medicine, I mean traditional treatments based on experience and on knowledge passed down across generations and often using plant-derived substances.)

Women were likely the healers in Israelite household, for several reasons:

1. Many plants used as condiments for flavoring food were also used to concoct healing potions or salves. In preparing meals, women became familiar with the properties of these plants. As many as twenty substances, many related to food preparation, would have been in the medicine chest of an Israelite household.[27] Hyssop, for example, can

flavor food or serve as a purgative (Ps 51:7). Women probably used the small stone mortars-and-pestles found in domiciles for preparing flavorings for food and also for compounding ointments.

2. Female imagery sometime accompanies the use of healing substances (e.g., Jer 46:11).

3. The Bible refers to women as herbalists. In warning people of the drawbacks of monarchic rule, Samuel says that kings would take their daughters to serve as "perfumers, cooks, and bakers" (1 Sam 8:13). "Perfumers" is a misleading translation. Its Hebrew root (*rkh*) refers more broadly to preparing ointments or spice blends for medicinal, culinary, or esthetic purposes. But perfume production in antiquity was largely done by specialists in workshops, not women in households.[28] Thus the daughters in Samuel's warning were those familiar with household procedures: cooking, baking, and the preparation of culinary and medicinal substances, not fragrances. They were herbalists, not perfumers.

4. Ethnographic information indicates that women typically have knowledge about using certain substances and techniques to care for ill or injured people. Across cultures, women are generally the healers.[29]

5. Sorcerers—specifically female ones—are condemned in Exodus 21:17, an indication that sorcery was practiced by women. Sorcery involves casting negative spells against someone, but spells can also be cast against evil forces. Note that rural Greek villagers used spells against forces thought to cause illness despite the condemnation of those practices by the church.[30]

6. Anthropomorphic imagery for God, sometimes attributing female qualities to God, appears sporadically in the Hebrew Bible.[31] A striking instance in Hosea 11:3-4 depicts God's maternal care for Israelites: teaching them to walk, and also holding, *healing*, loving, and feeding them. Caring for sick children was a mother's responsibility and likely signifies the wider household role of women as healers.

7. Women's experience with childbirth and child-care perhaps made them more aware than men of body processes.[32]

In short, health care in ancient Israel was primarily household-based and administered by women, often with the advice of female neighbors with greater knowledge of techniques and substances. Some knowledgeable women probably had a semiprofessional role as healers in their communities (see chapter 9), just as did women (midwives) competent in reproductive issues.

Reproduction

The maintenance of households depended on women bearing children and on children surviving to adulthood. But having successful pregnancies and viable newborns was fraught with difficulties; maternal and infant mortality rates were high (see chapter 5, pp. 98–99).

Like the health issues discussed in the preceding section, problems associated with reproduction are handled today by medical personnel, although prayers might also be offered. But in the ancient world and in traditional societies to this day, those difficulties were often considered the work of evil spirits and were treated by the use of devices and acts meant to protect mothers and infants by deterring the powers that threatened them. Babylonian medical texts, for example, include incantations along with pharmacological recipes in the instructions for dealing with childbirth.[33] Particularly menacing in Mesopotamian cultures were the malevolent female demons Lamashtu and Lilith, both believed to prey upon women giving birth or nursing their children, sometimes snatching newborns from the mother's breast.[34] Lilith also appears in the Hebrew Bible (Isa 34:14) and in postbiblical Jewish sources, indicating that Israelites too feared her.

Even when medical assistance is available, women in traditional societies characteristically turn to folk medicine to aid conception and protect pregnant women, new mothers, and infants. The Hebrew Bible offers relatively few clues about Israelite treatments for reproductive problems. Texts from other ancient Near Eastern cultures and early postbiblical Jewish literature provide information, and some archaeological artifacts can be associated with practices relating to reproduction. In addition, ethnography and travelers' reports indicate a rich array of practices. Particularly valuable is the two-volume work by the late nineteenth-century folklorist Lucy Garnett.[35] For a decade Garnett traveled throughout the Ottoman Empire and, as a woman, gained access to Muslim, Christian, and Jewish homes that would not otherwise have welcomed a Western stranger. All these sources are important, given the paucity of biblical information.

Reproductive success was a concern of both men and women.[36] Then, as now, barrenness was sometimes a problem. The barren-woman tales in the Hebrew Bible herald the children that are ultimately born (e.g., Isaac to Sarah, Samuel to Hannah) but also reflect infertility problems (cf. Ps 113:9 and Isa 54:1). In several instances men's petitionary prayers or sacrifices invoke divine aid for barren wives (e.g., Gen 15:2; 20:17-18; 25:21).

However, judging from ethnographic evidence, household religious activities meant to aid conception and protect the mother and child were largely the domain of women. The story of Rachel and the mandrake (Gen 30:14-17), involving a magic-medical use of a plant substance to aid conception, is an example.[37] So too is Hannah's successful attempt to conceive a child: she prays and makes a vow, and she offers a sacrifice after her son's birth in partial fulfillment of the vow or simply in gratitude (1 Sam 1). Her activities take place at a shrine; but the sacrifices of Samson's parents, in their quest for conception, take place in their own fields. Also, Samson's mother adheres to certain dietary restrictions (Judg 13:1-23). Other remedies for infertility and related problems included herbs, amulets, and incantations.[38]

Some biblical practices exhibit striking connections between texts, artifacts, and/or ethnographic reports.[39] The treatment of a newborn, according to Ezekiel 16:4, involved three procedures: (1) washing and anointing the infant; (2) rubbing it with salt; and (3) wrapping it tightly in cloths. All three were practical measures with apotropaic (protective) functions meant to keep away harmful spirits. They are mentioned in the Talmud as being so important that they must be done even if it meant violating sabbath regulations (e.g., b. Šabb. 129b), and all appear in ethnographic reports about Christian, Jewish, and Muslim women. Infants in Syria, Palestine, and Iran were washed with salt and oil and then swaddled; and similar practices were observed n Bulgaria and Macedonia. These practices have persisted in Mediterranean and Middle Eastern regions since biblical times, probably with the same sense that they keep newborns safe from malevolent forces.

Another widespread practice is the use of light, or metal jewelry that reflects light, to ward off demons thought to be lurking in the darkness and threatening newborns and new mothers. Terror and pestilence were linked with night and darkness (Ps 91:5-6), and so too were evil forces. But light represents divine protection (e.g., Job 29:3), as when parental guidance is likened to lamplight protecting children from danger (Prov 6:20-23). The discovery of small terracotta oil lamps in virtually every excavation is relevant to these beliefs. Keeping a lamp burning near sleeping children was arguably one use of lamplight. Today nightlights placed in children's rooms to assuage their fear of monsters is a response to the same kind of concern, one recorded in many cultures. Albanian Muslims and Moroccan Berbers, for example, keep a fire or candle burning continuously near an infant and its mother lest supernatural beings bring evil.

Talmudic and medieval Jewish tradition records the lighting of lamps or candles near a newborn to celebrate the birth and also to keep away the harmful demons of the dark.[40]

Amulets were also widely used as protection and are attested in archaeological materials and in texts. The ugly Egyptian dwarf-god Bes appears on amulets and other artifacts (including scarabs, seals, and ceramic appliqués) found at Israelite sites. In fact, several molds for manufacturing Bes amulets have been found, indicating that they were produced locally rather than being imported from Egypt. They apparently were in high demand. Why was Bes so popular? Undoubtedly because Bes, according to many Egyptian sources, was a guardian of newborns. His ugly countenance, along with the knife he often brandishes, was believed to fend off demons threatening infants and new mothers. Women who used these amulets were probably not Bes worshippers. Visual symbols, especially those considered apotropaic, could migrate across cultures, retaining their symbolic power but not necessarily their original theological meaning.

Another amuletic object found in some Iron Age households is the eye symbol, or *wedjat*, sometimes called the Eye of Horus. It was meant to ward off the "evil eye," seen as the source of infant mortality among other ills in Near Eastern cultures from antiquity to the present.[41] For example, a Kurdish Jewish woman in the early twentieth century repeatedly blamed the evil eye for the death of her infants and those of her mother.[42] As protection from the evil eye, the *wedjat* is found widely in Middle Eastern cultures and elsewhere to this very day. An eye symbol atop a pyramid appears on the back of a U.S. dollar bill. And the Rx symbol used in prescribing medications probably originated as a stylized *wedjat*, symbolizing the role of drugs in protecting against illness and promoting healing. Clearly, belief in Horus is not a factor in the eye symbol's current use, nor would an Israelite woman hanging an eye amulet around an infant's neck be invoking an Egyptian deity.

Amulets are not mentioned in the Bible except in a list of women's items of adornment (Isa 3:20). But their use by Israelites seems certain because archaeologists have found examples at Israelite sites and because they are widely attested in ancient Near Eastern literature, postbiblical Jewish texts, and ethnography. Mesopotamian sources, for example, instruct pregnant women to wear amuletic jewelry and also recite incantations to ward off danger; and Egyptian texts refer to certain kinds of jewelry with amuletic power. Talmudic passages attest to (by condemning) a lively involvement of women with magical practices meant to avert the evil eye and also advocate wearing amuletic stones to prevent miscarriage. Other ancient Jewish texts recommend amulets (*lamellae*) inscribed with biblical verses—especially Exodus 23:26, "No woman in your land shall miscarry or be barren"—as protection during childbirth.

Another kind of artifact is frequently related to fertility or lactation concerns: small (usually 3 to 6 inches high) terracotta figurines of standing women, naked from the waist up. Most have prominent breasts with the woman's hands placed under them. Known as "pillar figurines" because the lower part resembles a slightly flaring pillar, many hundreds have been discovered, almost always in Iron II household or tomb contexts at Judean sites. Ever since they were first discovered in the nineteenth century, most scholars have considered them fertility goddess figurines. An anthropological perspective, however, contests that supposition.[43] And an exhaustive archaeological and phenomenological study suggests they had general apotropaic or healing purposes.[44] Thus it now seems unlikely that they were used for pregnancy or lactation problems but rather were used by women (and men) in healing rites. I mention them only because they are well-known artifacts long—and perhaps erroneously—associated in biblical scholarship with fertility issues or goddess worship.

The ritual practices just described were concerned mainly with achieving reproductive success. Others marked or celebrated the arrival of a child and are considered below as part of Israelite life-cycle religious practices.

Feasts and Festivals

Celebrations are ubiquitous in human cultures. It would be difficult to imagine that people could live without events offering periodic relief from the stresses of the workaday world and without ways to celebrate milestones in their household and communal lives.

Food plays a role in all such events. Consider the etymology of "festival" and the related "feasts." Both derive from Latin—*festa* ("feasts, holidays"), the neuter plural of *festus* ("festive, joyful, merry")—via Old French and Middle English. And both words are related to *feriæ* "holiday" and *fanum* "temple."[45] Today "feast" is used for a special meal usually (but not always) held in a secular context, and festivals too are generally secular. But when these words entered English in the thirteenth century, both signified religious events and were virtually identical in meaning. And in biblical antiquity any special meal or celebration was inherently religious. Thus, for ancient Israel, the two terms are roughly interchangeable and

are often used synonymously by biblical scholars. Because Israelite celebrations, even funerary ones, involved feasting, women's participation in
them overlapped with the food-processing activities discussed in chapter 7
and also with the foodways described in the next section of this chapter.

Aside from their religious dimension, what else characterizes a festal
event? What is a feast? Social scientists have offered many definitions.
Simply put, a feast is a ritualized meal, with functions other than just
sustenance.[46] But other features are also salient:[47]

- Food and drink are generally more abundant and/or of better quality
  than at ordinary meals.
- The meal has a special purpose.
- A feast is usually longer than daily meals; sometimes it lasts several
  days and has a sequence of meals.
- The number of participants is typically (but not always) greater than the
  number of people in an individual household. A feast often involves several households connected by kinship or proximity, or even an entire
  community.

Social scientists usually classify feasts as either occasional events or regular ones. The former are typically associated with life-cycle events and
originate in the household in which that event occurs. (Other occasional feasts originate with community authorities and are not considered
here.[48]) The latter are feasts that occur at set times: annually, monthly, or
even weekly.

Life-Cycle Events

Cultures everywhere mark life-cycle events with rites of passage. Some are
linked to biological transitions: chiefly birth, puberty, and death. Others
signal social transitions, marriage being the most prominent example in
traditional societies. Biblical texts and sometimes archaeology provide evidence of celebrations marking stages in the life process, although there is
no mention of puberty rites in the Hebrew Bible.

Birth Rituals

Rituals surrounding childbirth overlap with the rituals and activities
meant to achieve reproductive success and were surely a central aspect of
household religion.[49] Women, like those attending the birth of Ruth's son

(Ruth 4:14-16), uttered prayers and blessings of gratitude. The song attributed to Hannah (1 Sam 2:1-10) is perhaps an example of a birth-song genre.[50] And, although not mentioned in the Hebrew Bible, feasts celebrating the birth of a child were probably held in conjunction with two birth rituals: circumcision and name-giving.

The circumcision of newborn males is a childbirth ritual apparently unique to the Israelites and their Jewish successors, for virtually every other culture practicing circumcision performs it on older boys or at puberty or marriage.[51] Circumcision festivities, with food and drink and also music, vary widely in postbiblical Judaism. Some, especially those with protective as well as celebratory aspects, surely have Israelite roots. Consider the cryptic and troubling account of the circumcision of Moses' son (Exod 4:24-26). God apparently tries to kill Moses or the son, and Moses' wife Zipporah comes to the rescue by expertly circumcising the son (or Moses?). Among all the references to circumcision in the Hebrew Bible, this one is notable because a woman with priestly competence performs it and also because it seems to be apotropaic rather than related to the covenant.[52] It suggests that the enigmatic origins of Israelite infant circumcision may lie in a mother's efforts to safeguard her family.

Name-giving, presumably accompanied by a naming feast, frequently acknowledges God's role in the birth of a child. Names in ancient Israel were commonly *theophoric*: they consisted of a divine name and another word indicating past or hoped-for divine help or protection. About one-fourth of the 1600-plus personal names found on Iron Age inscriptions allude to the birth process.[53] For example, "Mattaniah," found several times in the Bible and on many seal inscriptions, means "gift of Yah [short for Yahweh]." Women name their children in about two-thirds of the naming narratives in the Hebrew Bible, as when the matriarch Rachel names the four sons she considers hers and when Leah names the nine children she claims. The presence of male name-givers may reflect the Bible's androcentrism and mask a reality of mothers nearly always naming their offspring.[54] Names invoking God's role in birth and women as name-givers together indicate women's role in household religious practices related to reproduction.

One biblical reference to a religious aspect of childbirth relates to impurity. (Impurity makes a person ineligible to approach the central shrine, and bodily emissions of both men and women can cause impurity.) The period of impurity after bearing a daughter is double the impure period following the birth of a son (Lev 12:1-8), suggesting a preference

for male children. However, the reason for the difference in the duration of impurity is not specified, and other reasons are possible. Perhaps
a woman's impure state was shorter for a son because of the circumcision to take place on the eighth day; circumcision trumps maternal impurity. Moreover, the sacrifices a new mother must offer are the same for
infant girls and boys (Lev 12:6), thus indicating an equivalency of male
and female newborns.[55] Those sacrifices included purification offerings,
which became consecrated food—part of a sacrificial feast to which the
woman has access.[56] However, it cannot be determined whether the childbirth practices in this priestly text represent the experiences of most new
mothers throughout the Iron Age. Otherwise, household celebrations and
women's prayers were the likely birth-related religious practices in Israelite
households.

Marriage Celebrations

Marriage celebrations are a prominent marker of social transitions. But
identifying them as Israelite religious events is problematic. In the biblical
world there was no wedding—a religious ceremony joining a couple in
matrimony—as such; and the Hebrew Bible lacks a term for "wedding."
Marriage was simply a social occasion and also a legal process if property was involved.[57] Elites and perhaps all property owners probably had
marriage contracts (*ketubot*) delineating financial and other terms of the
marriage as negotiated by the parents, just as a bill of divorce marked
the dissolution of a marriage (e.g., Isa 50:1). Although signing those documents may have been formal and may have invoked divine witness, such
transactions would have borne little resemblance to today's ceremonies.
The religious dimension of marriage, expected and explicit today in most
weddings, is apparently a postexilic development.[58] Marriage in Egypt
and Mesopotamia too was an arrangement between two families with no
involvement of religious or state officials.[59] (Even in Christianity, marriages
did not require a priestly officiant until the early thirteenth century.[60])

Nonetheless, celebrations—feasting with music and dancing—accompanied marriage (i.e., when a woman moved to her husband's household
as agreed by both sets of parents), and perhaps sometimes betrothal too.
The Song of Solomon is often considered a set of love songs sung at these
celebrations, which may have lasted as long as seven days (see Judg 14:12).
Sacral sensibilities, even if absent from the marriage arrangements, probably did inhere in wedding feasts, with their festivities including praise to
the deity and prayers for the couple to have children.

Death Rites

Death rituals are as ubiquitous across cultures as are childbirth ones. Women have mortuary roles—as mourners or as providers of postmortem sustenance—in many Mediterranean cultures. Women's mourning practices were ingrained in classical Greek culture and continued into the Roman and Byzantine periods.[61] Funerary wailing and lamenting were the sacred duty of Jewish, Christian, and Muslim women in the nineteenth-century Ottoman Empire.[62] Women in rural Greece fulfill a family's sacral obligations to the dead, caring for people in death as they did in life.[63] This means washing them, grieving their passing with laments, and sometimes keeping them company by visiting their graves. They also provide offerings of food, which "symbolizes the continuing relationship between the worlds of the living and the world of the dead," at the graves.[64] Women in peasant households in ancient Israel probably had similar responsibilities. The Bible alludes to women lamenting (2 Sam 11:26; Joel 1:8), although elite households perhaps hired professional women mourners (see chapter 9). Women would also have prepared the funerary meal, at which kin and neighbors gathered to comfort relatives of the deceased (see Jer 6:7-8).

Dead ancestors were believed to exist in a semidivine or preternatural state and to have the power to help or even hinder the living, mainly in the realms of foreknowledge and fertility.[65] Foreknowledge is a factor in the narrative about a woman summoning the "ghost" of Samuel to help Saul with military problems (see 1 Sam 28:3-25 and chapter 9). Ethnographic evidence affirms the fertility realm: for many centuries Jewish women, hoping to overcome problems of conception or pregnancy, have visited the traditional tomb of the ancestor Rachel, who died in childbirth (Gen 35:16-21). Also, Isaiah's scorn for people who sought the assistance of deceased ancestors (Isa 8:19; cf. Ps 106:28) signals that people were doing that.[66]

Supplication to the dead because they might help the living meant providing nourishment in the form of offerings. Vessels used for food and drink intended for the ancestors have been found in all types of Iron Age burials.[67] Monthly festivals (see below) were the occasion for depositing foodstuffs at burial sites; also, deceased kin might be acknowledged at ordinary meals (see the last section of this chapter). Some Mesopotamian texts require women to provide special foods for deceased ancestors.[68] Ethnography also provides examples: Christians in nineteenth-century Anatolia occasionally held household feasts at which the deceased were invited to share special foods prepared in their honor; and women in rural Greece carried food offerings to the graves of deceased family members.[69] The biblical prohibition against providing sacral foods for the dead (Deut 26:14) is a sure sign that Israelites similarly gave certain foods to the deceased. Women as producers of food likely prepared those offerings and placed them at the burial sites, thus serving to connect the realms of the living and the dead.

Regular Celebrations

Feasting is associated with ancient Israel's regular or calendrical festivals, which took place annually, monthly, and weekly, and usually were community events transcending individual households. The three major Israelite feasts (Passover, Booths, and Weeks), as for traditional agrarian peoples everywhere, were keyed to the annual cycle of food production.[70] The late spring Festival of Weeks, for example, is called the Festival of Ingathering (Exod 34:22) or Day of First Fruits (Num 28:26). Calendrical considerations apparently underlie the other regular festivals. The Israelites were like their Near Eastern neighbors in having monthly festivals to mark the moon's miraculous reemergence after gradually disappearing over the course of a month.[71] But the weekly sabbath was apparently unique to the Israelites.

Relying on biblical texts for information about Israelite festivals raises several problems: (1) Pentateuchal priestly sources provide most of the information, but these texts are from late in the Iron Age. Do they reflect festivals held in the preceding centuries? (2) They mandate that celebrations be held at the central sanctuary. Does that mean people did not observe them in their own settlements? (3) How were the festival practices mentioned in the Bible observed and experienced by households?

The first two questions can be readily answered. First, the festivals described in the Pentateuch were likely held throughout the Iron Age—the annual ones because they were typical agrarian events, and the monthly ones because they were also common in the Near Eastern world. Moreover, all three kinds of regular festivals are attested in biblical texts outside the Pentateuch, notably by eighth-century prophets (Hos 2:13; Amos 8:5; cf. Isa 1:13).

As for the second question, most festivals probably originated in households and continued to be observed by households even when some people traveled to Jerusalem to celebrate them as mandated in Deuteronomy (e.g., 16:16).[72] The presence of archaeological materials related to feasting in many Iron Age domiciles indicates household festal celebrations.[73] So do biblical texts. Each household or group of households held the Passover feast (according to Exod 12:3-4); Job's family, women included, held house-hold feasts (Job 1:4-5); and Jeremiah (see below) mentions household rituals involving women, men, and children. David and Jonathan antic-ipate a new moon feast in Saul's household (1 Sam 20:5-29), but David begs off, celebrating instead with his own kin in Bethlehem. Deceased kin (discussed above) were venerated at new moon feasts, when household members shared a special meal with their ancestors at a shrine, the burial site, or even the domicile itself.[74] All household members (not just family) and even livestock (also part of the household; see chapter 6, pp. 104–105) are enjoined to keep the sabbath in the Decalogue (Exod 20:8-11; Deut 5:12-15). Wives are not specifically mentioned, probably because they are subsumed into the "you" (the male household head) to whom the sabbath commandment is addressed.[75]

The third question, about how households experienced the regular celebrations, is more complicated. Israelite festivals have been studied for over a century, but the focus has been on festival origins, the sacrifices offered, and Near Eastern parallels rather than the way households cele-brated festivals. This is not the place for a detailed examination of house-hold festal events, but a prominent festival feature can be emphasized: festivals, like life-cycle events, involved feasting—consuming food and drink, much of it prepared by women.

The three annual festivals featured seasonal foods, with harvested crops finding their way into the festal meal. For example, wine at Booths was likely connected to the fall grape harvest (Deut 16:13; cf. Judg 9:26-27). The "meal" of the new moon festival is equated with a family feast/sacrifice (1 Sam 20:24, 29). The sabbath regulations mention animal and other offer-ings, a signal that celebratory meals are part of sabbath observance, as they have been since postbiblical times and likely since the inception of a weekly day without work, whenever in the Iron Age that might have been.

Feasts also provided an opportunity to consume foods not ordinarily eaten, foods specific to a given festival but also meat, which was not part of daily fare (see chapter 3, pp. 48–49). The Bible specifies animal sacrifices at all the regular celebrations. Some animals were burnt offerings, fully consumed on the altar. But others apparently became food for the cel-ebrants (Exod 12:8; Lev 7:15; Deut 16:6-7), as archaeological evidence also suggests. The conceptual and actual relationship between festival sacrifices and household feasts probably varied, but festival sacrifices, whether at local or regional shrines or at the central one, meant that those bringing the offerings consumed some meat, whether in special rooms or outdoor spaces of local or regional shrines or in their own domiciles.

IN ORDER TO appreciate the role of women in festal events, the functions of such events in traditional societies, as identified by social scientists, must be considered briefly.[76]

Religious functions underlie all others. Gratitude to the deity was often part of festal prayers, songs, offerings, or sacrifices. The festal repast might be experienced as a meal shared with the deity or ancestors, whose blessings were sought or acknowledged. The dynamics of reciprocity—in which someone's positive action toward another elicits a positive response in return—were also incorporated into ritual practices.[77] Offerings to a household's god(s) and ancestors were meant to motivate the deity and ancestors to provide what people needed: good health and fertility of the soil and the body.

Social and socioeconomic functions are important in several ways. Festivals are powerful mechanisms for solidifying relationships, for food "is part of a general idiom in which relationships are expressed."[78] Moreover, ancient Israel's annual festivals were "historicized," with festal foods related to past events. For example, the consumption of lamb, bitter herbs, and unleavened bread at Passover commemorated traditions about the exodus from Egypt (Exod 12:8; Num 9:11). Some foods were thus mnemonic devices, linking people to foundational experiences associated with their ancestors, making festivals a "key site where food and memory come together."[79] People eating the same foods, which were linked to the idea of a common past, and enjoying the same festivities identify with each other. Shared festal occasions shape and strengthen group identity and community solidarity.[80]

In contributing to group cohesion, Israelite feasts thus increased the likelihood of the inter-household mutual aid so vital for household and community survival (see chapter 3, pp. 56–57). The gathering of kin-related households also provided an opportunity for women to activate connections that would lead to marriages for offspring (chapter 7, p. 142). The social function included a psychological one: the special food, the break from daily toil, the opportunity to see distant kin, the music and dance of rejoicing, and the general revelry (see Exod 32:6) made feasts highly pleasurable social events, bringing enjoyment to the often tedious and monotonous lives of Israelite peasants. And on an economic level, festival gatherings allowed people to share resources. Commodities could be bartered and exchanged, thus expanding the rather limited diets of individual households (described in chapter 3).

Political functions are intertwined with economic ones and would have had both negative and positive effects. Part of the offerings at shrines supported the priestly or political elites who organized (and required?) festivals; that is, festivals were one way for those in power to extract resources from the populace. Yet clan, tribal, or national officials might contribute some festal foods (e.g., 2 Sam 6:17-18); such largesse helps them to gain or maintain group loyalty and legitimize their power. Also, feasts are modes of communication, whether in a tiny village or a nation-state. In a world without newspapers, electronic media, or other modes of communication we take for granted, feasts were an important mechanism for leaders to gather information, discuss strategies, and announce policies. Finally, they provided the opportunity for related households and clans to gather, interact, and identify with each other, thus fostering the alliances necessary for group stability and survival. Traditional feasting is essential for the functioning of sociopolitical units at all levels.

These functions of feasting tend to go unrecognized in considering Israelite life. But their importance cannot be underestimated, nor can the significance of the work of household members, especially women, in producing festal foods. Women shared in sacrificial meals, as suggested by biblical texts (e.g., 1 Sam 1:4-5, 18) and by information about ancient Greek sacrificial feasts.[81] But just as important, in preparing the foodstuffs that were the mechanisms for the various and interrelated dynamics of life-cycle and festal events, women played an integral role in household religious life. Women thus "symbolize, create, and sustain those bonds necessary for social order."[82] Just as providing food for daily consumption was a maintenance activity that sustained household members biologically, providing foods for the celebration of life-cycle events and festivals was a maintenance activity that sustained the household in its relation to god(s) and ancestors and as a social unit in the larger community.

What the experience of providing food and participating in festal and life-cycle celebrations meant to women can be suggested on the basis of ethnographic materials, which are considered in the next section—for women's adherence to foodways overlapped with their culinary roles in celebrations.

Foodways

The food-processing tasks described in chapter 7 were a major component of the maintenance activities of Israelite women because they took considerable time and energy and because food is essential for life. In preparing food and drink, Israelite women also observed certain culinary customs, or foodways. (*Foodways* is a term denoting a people's food practices—what they eat, how they prepare it.) The foods consumed by a traditional society are determined largely by environmental constraints, but they are also cultural constructions. People eat some foods and avoid others, and the specific features of a group's cuisine embody its identity and beliefs. Food, according to an anthropologist specializing in the study of food and gender, is "a prism that absorbs a host of assorted cultural phenomena and unites them into one coherent domain while simultaneously speaking through that domain about everything that is important."[83]

Israelite foodways have inherent religiosity. The components of sacrificial feasts—meat plus elements of the Mediterranean triad—were considered a divine gift (e.g., Hos 2:8, [Heb. 2:10]). And sacrificial foods were virtually the same as a household's daily fare except, of course, that festivals meant greater quantities, special foods, and meat. The sacrificial regime, in other words, replicated the household regimen: the basic components of the household diet became the foods and drinks of the sanctuary. Well over a century ago, Wellhausen observed in reference to Israelite practices that "A sacrifice was a meal."[84] Ceremonial feasts and daily repasts both reflect the economic basis of society.

Mary Douglas, a British anthropologist whose work on food has been influential in biblical studies, has argued that everyday meals and special feasts have intertwined meaning, each serving as metaphors of the other.[85] She famously declares that "a very strong analogy between table and altar stares us in the face."[86] Although there are differences between feasts and everyday meals, the two are not as oppositional as they might seem. Food is the medium whereby opposites—quotidian consumption and festival repasts—meet.[87] The food and drink offerings at shrines can be considered household practices writ large, for they originate in the household, not vice versa: festival meals and sacrificial practices at sanctuaries were developments of the family meal.[88] That is, the festivals and feasts described in the preceding section were elaborated versions of ordinary household foodways.

Because food was fraught with meaning, daily meals were likely marked in some ways with religiosity. But how? Ethnographic and archaeological data and some biblical allusions are helpful, together indicating the presence of household religious activities related to food.

Consider the command that a piece of bread dough be removed as a "gift" or "donation" (*terumah*) to God before the dough is baked (Num 15:17-21). This household ritual practice apparently was meant to secure a blessing on the household: a dough donation is made "in order that a blessing may rest on your house" (Ezek 44:30b).[89] Although these biblical texts are relatively late, they arguably reflect ancient ritual practices connected with the preparation of bread. Ethnographic observations of Middle Eastern peoples in the late nineteenth and early twentieth centuries, while not reporting this specific practice, indicate that bread preparation typically involves ritual activity. For example, some Muslim and Christian peasant women allayed their fears of tainted flour, believed to be caused by evil spirits, by saying brief prayers when bringing flour to the mixing bowl and by reciting certain phrases when preparing bread dough.[90] Palestinian villagers in the mid-twentieth century considered bread sacred, and handling it improperly was sacrilegious.[91] These and other household rituals likely go back to antiquity, given that other late nineteenth- and early twentieth-century practices, like some associated with childbirth and mentioned above in this chapter, resonate with information gleaned from biblical texts, archaeological remains, or both.[92] Traditional ritual practices can persist for millennia, especially for a foodstuff—bread—central to the diet.

The dietary regulations of the Pentateuch (Lev 11; Deut 14:3-22), mainly restricting the kind of animal protein that could be consumed, are suggestive of other foodways. Many theories about their origin and function have been proposed, none entirely satisfactory.[93] The prohibitions of some species (notably pig) probably originated because of environmental and economic constraints and only later were encoded in notions of "unclean" (impure) animals.[94] Although it is difficult to determine how widespread the avoidance of forbidden animals was in the centuries preceding the formation of Leviticus and Deuteronomy, the categories of clean and unclean animals in those books may well reflect ancient foodways and rituals. After all, other biblical texts (e.g., Gen 7:2-3; Judg 13:7; Hos 9:3) assume that some animals were impure (unclean); and archaeologists have found very few remains of forbidden animals at Israelite sites.[95]

The instructions about draining the blood of butchered animals (Deut 12:16) and refraining from cooking a young animal in the fat of its mother (Exod 23:19) are similarly obscure.[96] But adhering to these instructions—whenever and wherever they became part of Israelite foodways—added a sacral dimension to household food preparation on the occasions when animals were slaughtered by household members, whether male or female (1 Sam 28:24).

Archaeological remains also indicate a religious dimension of household meals. The best materials in this regard come from the Tell Halif excavations, which have provided data that are conducive to the reconstruction of household activities (see chapter 2, p. 29). The excavators carefully recorded the find-spots of all artifacts and also analyzed samples of the debris embedded in the floors of a pillared dwelling. The artifacts and debris samples found in one of the interior rooms indicate household religious practices:[97]

1. The pottery consisted of forms used for food consumption rather than food storage or preparation.
2. Micro-analysis of the debris samples yielded remnants of foods (fruits, legumes, and grains) that would have been components of daily meals and also animal bones that would have been part of special meals.
3. Artifacts identified as having ritual use were also found in this room: a small stand for incense or food offerings; two small, finely shaped stones, perhaps altars or markers of ancestral or divine presence.
4. Part of the room had no artifacts at all but apparently was covered by mats or textiles on which people sat at mealtimes, just as in traditional Palestinian villages.[98]

This set of features, and similar ones at other sites, indicates that people in at least some pillared dwellings sat together for meals that included ritual acts.

What might those mealtime rituals have entailed? Data from ancient Near Eastern texts are suggestive. For example, some texts refer to small portions of bread (*kispu*) that were set aside for deceased ancestors whose names were invoked at household meals.[99] Monthly offerings (at the new moon, discussed above) may have been more elaborate. In Israelite households, small amounts of the daily fare of fruits, vegetables, oil, or grains were probably poured out as libations or set on small altars or bowls.[100] Like festival offerings, they involved the concept of reciprocity. Daily offerings acknowledged that divine or semidivine forces as well as household labor were the source of food; they would also have served to enlist help from deities or ancestors in securing sufficient food. Daily meals were thus marked as religious through offerings or in other ways not visible or familiar to us. An influential contemporary theorist of religion, Jonathan Z. Smith, emphasizes the ubiquity of household religion in noting that "elaborations of quotidian acts of eating, drinking, cooking, serving, pouring" might signify any meal as "religious."[101] Anthropologists observe that "food has a spiritual aspect" and that "a family meal is a sacred event."[102] In short, the discovery of both vessels of consumption and ritual objects in an area of a pillared building used for household meals signals that foods (prepared by women) were offered to the deity and/or ancestors.

The very act of consuming foodstuffs produced by household members on household land using household implements has importance transcending whatever ritual acts accompanied meals. The act of eating solidifies the connection of the human and material components of a household. Even the simplest meal embodies the relationship of the occupants of a household with their ancestors as well as with the patrimonial land that sustains them.[103] Meals also engage religion in that livestock and crop fertility were believed to be dependent on divine providence (which in turn was contingent upon human obedience—at least according to biblical texts, e.g., Lev 26:3-5; Deut 28:1-5; Ps 128). Thus food at daily meals, as at festal ones, was considered the result of the divine bestowal of fertility. The passages in Jeremiah (7:18; 44:15-19, 25; cf. Jer 19:13) about women preparing cakes and libations for offerings are especially relevant, not only because they show women presenting libations and offerings in household space but also because those ritual acts were understood to assure household prosperity.

ISRAELITE WOMEN WERE surely responsible for many household food rituals accompanying daily meals. Similarly, through their food-preparation tasks and their special connections with deceased ancestors, they were among the "leaders" of household religious celebrations—life-cycle events and regular holidays—as are women in traditional Mediterranean cultures.[104] Women also performed many of the rituals accompanying the reproductive process and carried out the ritual processes related to health care. Everywoman Eve clearly had a prominent role in many household religious practices.

The importance of women's role in household religion has been obscured by masculinized approaches to the study of Israelite religion. Until relatively recently male religious professionals or scholars were the chief interpreters of Israelite religion, and their perspectives generally marginalized women's experiences and practices as not being the "real religion" carried out by male priests.[105] Women's practices were deemed responses to "the minor distresses of everyday life."[106] Even feminist biblical scholarship, influenced by the prominence of male cultic officiants in the Bible and the lack of information about household practices, tends to adopt an androcentric stance, looking at the religious lives of Israelite women as having been circumscribed by male religious culture. This has the effect of privileging male roles as being more important. Could the seemingly mundane food-preparation or lamp-lighting tasks, among others that were part of household religious practice, really have been as important as the explicitly sacral actions of priestly officiants at community shrines?

Anthropological perspectives provide compelling positive answers to that question. For one thing, they emphasize the centrality of the household. Thus religious activities of Israelite households, carried out mainly by women and dealing with health issues, reproductive concerns, and agrarian fertility, would have been considered critical for its well-being. Religion would have been emotionally and conceptually comprehensible for people first and foremost in terms of the religious practices encountered in daily life and only secondarily in terms of the participation of households in the community festivals that integrated households into larger social and political systems. The women who performed household food rituals were well aware of the stakes involved, and Jeremiah's account (Jer 44:15-19, 25) of a household religious practice indicates that women were able to articulate the importance of their acts. Indeed, women were not only critical actors in household religious life but might be considered "theologians who gave voice to some of household and family religion's most constitutive beliefs."[107] Women, rather than men, held the "leadership role" in household religion.[108]

Household rituals, many involving food prepared and offered by women, may seem trivial to us from our twenty-first century perspective. Most biblical scholarship has failed to grasp the importance of food in the religious lives of premodern peoples and thus has not recognized that the women in charge of food practices were performing rituals. Rituals by definition are stereotyped behaviors that must be performed in prescribed ways in order to be efficacious. Performing them meant adhering to a body of knowledge, passed from generation to generation. It also meant transmitting the values encoded in them. A hallmark anthropological study of the religious lives of Middle Eastern Jewish women reveals that the preparation and use of food and herbs for religious purposes, rather than being experienced as drudgery and extra work, was experienced as ritualized behavior with sacral meaning.[109] With their knowledge and control of food-producing technology and household religious procedures, Israelite women were ritual experts for many household religious practices no less than were priests for the rituals of shrines. In performing household rituals believed essential for the well-being of its members and thus for household survival, women's religious lives were enriched in ways not often recognized.

9

Excursus: Professional Women

IMAGINE THAT YOU could step back in time and visit Everywoman Eve's household. One of her children is seriously ill, and a health-care consultant is summoned. At the same time, because of drought conditions, her household is short of grain; a messenger is sent to borrow a small amount of this commodity from kin in the next village. Then her elderly father-in-law dies, and she sends for a funerary specialist.

Most people reading this account would assume all the characters in this scene, except Everywoman Eve and perhaps her sick child, were male. But that would not be true—some may have been women. Household maintenance tasks were a full-time job for Everywoman Eve. Does that mean that women had no other roles in Israelite society? Not at all. Some women in fact held "professional" positions—ones requiring special knowledge, skills, or both—that served people beyond the household. Although these supra-household roles were probably found mainly in large or urban settlements, at least some peasant women likely moonlighted with extra-household roles. Some of those roles have features relevant to the discussion of social hierarchies in chapter 10.

Identifying professional roles means relying mainly on biblical texts, although ethnography, archaeology, and ancient Near Eastern texts also provide some data. The Hebrew Bible is a problematic source for information about average women and their daily lives (as noted in chapter 3). Yet "professional" women serving the larger community are more visible than their Everywoman Eve sisters because of the Bible's national interest. Moreover, biblical information about them seems reliable, judging from its resonance with what is known from ethnography and other ancient texts.

The positions held by women were both numerous and varied.[1] About twenty different roles are mentioned in the Hebrew Bible. Some were carried out by women as individuals, some by women working in groups, and some by women working either alone or with others. Certain jobs were related to class, specifically to membership in the royal family. Many positions were held exclusively by women, others by both women and men.

The position mentioned most often in the Hebrew Bible is prostitution, arguably the world's oldest profession. Biblical texts tend to discourage sex for hire (e.g., Lev 19:29; Deut 23:18) and consider prostitutes a danger to society (e.g., Prov 29:3). Moreover, prostitution (like adultery) serves as a metaphor for Israel's unfaithfulness to Yahweh (e.g., Hos 9:1). Yet it is never categorically forbidden. Indeed, it was apparently tolerated, for it seems somewhat less problematic than adultery (Prov 6:26). And, unlike in many contemporary societies, it is not criminalized in biblical legal texts. Moreover, both the prostitute Rahab (who saves Israelites sent to scope out the land in Josh 2; 6:17-27) and Judah's daughter-in-law Tamar (who poses as a prostitute in order to bear an heir for her deceased husband in Gen 38) are heroic figures.

Women's expertise in household maintenance activities translated into professional work for some. Food-processing skills meant that, perhaps against their will, women might be conscripted to work as cooks or bakers in the royal household (1 Sam 8:13); or perhaps young women were drafted for those jobs, where they were taught by experienced members of the palace kitchen staff. A related kind of proficiency—knowledge of herbal substances—served both culinary and healing purposes (see chapter 8, pp. 151–152) and is also mentioned as a role held by women brought to the royal household. Some female herbalists would have served as health-care specialists, visiting households whose own efforts to care for the ill seemed to no avail.

Household textile work also translated into professional expertise. Widely associated with women in ancient Aegean and Near Eastern cultures, it is represented by the Bible's "skillful women," who produced special yarns for the tabernacle's sumptuous fabrics (Exod 34:25-26), and by the women who wove fabrics in temple workshops (2 Kgs 23:7). Because several looms were sometimes set up in a single household, as archaeology has shown (see chapter 7, p. 133), textile production was a cottage industry for some. The biblical references to an elite woman making and selling textiles certainly suggest that: "She seeks wool and flax, and works with willing hands....She puts her hands to the distaff, and her hands hold the spindle....She makes linen garments and sells them; she supplies the merchant with sashes" (Prov 31:13, 19, 24).

Women producing more textiles or other commodities than their households needed became entrepreneurs. Stamp seals or seal impressions inscribed with women's names similarly indicate that some women were businesswomen.[2] These artifacts usually bear their owners' names and were used in economic or legal transactions. They would be pressed onto wet clay affixed to documents, thus serving as their owner's "signature." Of the more than 1,200 known seals or seal impressions, about three percent have women's names. Similarly, several ostraca (potsherds with a brief inscription, usually written in ink) with women's names, all dating to the late Iron II period, indicate that women were recipients or owners of commodities transferred in economic transactions.[3]

Women's knowledge of medicinal substances as well as their familiarity with childbirth meant that some, usually older women, served as midwives (Gen 35:17; 38:28; Exod 1:15-21), although elite women were more likely than ordinary peasants to use them. (Most peasant women were attended at delivery by their network of female friends, neighbors, and kin; see chapter 7, pp. 139–141). Midwives were health professionals—experts in the techniques of delivering babies and the afterbirth, then tending to the mother's recovery and the newborn's vitality. They were also religious specialists who recited appropriate prayers, blessings, or incantations, as did midwives in other Near Eastern cultures.[4] The pronouncement of Rachel's midwife (Gen 35:17) has been called a salvation oracle.[5]

A related profession was that of "nurse"; the biblical term for this appears three times (Gen 24:59; 35:8; 2 Kgs 11:2-3) and probably designates a wet nurse rather than a medical attendant. Like midwives, wet nurses served the elite and royal women who could afford them. The children of peasant women who found themselves unable to suckle their infants or who died in childbirth were perhaps fed by a lactating woman from the mother's network of friends, neighbors, or kin; but all too often these babies did not survive.[6]

Women held other professional positions in the religious realm besides midwifery. The women serving at the tent of meeting (Exod 38:8; 1 Sam 2:22) were probably conveying messages from God.[7] Also, a somewhat enigmatic biblical word, *qedešah*, is from a root meaning holiness and may refer to a group of female religious functionaries. This word, although usually translated "temple prostitute" (e.g., Deut 23:17 [Heb. 23:18]), probably denotes a class of cultic personnel rather than women (or men, in the case of the equivalent masculine biblical term) who perform sexual acts in a sacral context. Although several biblical references do not fit this interpretation, the possibility that the term refers to a sacral female position cannot be discounted. The women "weeping for Tammuz" (Ezek 8:14) were cultic personnel too. But they were not participating in a rite mourning the Mesopotamian god Tammuz, as is often supposed. Rather, "weeping for Tammuz" is used in an extended sense for women engaged in a mourning ritual, just as bacchanalia refers to drunken revelry but does not mean the worship of Bacchus. Moreover, this ritual was not a discrete act but rather part of a complex of ritual activities, the rest carried out with male priests within the temple precincts (Ezek 8:16-17). The weeping women were part of a mixed-gender group performing a sequence of temple rites.[8] Their leadership in mourning rites may be related to general female expertise in lamenting (see chapter 8, p. 160, and below).

A more prominent religious role, given the importance of prophecy in the Hebrew Bible, was held by the women bearing the title prophet: four notable named women (Miriam, Deborah, Huldah, and Noadiah), and several unnamed ones (Isa 8:3; Joel 2:28 [Heb. 3:1]; cf. Ezek 13:17-23). These few female prophets in the androcentric Hebrew Bible are probably the tip of the iceberg—the small visible part of a large cohort of other Israelite women performing prophetic functions, as elsewhere in the ancient Near East.[9] The masculine plural word for prophets, *nebi'im*, sometimes designates groups of prophets and is probably a gender-inclusive term in some biblical texts. Except perhaps the named ones, female Israelite prophets would have been versed in divinatory technique, thus serving the same predictive functions as their male counterparts. Most Israelite prophets, like those elsewhere in the ancient Near East, were professional prognosticators rather than spokespersons for the divine will. They used a variety of techniques (see Num 22:7 and Ezek 21:21-23 [Heb. 21:26-27]) in response to requests from clients for information about the future. The work of these prophets apparently overlapped with that of other professionals. If we suspend the critical stance of the text, we can see that the female prophets of Ezekiel 13:17-23 are performing complex rites, probably "medical" ritual praxis for treating difficulties of pregnancy and childbirth or perhaps rites to summon the dead.[10]

Some specific divinatory modes are criticized in the Hebrew Bible—a sure sign that these techniques were entrenched features rather than fringe elements of Israelite society. For example, dream analysis involving omens and portents is condemned (Deut 13:1-3 [Heb. 13:2-4]), as are soothsaying, auguring, being a sorcerer, casting spells, consulting "ghosts or spirits," and seeking information about the future from the dead (Deut 18:10-11;

see also Exod 22:18 [Heb. 22:17]; Lev 20:27). This list of forbidden practices is gender inclusive, for practitioners of several of them are women:
Exodus 22:18 (Heb. 22:17) mentions female sorcerers, and the Ezekiel
text just cited criticizes female prophets who were using various devices.
Moreover, a female necromancer—someone who consults or calls up a
dead person and thus serves as a medium, or intermediary, between the
living and the deceased—has a prominent role. In 1 Samuel 28 Saul has
the "woman at Endor" summon the ghost of the dead prophet Samuel
and apparently escapes biblical censure, perhaps because criticism of divinatory activities was not universal among biblical authors.

Another profession in the realm of religion was a funerary one.
Professional mourners in the ancient Near East and Aegean were almost
always women, and in Egypt they were exclusively women.[11] Depictions
of women performing typical mourning gestures—beating their breasts
and tearing their hair—appear on a royal Phoenician sarcophagus.[12] Also,
ethnomusicological research shows that funeral lamentations are typically
chanted by female specialists.[13] Male mourners are mentioned once in the
Hebrew Bible (lamenting the prominent king Josiah; 2 Chr 35:25); but
women are the lamenters in other texts and probably were more numerous, given the preponderance of female mourners across cultures. One
biblical passage (Jer 9:17-20 [Heb. 9:16-19]) is especially significant:

> [17]*Thus says the LORD of hosts:*
> *Consider, and call for the mourning women to come;*
> *send for the skilled women to come;*
> [18]*let them quickly raise a dirge over us....*
> [20]*Hear, O women, the word of the LORD,*
> *and let your ears receive the word of his mouth;*
> *teach to your daughters a dirge, and each to her neighbor a*
>   *lament.*

Note that the lamenters summoned to chant the dirge are called "skilled,"
a term that designates an acquired competency. Also, these skilled women
are urged to impart their knowledge to others. "Daughters" in v. 20 may
refer to biological daughters of mourning women, who will learn this profession from their mothers; but it perhaps is used in an extended sense to
represent an association or professional "guild" of women lamenters (cf.
2 Sam 1:24), just as "sons" denotes a "company [literally, sons] of prophets" (e.g., 2 Kgs 2:3, 5, 7, 15). Either way, an expert mourning woman is

enjoined to instruct others, including her "friend" or "companion" (rather than NRSV "neighbor"). Note too that parts of Lamentations present two gendered figures: an unnamed male and "daughter Zion," the latter portrayed as a lamenting mother.[14] The poignant prayers of daughter Zion may be those of a professional mourning woman.[15]

Both religious and secular settings characterize another profession: musical composition and performance (singing, playing instruments, and dancing). In attributing songs with significant religious themes to Miriam, Deborah, and Hannah, biblical narrators show awareness of female composers. The songs of Miriam and probably Deborah are accompanied by dancing and playing the frame drum (anachronistically called "tambourine" in most English translations); similar groupings of song, dance, and drumming appear elsewhere (1 Sam 18:6-7; cf. Judg 16:1-2; Jer 31:4). In all of them women lead the people in celebrating military success against great odds. Their songs give credit for the victory to Yahweh's intervention in human affairs. Women thus serve not only as accomplished performers but also as "theologians" who portray an important aspect of Yahweh's relationship with the people.

Dozens of different musical instruments are mentioned in the Hebrew Bible, but only the frame drum (Hebrew *top*) is explicitly connected with musicians of a specific gender, in this case women. The corpus of small terracotta figurines found in the east Mediterranean includes many statuettes of people playing musical instruments; virtually all those playing the frame drum are female, similarly indicating that the frame drum was mainly a woman's instrument. Thus the eleven biblical texts in which frame drums are part of instrumental ensembles (e.g., Gen 31:27; 1 Sam 10:5; Isa 5:12) likely refer to mixed-gender groups in both religious and secular contexts. In one instance, women (not men) play the frame drum in a procession to the temple (Ps 68:25 [Heb. 68:26]). And female vocalists are mentioned alone or together with men in both secular and religious settings (e.g., 2 Sam 19:35 [Heb. 19:36]; 1 Chr 25:5-6; Eccl 2:8).

Women served as couriers, either memorizing a dispatch or carrying it in written form. To be sure, most messengers in the ancient world were men. However, a woman bears messages exchanged by David and Jonathan (2 Sam 17:17). And personified wisdom sends female servants to summon people to a banquet (Prov 9:1-5). Also, although not apparent in English translations, female heralds ("those who bear tidings," a feminine participle) appear in metaphoric language (Isa 40:9; Ps 68:11 [Heb. 68:12]) and suggest the existence of female heralds in ancient Israel.

Women holding prominent leadership positions are represented by Deborah, who both adjudicates and is called a prophet (Judg 4:4); in fact, she is the only leader in Judges so designated. She also plays a decisive role in a military victory over the Canaanites, which she then celebrates in song. Several unnamed women—the wise women of Tekoa and Abel of Beth-maacah (2 Sam 14:1-20; 20:14-22)—are also community leaders. Their sagacity helps solve tensions in the palace and kingdom during King David's reign. These wise women command the respect of male leaders, and their words lead to important outcomes. They surely represent the presence of female village sages whose knowledge and judgment served their communities. The sagacity of community wise women is arguably an extension of the household wisdom of women like the "sagelike matriarchs" in Genesis, who exhibit elements of knowledge and persuasive speech otherwise associated with sages.[16] Moreover, the personification of wisdom as Woman Wisdom in Proverbs is part of the strong association of biblical wisdom traditions with women.[17]

Finally, royal women had managerial roles on a national level. The managerial aspect of the maintenance activities of agrarian women (see chapter 10) was even greater for elite women, as in Proverbs 31, where the "strong woman" organizes her household's productive and commercial activities. Take this to the royal level and we see the wives of Israelite kings, like their sisters in other Near Eastern cultures, managing the palace staff (both male and female) and thus the productive and commercial enterprises of the monarchy. At least some royal women—perhaps just those called *gebirah* (a title meaning "great woman" and used for several queen mothers)—were responsible for a wide range of administrative, religious, and diplomatic activities.[18] When King Jehoiachin surrenders to the Babylonians in the sixth century BCE, he and his mother head the list of people carried into captivity (2 Kgs 24:15-16). Because of her powerful position in the royal household, the queen mother apparently outranks all the others.

A CLOSE LOOK at household maintenance tasks (chapters 7 and 8) helped negate the facile assumption that Israelite women were "only wives and mothers"; so too does the identification of their many extra-household roles. Considering the dynamics of those roles is also important. What did it mean for women to be professionals? The answers to that question will not necessarily apply to all the positions described in this chapter— prostitutes and sorcerers, for example, would have been unlikely to garner the esteem that accompanied other professions—but positive characteristics of expertise and community service would have pertained to most of them.

On a personal level, women performing professional roles would have experienced the gratification of serving a constituency beyond their households and also contributing to the household economy when their service or entrepreneurship brought remuneration. To the extent that their services were essential and appreciated by their clients or audiences, professional women were accorded a modicum of prestige. To be sure, some women performing professional tasks did so as servants in the palace or shrine; little can be said about their experiences, especially if they lived in the palace or temple compound, away from their households.

Women's professional roles also had important social qualities. Some professions—such as music (singing, dancing, and/or playing instruments), divination or some kinds of prophecy, and lamenting—are notable for being group enterprises. Women in these occupations experience the camaraderie of sustained contact with the others in their cohort. Moreover, women in gender-specific groups exercise exclusive control over themselves and the contexts in which they carry out their work; they thereby experience a sense of power rather than powerlessness.[19] Women's professional groups become, in a sense, "guilds." This term usually designates a formal union but can also be used, as here, to denote more loosely a group of people who come together in the common pursuit of a craft or trade that provides a service to people in their community. These groups have their own hierarchies, depending on the age or skill level of their members.

Most professional roles involved expertise. Women had to learn appropriate technologies, techniques, songs, dance moves, laments, chants, divinatory procedures, or sapiential materials. And those involved in performance had to practice their skills. The acquisition of specialized knowledge came from others and from experience. Group functions mean group meetings and, in some cases, rehearsals. Women carrying out their professions individually learn as apprentices to experts. Either way, those knowledgeable became mentors to novices. Those with special proficiency thus experience the esteem of their less skilled colleagues and also the satisfaction of helping younger women acquire essential skill, bodies of knowledge, or both.

A special dynamic was operant for those in performance groups. The audience becomes part of a communicative flow; it acknowledges the performers' skill and also is part of a power dynamic in which the performers have control over members of the audience, at least during the duration of the performative acts.[20] Given the frequency of festivals, with their entertainment component, as well as funerary events, female performers exerting performance power would have been familiar figures. Perhaps the leadership positions visible in the Hebrew Bible entailed a similar power dynamic. The wise women, named prophets, Deborah as judge and general, and royal women managing palace operations all are portrayed unproblematically exerting control over others as they make decisions or otherwise render services with national consequences.

In the aggregate and in a variety of ways—some accepted in the Hebrew Bible and others condemned—the professional women described in this chapter served individual households, local or regional communities, and the people Israel.

Gender and Society: Reconstructing Relationships, Rethinking Systems

NEGATIVE STEREOTYPES AND judgments about the relationships between women and men in ancient Israel abound in biblical scholarship. Israelite women are thought to be inferior to men, the chattel of men, even enslaved by men.

Literary critics, who tend to work directly and solely with biblical narratives, have persistently identified male dominance in biblical texts and often therefore claim to see it in ancient Israel too. One of the most pointed examples is the assertion that ancient Israel's social system was patriarchal and that it was "a male-supremacist social and cognitive system."[1] Supremacist is a powerful word, indicating that members of a group (in this case, men) believed themselves to be supreme and superior to others (in this case, women) and thus have the right to rule over them or otherwise control them. Patriarchy would thus be a form of supremacism—granting special rights and privileges to men and denying them to women.

This perspective echoes one made several decades ago by the prominent feminist theologian Rosemary Ruether, who chastises the biblical prophets for not objecting to the "enslavement of persons within the Hebrew family itself: namely, women and children."[2] And it resonates with more recent assertions that Israel was "rigidly patriarchal" and that women were "subordinated to men."[3] These extreme views, alluded to in chapter 1, are present in milder but nonetheless negative assessments that continue to label Israelite society patriarchal and to assume general male dominance.[4] The lead essay in the well-regarded *Women's Bible Commentary* refers to the "patriarchal values embedded in all of the biblical writings" as mirroring Israelite society.[5] Even Frymer-Kensky, who heralds prominent biblical women and defends the Bible against charges of misogyny, uses the patriarchy label and asserts that women were dominated by their husbands.[6] The patriarchal social and cultural world of Israelites, it is assumed, was arranged to benefit men directly and to always give men power over women.[7] In short, scholars generally view women in biblical antiquity as powerless pawns in an all-pervasive, male-dominated hierarchical structure.

Popular views are much the same. Here are some examples of what students in my course on women in the Bible and its world (mentioned in chapter 7) say when asked in the first class to jot down their notions about women in ancient Israel:

- Women were to be seen, not heard.
- Women were shrouded and quiet.
- Are women as devalued in the Bible as they seem?
- I have very few impressions of women's roles.... However, subservience is what comes to mind.
- I have always assumed that women were vastly inferior to men in biblical times.
- I think of women in the biblical period as being oppressed.

These unexamined notions stem from traditional interpretations of the Bible and its world in institutional religion, which draws on scholarly appraisals like those just mentioned. Cultural productions, including contemporary media, are also influential. For example, the website of an organization advocating religious tolerance alerts us to the status of women in biblical antiquity: "Women were generally viewed in a negative light.... Women were considered inferior to men."[8]

But are these views legitimate? They are typically based on biblical texts taken out of context and pay little or no heed to information about Israelite society from other sources. And they employ the term patriarchy without attending to its origins or considering its legitimacy as a descriptor of ancient Israel. Assumptions that Israelite gender relations are marked by systemic male dominance in a patriarchal society are problematic in light of what is now known about the social reality of ancient Israel and in consideration of the deficiencies of the patriarchal paradigm. They can be contested.

In contesting the typical perspectives, this discussion first uses information about the maintenance activities of agrarian women, arguably the majority of women throughout the period of the Hebrew Bible, to reconstruct Israelite gender relationships and thus determine whether traditional negative assessments are legitimate. It then examines the concept of patriarchy—its origins and the ways in which using it for ancient Israel are inappropriate—and also considers other possibilities for characterizing Israelite society. Finally, in accord with my claim in chapter 1 that this study would engage an anthropological perspective by looking at ordinary Israelite women apart from the admittedly biased biblical text, I engage another aspect of an anthropological perspective: the issue of evaluation. Anthropologists studying other cultures struggle with the problem of evaluation. They ask whether, as outsiders, they can or should make judgments about the group they are studying. I believe it is fitting, given the authoritative position of biblical texts for so many people and the concomitant problem that it poses for contemporary Christian and Jewish feminists, to conclude this project by confronting the problem of evaluation in relation to Everywoman Eve and her context.

Gender Relationships

The life of an Israelite agrarian was not compartmentalized, as it is for most of us, into separate domains of work and family, public and private. The domicile was the workplace, and its occupants were the workers. Although the activities of women and men overlapped at certain times and under certain circumstances, they were not the same. Texts and archaeological data along with ethnographic observations have enabled us to reconstruct women's household activities. Ethnographic examples and anthropological discussions now provide the opportunity to understand the gender dynamics embedded in women's contributions to household life and to consider the meaning of those activities for Israelite women. Recourse to several biblical passages is also illuminating, for these texts tend to corroborate what the anthropological perspective reveals—that the negative image of Everywoman Eve in academic analyses and popular conceptions is flawed.

An Anthropological Perspective

The negative assumptions about women in ancient Israel are hardly unique. Whether expressed implicitly or explicitly, assumptions that "women virtually everywhere play a subordinate role" appeared repeatedly in anthropological literature until the rise of feminist anthropology (described in chapter 1).[9] Those conventional views about gender relations in premodern cultures were rooted, as are some of the presentisms discussed in chapter 6, in Victorian gender ideology, which "identified men as public, active, powerful, and dominant over women, who were considered intrinsically subordinate, domestic, passive, and powerless."[10] That hierarchical ideology was projected onto the past to interpret "all men's activities and roles as powerful and high status, while devaluing women's roles and activities as unimportant and low status."[11] Earlier generations of anthropologists carrying out ethnographic research, mainly men who either were oblivious to the possibility of female power or who did not have access to the internal workings of a household, perpetuated these views.

More recent ethnographic studies have provided fresh data and a different perspective. In small, traditional, Mediterranean societies where—as in ancient Israel—the household is the basic economic unit of society and where women and men work very hard in mostly different sets of maintenance tasks, female power has been repeatedly documented. This documentation began in the 1960s, when a report on household life in a small Greek village (population 216) appeared in a special issue of *Anthropological Quarterly* on "Appearance and Reality: Status and Roles of Women in Mediterranean Societies."[12] The author was not surprised to find that women and men contributed about equally to household labor. But because she held mid-twentieth-century views about women as powerless and subordinate in traditional societies, she was surprised to discover how influential women were. They exerted considerable power in household decision-making about economic matters and also about choosing marital partners for their children. Despite appearances to the contrary, male dominance was not a functional reality in household life.

Other research has similarly shown a striking absence of hierarchical male control of women. A study of rural Greek households revealed women to have as much decision-making power as their husbands, if not more.[13] Peasant women in France were observed to control "the major portion of important resources and decisions"; and, in considering the "actual power of peasant women and men relative to each other…women appear to be generally more powerful."[14] Research on Sardinian households similarly showed facile assumptions about women's subordination to be simplistic and misleading.[15]

These and other studies indicate that the usual views of household power dynamics require modification when considering any traditional society.[16] Analysis of power tends to focus on institutional forms, thus highlighting visible and often coercive male power. But power can also be less visible and noncoercive, achieved (often by women) through a variety of interpersonal interactions—including affiliation, cooperation, collaboration, negotiation, and inspiration. Small-scale, noncoercive power exerted by women is no less important than male power, especially in terms of the daily functioning of households and their communities. To put it another way, shared power, or "power with" is as important, maybe more important, than "power over."[17] Forms of female power may look different than forms of male power, but they cannot be discounted. Conventional ideas that see women as passive and powerless in all premodern societies thus misrepresent the reality, namely, that women's maintenance roles in traditional agrarian societies translate into certain kinds of power that overlap with or complement male power.

Awareness of the presence and function of female power is critical for understanding gender relations in agrarian Israelite households. The maintenance roles of Israelite women described in chapters 7 and 8, which are much the same as those in the studies just mentioned, suggest a similar power dynamic. Virtually all of women's maintenance activities were likewise vital and indispensable to the social and economic survival of the household and contributed, in ways described below, to their household power. Carrying out household roles determined the organization and relationships of household life.

Women's maintenance activities were time-consuming and energy-demanding; they also involved complex technologies. In the aggregate, they probably required more technological skills than did men's. In even the simplest societies, women who transform raw products into cooked foods and produce other household commodities, as did Israelite women, are seen as having special knowledge—the ability to "work...wonders."[18] In contrast, the food-preparation task men are most likely to perform—cooking meat at sacrificial feasts—is perhaps the least technologically complex, especially if it involves roasting over an open fire. From time immemorial, men have put the steaks on the grill and women have concocted the stews. Women's other maintenance activities similarly required specialized knowledge and skills. Textile work, for example, was "one of the most complex and multi-phased processes" of any of the ancient technologies.[19] And making pottery, a five-stage process, each step of which requires special knowledge and skills, is considered "a very difficult task."[20] Technological expertise certainly figured in the agrarian tasks of Israelite men, but those tasks were rarely daily ones. For example, men plowed and planted grain seeds several times a year and sheared sheep annually; women converted grains into edible form virtually every day, making their technological proficiency visible in daily life.

Women's control of and expertise in household technologies—transforming the raw into the cooked and producing other household foodstuffs and commodities—affords them both *personal* and *social* power. A little-recognized concomitant of women's technological skills is the valued sense of self that is afforded by providing items necessary for survival. Moreover, many women's tasks produced direct results, providing the gratification derived from making items that are immediately consumable or usable. The collective mindset described in chapter 6 does not preclude this self-awareness and self-satisfaction.

Because commodity production in subsistence households is central to their economic and social life, women's maintenance tasks positioned them to exercise certain kinds of household power. Women in traditional cultures make important household decisions by virtue of their dominance of essential household processes.[21] How is this manifest? Take, for example, the production of life-sustaining foodstuffs. Women's control of their production means the control of their distribution under most circumstances (see Prov 31:15). Those who spend considerable time and energy converting raw foodstuffs into edible form have much to say about how, when, and how much food is consumed. Across cultures, people tend to control the distribution of the fruits of their labor.[22] Because their maintenance tasks generally take place in or near the domicile, women also determine the allocation and use of household space and its implements, as in traditional Palestinian villages.[23]

Women's power in household decision-making is not a trivial matter. Because the household is the most significant social and economic unit, household power has important consequences for the community as a whole. Ethnographic evidence indicates that when women have essential information about household or village matters, they also participate in discussions about how to solve household problems or deal with community issues.[24] Their economic contributions to household life conferred "a juridical position" on Sardinian women.[25] The networks of communication with other women, established in their pattern of joint work, gave Israelite women access to certain kinds of information that similarly would have figured in household, and also community, decisions about economic and political issues (see chapter 7, pp. 143–146).

Highlighting their household power means rescuing Israelite women from mistaken notions of female powerlessness and subordination in household life; it also means recognizing the gender balance in Israelite households. Women in peasant households dominate in certain kinds of household activities and men in others, with significant contributions by both. As a result, female-male relationships are marked by interdependence, with a relative symmetry between the positions of women and men.[26] The marital union of women and men in rural Greece has been called an economic, social, and moral partnership because of their mutual dependence on each other.[27] The designation "partnership" resonates with the term "partner" in the Eden tale, which portrays the woman as the "powerful counterpart" of the man (see chapter 4, pp. 73–74).

Overall, gender interactions in peasant households are largely complementary. In some instances women may have greater decision-making powers, and in other matters (see below) men are in control. Their combined efforts are signified in ancient Israel by bread production. In most settlements bread could be obtained only by household production; and, as the fundamental nutritional commodity (see chapter 3), bread was the sine qua non of food. Bread production and consumption were thus the nexus of household economic and social matters. Bread was a social and economic substance as well as a physical one for the Israelites.[28] It signified the social and economic processes that produced it and, as in traditional Mediterranean societies, "confirm[ed] the complementarity of men and women" as its producers.[29] Women and men in agrarian Israelite households together were "breadwinners" responsible for the livelihood of their households. Complementary gender-linked responsibilities as parents (see chapter 7) as well as providers were woven together into the overall fabric of daily life.

I have avoided looking beyond the Mediterranean basin for analogues to ancient Israelite life. But information about American frontier households, which, like Israelite ones, were largely self-sufficient, may be relevant. Diaries and other writings show that frontier women functioned in a "partner model" with respect to household dynamics.[30] They regarded their participation in decision-making to be important, for pioneer homesteads were understood to be viable only through the considerable cooperative efforts of a marital pair.

The ethnographic evidence for the complementarity of women and men in traditional agrarian households overturns the traditional views of gender hierarchy, with men controlling women in all respects. It also provides compelling evidence that the dichotomy between public and private that characterizes industrial societies (see chapter 6) and the associated view that low-status, female household tasks give women secondary status cannot be applied to small-scale premodern settlements.

The idea that women's maintenance activities were not valued (see the discussion of presentism in chapter 6) is similarly invalid. The significant economic, social, and political value of women's maintenance tasks likely afforded Everywoman Eve not only substantial household power but also the respect that accrues to any household member whose labors are essential for survival. When women are skilled managers of household production systems, they are accorded prestige and experience self-esteem. The idealized woman of Proverbs 31, after all, is praised by her husband and children for her household work. Because technical expertise was considered a form of wisdom in ancient Israel, women's technical skills and their ability to impart them to the next generation made them "wise women." And their tasks of socializing and educating children made women household sages.[31] Finally, the religious maintenance roles presented in chapter 8 would have not only enriched women's lives but also earned them respect for performing ritual activities considered essential for achieving biological and agricultural fertility.

This anthropological perspective of the gender dynamics implicit in women's maintenance activities suggests that Everywoman Eve was no less powerful than her partner, and perhaps more so in some ways. Does any biblical information, apart from the possible depiction of Eve as the powerful counterpart of Adam (see chapter 4, p. 74), support the anthropological view? Biblical sources do not provide directly relevant information about the gender dynamics of average Israelite women. But sometimes elite women are visible in biblical texts, and several exhibit the decision-making power evident in ethnographic reports. These texts are important, for the activities of these women resemble those of their less affluent sisters; they both supplement and confirm the ethnographic information about women's household power. (The lives of royal women were too distant socially and economically from the lives of peasant women; thus narratives about kings' wives and mothers are not examined.)

Biblical Evidence

Most of the power described in the ethnographic studies cited above was exhibited by older women with considerable experience in household maintenance tasks. Senior women, especially when extended or complex families are involved, held what today we would call managerial roles. Their household responsibilities and expertise meant that they oversaw the assignment of tasks and use of resources. They were responsible for organizing the work of those junior to them, including adult sons. In today's terms, the senior Israelite woman functioned as the household's "COO" (chief operating officer) and, if the senior male was away or incapacitated, as the acting "CEO" (chief executive officer).[32] Household hierarchies were based on age and experience as much as on gender.

This managerial feature is visible in several texts. The relevant biblical figures are three narrative women—Micah's mother, Abigail, and the great woman of Shunem—and the woman of Proverbs 31 (already mentioned in several chapters).[33] A pair of stipulations in the legal section of Exodus is also considered. The narrative women may not be fully historical figures, and Proverbs 31 probably presents an idealized woman. Yet these images still have "historical and sociological value" for reconstructing the lives of Israelite women.[34] Narrative details can be manipulated to produce desired effects but still reflect social conventions.

The story of *Micah's mother* (Judg 17) is about an unnamed woman who discovers that 1,100 shekels of silver have been stolen from her. Hoping to recover this considerable amount, she utters a curse in the hope that God will punish the thief. In the biblical world curses (and blessings) were believed to be efficacious. Thus when the thief, who happens to be her son Micah, hears it, he fears divine punishment and so confesses and returns the stolen property. But the story doesn't end there. Micah's mother decides that at least a portion of the silver (200 pieces) should be "consecrated" to Yahweh. She commissions a metalsmith to make items for the household shrine.[35] Presumably she retains the other 900 pieces of silver.

This narrative, probably meant to critique the family's behavior, in the process provides interesting details about women's decision-making powers and other behaviors. This well-to-do woman, perhaps a widow because Micah's father is not mentioned, has resources that she can use at her own discretion. She also has the right to make oaths, whether curses or blessings. She performs efficacious religious acts in uttering a curse about the theft and later offering a blessing: forgiving her son or perhaps rewarding him for his honesty, she says "May my son be blessed by the LORD!" (Judg 17:2). Like the father of the prodigal son (Luke 15:11-32) she harbors no parental anger. Finally, she decides to commission cultic objects, which contribute to the value of the household shrine.

Another fascinating narrative (1 Sam 25) is about *Abigail*, the wife of a wealthy but "surly and mean" man named Nabal, meaning "fool" (v. 3). In contrast her name probably means "her father rejoices," and she is described as "clever and beautiful" (also v. 3). The story takes place in the days of King Saul and relates an interaction with David, who is an outlaw at the time. Boorish Nabal has insulted David. The young men working with Nabal tell Abigail about this incident, and she decides to make amends lest retributive harm come to her household. At her own initiative, and without consulting her husband, she prepares gifts for David: "two hundred loaves, two skins of wine, five sheep ready dressed, five measures of parched grain, one hundred clusters of raisins, and two hundred cakes of figs" (1 Sam 25:18). She loads them on donkeys and instructs the young men in her household to go ahead of her as they set out to bring the gifts to David. When they find him, Abigail's impassioned plea and diplomatic address to the future king (1 Sam 25:24-31) succeed in averting David's ire. When she tells her husband what has happened, he suffers what seems to be a *stroke*. Appropriately, ten days later "the LORD *struck* Nabal" (1 Sam 25:38; my emphasis) and he dies. David learns of this and sends messengers to Abigail asking if she would become his wife. She agrees.

Abigail is the principal character in this story about a woman in an affluent household. The young men come to her to report the unfortunate encounter with David's men. She senses the danger to her household and takes swift action. She has access to resources—large quantities of foodstuffs—and makes a decision about how to use them. She does this on her own, without consulting Nabal; and she enlists others from the household to accompany her to meet David. Unlike the case of Micah's mother, whose words are not reported except for a brief blessing, Abigail's lengthy speech is presented. It exemplifies wisdom and diplomacy. In its use of imperatives and in the directness of its rhetoric, it displays authority and creates "a picture of a woman used to being in charge."[36] Abigail's intelligence, mentioned *before* her beauty at the beginning of the narrative, as well as her beauty make her a welcome member of what eventually will be the royal household. She functions as a mediator, empowered by her skill as a negotiator rather than by recourse to force. And, as is likely the case in village politics, she provides desirable food to enhance the receptivity of David to her entreaty to forego violence. She is a sagacious woman no less than the wise women described in chapter 9.

The third narrative (2 Kgs 4:8-37; 8:1-6) has been called "one of the most remarkable in the Bible."[37] It's about an affluent woman identified as a resident of Shunem and thus called the *Shunammite woman* (2 Kgs 4:12). Unlike virtually all women in biblical narratives, she is not presented as the "wife of" someone. This unnamed figure is described by the adjective *gedolah* (2 Kgs 4:8), a word used in the Hebrew Bible in reference to people "of esteem and status."[38] The usual translation, "wealthy," is not incorrect yet does not do justice to the term's connotation of respect.

The prophet Elisha is visiting her town; the Shunammite, who happens to be childless, invites him to a meal. Moreover, noting that he is frequently in the vicinity, she decides that he should have his own room in her house. Informing her husband of this, she has a room prepared for him. In gratitude, Elisha offers to commend her to the king or his general. She declines, claiming that her standing among her people needs no such intervention. The prophet then says he will see to it that her infertility problem is solved, which he does—she bears a son. Some years later, the child is in the fields with his father and becomes ill. He is brought to his mother and dies on her lap. The Shunammite immediately has a donkey saddled and sets off to fetch Elisha, who comes to her domicile and revives the deceased lad.

This happy result is not the end of the Shunammite's story. Sometime later Elisha instructs her to take her household to another place to get relief from a severe drought, and she does so. When the drought ends and she brings everyone back to Shunem, she finds that her property has been taken by someone else. She goes directly to the king, requesting that her property be restored. The king's favorable response brings not only the restoration of the domicile and land but also what it would have produced during her absence.

Several features about the Shunammite's story are notable. First, she makes decisions autonomously: inviting the prophet to her household, reconfiguring household space, moving away to escape the consequences of drought, and appealing to the king for restitution when the household is taken over by others. Second, she is the one who tends, albeit unsuccessfully, to an ill member of the household. Third, it is her status in the community that convinces the prophet that she needs nothing special from royal or military officials. Fourth, she interacts readily with a leading prophetic figure and with the king. Fifth, she is the one to whom the prophet turns when he wishes to warn her family to leave Shunem because of the drought. Does this autonomy and standing in the community mean that the household is her property?[39] Not necessarily. As the competent COO of the household, she manages its affairs, looking after its property. The designation "mother's household" (discussed in chapter 6) would surely apply to the Shunammite. When an Israelite woman entered a man's household as his wife, she identified with that household and it became hers as well as his. The household is viewed as corporate property, given the collective identity of Israelite households (see chapter 6, pp. 118–121).

This image of a woman running a household and making decisions about the use of resources also appears in a passage already cited several times—the depiction of a *strong woman* in Proverbs 31:10-31. These 22 verses portray the full life of a household manager. More than half refer to specifically economic processes. She provides food and engages in textile production—maintenance activities highlighted in chapter 7. In addition, she purchases land (v. 16), takes care of her profitable business (v. 18), and sells to merchants the textiles she has produced (v. 24). Moreover, she uses some of her household's resources as charity to the poor (v. 20). Indeed, the very language of this passage "ascribes to her physical, emotional, and intellectual strength, while the male is a bystander."[40] For example, the woman "girds herself with strength, and makes her arms strong" v. 17). The overall portrait resonates with the narrative images depicting women's autonomous resourcefulness and decision-making power.

It also resonates with a somewhat later Greek text, Xenophon's *Oeconomicus*, a treatise on household management that reveals gender relationships in elite Greek society. Xenophon does not polarize the relationship between wife and husband but rather "views their familial and economic roles as complementary"; their powers are divided, with a woman in some instances exercising authority over her marital partner.[41]

The managerial power of Israelite women and men also appears in two verses in the Covenant Code. Most stipulations in the Covenant Code reflect urban contexts (see chapter 2, pp. 20–21), but a small group of cases originated in village life.[42] These include Exodus 21:15, 17, which mandate the death penalty for offspring who curse or strike their father or mother. Capital punishment, which seems so harsh to us, is directed not toward children but to young adults in the household who threaten those above them "on the authority ladder."[43] These cases thus indicate that both parents have authority over adult children. So does Proverbs 20:20, part of the proverbial materials originating in ordinary family settings (see chapter 7, pp. 137–138); it proclaims that cursing either parent brings death ("your lamp [signifying life] will go out"). In the Covenant Code and Proverbs the dire consequence for threatening parental authority is specified for acts against both mother and father.

The legal provisions in Exodus and the related admonition in Proverbs make sense in the complex multigenerational families that were the norm in Israelite agrarian households. We tend to romanticize these large family configurations, which were economically essential in biblical antiquity and which indeed offer some advantages even today. But there is a downside, in that internal tensions can be more complicated than in nuclear families because more people are involved. Moreover, adult children—notably sons, for daughters marry out—at times challenge their parents. The threat of harsh punishment functions as a deterrent. At the same time, adult children have a responsibility to sustain their parents in old age. The translation "honor" in the biblical commandment to "honor one's father and mother" (Exod 20:12; Deut 5:16; cf. Lev 19:3, where "mother" precedes "father") is not quite accurate in this context, for the Hebrew term for honor (*kabod*) denotes the obligation of offspring to provide food, clothing, and shelter for elderly parents no longer able to support themselves.[44]

The Covenant Code and Proverbs texts affirming the authority of both parents come from village or family contexts, making it likely that the decision-making power of the women in the narratives described above was not unique to these elite individuals but rather reflects the dynamics in agrarian households working their own land, whatever their economic level. In fact, the biblical terms *ba'al* (m.) and *ba'alah* (f.) reflect this reconstruction.[45] Usually translated "master" or "lord" and thought to indicate sexual possession, *ba'al* can better be understood as a designation for the senior male in a household, the one who "owns" the household's property—the *nahalah* ("inheritance") mentioned in chapter 6. His wife, the senior woman in a household, is thus the *ba'alah*, the female head of a household, the manager responsible for administering the family household.

ETHNOGRAPHIC DATA AND biblical texts attest to female household power within an overall situation of gender complementarity in Israelite agrarian households. But households were the basic unit of a larger social system in which male figures dominated. Moreover, the term *patriarchy* is typically used to label the entire social system, household included. What does the lack of gender hierarchy within households mean for understanding Israelite society beyond the household? To answer that question, the meaning and adequacy of patriarchy as an analytical concept must be addressed.

The Larger Social System

First-wave feminist anthropologists in the 1970s and 1980s drew on the Weberian binary of informal power and legal authority in their analysis of social systems; women were associated with the former and men with the latter. My earlier work was heavily influenced by those models.[46] Since then a decided shift in thinking about power has occurred. Weberian (and Marxist) ideas about power focused on institutional forms and failed to take into account the way people interact with each other apart from formal structures. Power relations, it is now recognized, are not universally hierarchical or static but are rather circumstantial and continuously being negotiated.[47] Moreover, gender is not always the most useful category of power differentials. Age and social class are frequently more relevant, especially in societies where most men as well as women are excluded from institutional positions of power. Yet societies are repeatedly deemed patriarchal, a term related to male power. The relevance of that designation is clearly problematic.

The Patriarchy Problem

Defining patriarchy is not easy. As a theory meant to account for widespread gender stratification in human societies, it is often understood to be a general system in which power is held by adult men; and it usually implies near total male domination at the micro level of personal relationships as well as in macro institutional forms.[48] The influential feminist historian Gerda Lerner sees it as a term encompassing the "manifestation and institutionalization of male dominance over women and children in the family and the existence of male dominance over women in society in general."[49] This definition appears in her widely acclaimed book asserting that patriarchy as a universal condition originated with the rise of civilization in the ancient Near East. Her methodology is now considered seriously flawed.[50] Moreover, this understanding of patriarchy has been challenged by some social scientists, especially the third-wave feminists mentioned in chapter 1, who hold that one cannot call an entire culture patriarchal, for doing so means obscuring other, possibly more pernicious inequalities.[51] They argue that "the concept of patriarchy fails when the binary categories on which it depends are dismantled."[52] A glimpse at the origins and meanings of the term (not the system) is thus in order.

The term *patriarchy* comes from the Greek words *pater* ("father") and *archein* ("to rule"). Its use to denote a hierarchical social system became common in the writings of nineteenth-century European social scientists. Marxist political theorists drew on newly available translations of classical literature in their claim that the rise of private property in antiquity caused an original gender equality to be replaced by women's virtual servitude. The legal authority (*patria potestas*) of the male head of the ancient household (*pater familias*) was generalized to represent pervasive male control throughout society. Patriarchy was considered a system that systematically and structurally oppresses women and gives men authority over political, social, and economic institutions.[53] I would add religious institutions to this list.

This ideology of patriarchal dominance was aligned with nineteenth-century theories about the evolution of human societies from primitive (matriarchal or egalitarian) to a series of civilized (patriarchal) forms: tribe, chiefdom, state. It entered biblical studies in the 1880s, when two renowned biblical scholars (see chapter 1, p. 11)—William Robertson Smith and Julius Wellhausen—asserted that ancient Israelite society was dominated by the universal form of the patriarchal family as it evolved from tribe to state. Fast forward to the twenty-first century, when one of the most recent studies of Israelite society adopted the notion that Israelite patrimonialism (in which all power flows from the leader down through nested units of society) originates in the "patriarchal household government."[54] Feminist biblical scholars too, as noted at the beginning of this chapter, use patriarchy as a designation for both the Bible and Israelite society.

Although the term continues to be used, patriarchy is an inadequate and inappropriate designation and can no longer be seen as a cultural universal. Among the reasons for this assessment are the following:[55]

- Classicists question the validity of the model from ancient Rome that gave rise to modern notions of patriarchy in the first place.[56]
- Ethnographic reports from the Mediterranean world (like those cited in this chapter) and from other traditional societies indicate that much household power resides with senior women.
- When the household is the central unit of society, as it is in societies (like ancient Israel) in which production is at the subsistence level

and supra-household structures (clan, tribe, state) impinge relatively little on household life, women have significant agency not only in the
household itself but also in supra-household matters. The latter include
the political-economic aspect of women's maintenance roles discussed
in chapter 7.

- Informal organizations of female specialists in ancient Israel (see chapter 9) had their own hierarchies, independent of those in the general
social system. Women professionals would have operated outside of
other hierarchical structures.[57]

- Patriarchal models have been developed largely by analyzing modern
industrial societies and do not fit the interlocking social, economic,
and political structures of premodern groups.

- Using the patriarchy paradigm implies a fixed set of relationships,
when in fact social arrangements are rarely static and power relations
can shift over time.

- The focus on the subordination of women overlooks the fact that
inequalities are a function of class or age as much as, if not more than, of
gender. For example, insufficient regard is given to the inferior position
of servants, slaves, and strangers (or "aliens," probably people of different ethnicity) in ancient Israel. And male hereditary institutions, like the
Israelite priesthood, are a little noticed form of exclusion that excludes
most men as well as women from arenas of community religious power.

- Patriarchy is a hierarchical model that cannot be uniformly applied
to ancient complex societies (those with several levels of sociopolitical
organization).[58]

In short, patriarchy is a value-laden and diffuse term that is probably
unsuitable for characterizing any society, and there are ample reasons to
discard it as a designation for Israelite society. Yet critiques of the patriarchal model have had little impact on biblical studies, and feminist biblical
scholars continue to characterize Israelite society as patriarchal. However,
several biblical scholars now suggest other terms:

- Schroer would actually keep the term but define it somewhat differently
and use it to designate a system in which both women and men of
certain classes or groups "exercise domination over other men, women,
and children."[59] Recognizing some female domination is important, but
seeing it as limited to certain classes obscures gender complementarity
and women's power in ordinary households.

- Block says that patriarchy "places inordinate emphasis on the power a father exercised over the household" and too often connotes abusive behavior. He then suggests that *patricentrism* would be a term that better reflects "the normal biblical disposition" toward the senior male.[60] This may be suitable for describing biblical texts, but it would not be accurate in depicting household life.

- The term *patrilineal*, which I proposed in my earlier work,[61] certainly is important in describing the transfer of property across generations along the male line (see chapter 6); but it is an inadequate descriptor of household gender dynamics.

- Schüssler Fiorenza offers an intriguing proposal. She acknowledges the power inequities of monarchic rule in ancient societies and uses the term *kyriarchy*, from Greek *kyrios* ("lord") and *archein* ("to rule"), to designate "a sociopolitical system in which elite educated propertied men hold power over women and other men." She emphasizes that it is a system that subordinates men as well as women, and she focuses on the "exploitation, dependency, and inferiority and obedience of wo/men."[62] Her point is well taken with respect to national and regional governance systems, but it fails to capture the gender dynamics of households and small settlements or acknowledge the agency of specialists outside hierarchical systems.

The Heterarchy Alternative

Is there another, less value-laden and more suitable way to characterize social organization in ancient Israel? To answer that question, it is important first to recognize the nature of patriarchy as a hierarchical system. As anthropologists define it, *hierarchy* designates an organizational structure in which, on the basis of certain factors, some elements are subordinate to others and are usually ranked accordingly.[63] Hierarchies are often represented spatially as conical vertical structures, giving rise to phrases like "moving up in the hierarchy."[64] Recognizing that not all social systems are organized hierarchically, some of the social scientists who challenge the evolutionary models underlying the concept of hierarchical systems offer a more nuanced and adaptable model: *heterarchy*.

This is hardly a household term, even though it has been around since the middle of the last century.[65] A combination of Greek *heteros* ("different, other") and *archein* ("to rule"), heterarchy was introduced in the

1940s to describe neural structures, which aren't always arranged hierarchically, and then was used in the 1970s to represent the diverse rankings in computer systems. It first appeared in the anthropological and archaeological literature in 1979, when Carol Crumley used it to denote an "organizational structure…in which each element possesses the potential of being unranked (relative to other elements) or ranked in a number of different ways, depending on systemic requirements."[66] More simply, it is a term that can account for the fact that past societies had multiple sources of power that did not necessarily line up in a single set of vertical hierarchical relationships.[67] With respect to gender, it can accommodate arenas of activity in which women have power and agency; it can also incorporate the intersection of gender with other variables like age and class.

The heterarchy model takes into account many of the flaws, noted above, in the hierarchical (patriarchal) model. For example, it does not assume that ranking is permanent or that the ranking of elements according to different criteria will always coincide. As a much more flexible concept than hierarchy, it provides a way to accommodate the variety of patterns in organizational structures across cultures and to acknowledge different rankings of structures or elements of structures vis-à-vis each other.[68] Not surprisingly, heterarchy has been interpreted and employed in many different ways.[69] One of the most promising for this project is the integration of heterarchy and gender.[70]

Heterarchy provides a compelling concept for representing ancient Israelite society in the Iron Age. Perhaps its most attractive feature is that it does not eliminate hierarchies but rather recognizes that there can be a variety of hierarchies that may or may not intersect with each other. That is, heterarchies and hierarchies are not mutually exclusive concepts but rather interactive or dialectical ones.[71] A heterarchical society can be composed of various social units—including individuals, households, guilds of professionals, village communities, and kinship groups—that are involved in multiple horizontal as well as vertical relationships.

In the heterarchical model, this interweaving of differently structured patterns of relationships means that an individual—an Israelite woman in an agrarian household, for example—can rank high in one modality but low in another. The maintenance activities and social structures of ancient Israel meant that daily life was rarely structured according to fixed, hierarchical gender patterns. A woman's position would vary over time, according to other factors, such as age, participation in community activities, and role in the informal network of women formed by her work patterns. And certain systems associated with women holding extra-household professional positions (see chapter 9) would have their own hierarchies and cultural authority vis à vis other systems. All these factors contest the existence of Israelite patriarchy, which assigns general subordination to women. Interpretative traditions that anachronistically read the gender hierarchies in biblically based Judaism and Christianity (see the epilogue) back into Iron Age Israel can thus be challenged.

In other words, the perceptions cited at the beginning of this chapter about male dominance in pervasive hierarchical structures affecting all domains of human interaction and subordinating women should be replaced with the recognition that there were intersecting systems and multiple loci of power, with women as well as men shaping society. The heterarchy model allows for a more nuanced and probably more accurate view of Iron Age Israel—a view that acknowledges significant domains of female agency and power. The term patriarchy obscures the way individuals and groups were organized in complex and interlocking spheres of activity; it is not an appropriate designation for the Israelites.

The heterarchy model is important not only for understanding gender relationships. It also has great potential for understanding the diversity and complexity of Israelite society in general, as several biblical scholars have noted. Gottwald, a strong proponent of engaging social science research in the study of ancient Israel, calls heterarchy a more flexible term than the "stark choice" of either egalitarian or hierarchical to describe Israelite social arrangements in the Iron I period.[72] In his extensive study of Israelite religion as part of a dynamic and complex society, Zevit sees power throughout Iron Age Israel as heterarchical rather than hierarchical.[73] And Nakhai refers to ancient Israel's social structure as heterarchical."[74]

It is important to keep in mind that, like any model, the heterarchic one is a heuristic tool that cannot be deemed either true or false.[75] Rather, its value lies in helping us to understand a society that cannot be directly observed by allowing us to interpret existing data in new ways. Models must be modified or replaced if they are no longer helpful or if another one becomes more relevant. The hierarchy model has outlived its usefulness, especially in the way it sustains the notion of patriarchy. Perhaps the heterarchy one will endure.

Invoking heterarchy in this reconstruction of gendered life in Israelite households allows us to overcome the stereotypes of presentism and the distortions of patriarchy. The life of Everywoman Eve was difficult because of the demands on her time and energy, but it did not entail all-pervasive oppression and subordination. In carrying out a wide range of maintenance activities and in managing her household, she produced life-sustaining foods and materials, performed religious acts thought essential for household survival, and was enmeshed in relationships that contributed to the vitality of her household and community.

Yet the heterarchy model does not mean that no hierarchies existed. Women's household power was significant, given the centrality of the household in the lives of most Israelites. And women held some extra-household professional positions. But these features do not mean general gender equality or the absence of male privilege. Male dynasties and priest-hoods, and their bureaucracies, were the norm, excluding women and also most men. The male military brought men into positions of community power. Immovable property (land) was owned mainly by men. Female sexuality was controlled by men. And perhaps most important in the long run, the small group of educated elites responsible for creating or recording the Hebrew Bible was male. Whether, or how, these aspects of male position and power can be evaluated or judged must be addressed.

Evaluating Inequalities

Should we judge the world in which Everywoman Eve lived and the hier-archies that excluded or subordinated her? This question cannot be easily answered, given the overall anthropological approach of this project. That is, anthropological research generally applies the principles of *cultural relativism*.[76] This means not only trying to gain an emic (insider's) per-spective—considering Israelite culture as Eve would have experienced it. It also means trying to avoid making value judgments about her culture even though aspects seem unacceptable. It means avoiding ethnocentrism, that is, considering the values of the researcher's culture to be superior to those of the culture being studied. Although the Hebrew Bible provides a connection of sorts between the twenty-first century academy and Iron Age settlements in the Levant, the Israelite way of life was vastly different and should be accepted as such. In short, the anthropological approach means suspending judgment.

But this is not as easy or straightforward as it may seem. Anthropologists indeed attempt to be neutral in understanding the customs and structures of groups they study. But inevitably some aspects seem wrong, no matter what the culture.[77] Can anthropologists studying cultures that practice cannibalism or honor killings really consider them morally defensible customs? Must they refrain from criticizing blatant violations of human rights? As a philosophical stance valuing the customs and norms of all cultures equally, cultural relativism is often rejected in anthropological research. From a feminist perspective and from the perspective of an academic institution valuing diversity and equality, many aspects of Eve's life are indeed unacceptable. But the same could be said about many aspects of Everyman Adam's life, for class and ethnic inequities excluded most men from positions of power and exploited many men. Like other cultures in the ancient world, Israel had a monarchic system and a general acceptance of servitude and slavery that should be deemed intolerable.[78]

Having said this, a closer look at two examples of Israelite gender inequity mentioned above may be helpful. These examples—male property ownership, and male control of female sexuality—are interrelated. A household's land, as noted several times, was its life and livelihood. This property, or "inheritance" (*nahalah*), was transmitted along male lines, from father to son or sons and occasionally to daughters, if there were no sons. In principle, land could never be sold or transferred from one lineage or person to another. Although this principle seems to have been violated over time, with estates formed and controlled by elites, men generally did not have the option of buying or selling real property. Women were disadvantaged in this respect only slightly more than most men. It is even possible, insofar as the Israelite family household was a "corporate household,"[79] that household property was considered a corporate possession and not the individual domain of the senior male.[80] Women took on the identity of their marital household, sharing the sense of ownership.

With a household's land being not only its life but also its identity, maintaining it within the household patrilineage was highly valued, making it critical that a man's offspring were his own. Thus property/inheritance concerns hover in the background of many sex regulations. If a woman engaging in extramarital sex became pregnant, the heir to household property might not be her husband's son. Without DNA tests, strong cultural incentives to refrain from extramarital sex—like the death penalty for adultery (Lev 20:10; Deut 22:22)—were inevitable. (But note that the death penalty for adultery applied to married men too.) Thus many biblical texts favoring men involve male control of female sexuality for reasons of inheritance or procreation. They include the divine mandate in Genesis 3:16 for men to be sexually dominant (see chapter 5) and

the Pentateuchal legal stipulations concerning virginity, adultery, prostitution, levirate marriage, and childbirth.[81] Property transmission was at stake
for Israelites in ways that rarely exist in the developed world. Land was
the chief resource, and strategies safeguarding the inheritance of household property had essential functional value. Understanding the context
helps temper judgment. All told, the biblical texts in which men control
women arise from socioeconomic factors "rather than from a condemnation of female sexuality per se."[82] It must also be kept in mind that these
legal texts, like ancient law codes in general, were not codes for ordinary
conduct or adjudication of ordinary disputes and that most stipulations
were meant for urban elites.

An emic perspective provides another example of context mitigating
judgment. When people's lives are merged together in social units, as in a
society like ancient Israel with collective group identity, women experience
life not so much as individuals but as household members. The concept
of either women or men striving for personal independence is antithetical
to the dynamics and demands of premodern agrarians. Indeed, analysis of
biblical legal materials indicates that the household and not the individual was the reigning legal entity.[83] Moreover, gender differentials in life
patterns meant complementarity and interdependence and were essential
for the welfare of the household. Can we object to social arrangements
that contributed to household and also community survival? To put it
another way, is it really fair to criticize the past for not having the values
of the present?

But offering judgment is still in order. However, I direct judgment not
to Israelite society, which no longer exists, but rather to the interpretive
traditions that all too often equate biblical androcentrism with social reality. I agree with some feminist theologians who insist that biblical texts
themselves neither oppress nor liberate and assert that it is those who use
them and the way they are used that can become oppressive or liberat-
ing.[84] And I concur with feminists who emphasize that postbiblical interpretations are sometimes more powerful and problematic than the biblical
texts themselves.[85]

Once the Hebrew Bible became authoritative, it was interpreted
according to the post-Hebrew Bible context and ideas of its interpreters (see epilogue). Its male perspectives and interests become the vehicle for excluding women from certain roles and otherwise restricting
them. Interpreted in increasingly sexist and misogynist ways, biblical texts
often became the ideological justification for the sexism and misogyny

permeating many postbiblical texts (see the examples at the beginning of chapter 4). Knowledge about ancient Israel was mediated through the biblical lens and with little awareness of how the Israelite context differed from that of early Jews and Christians. Morally problematic claims about women were the result. Those patterns of interpretation grounded in biblical androcentrism are too often antithetical to current egalitarian values.

ALTHOUGH TRADITIONAL VIEWS have occluded or distorted Eden Eve and Everywoman Eve, research into their world using not only the Bible but all available sources has helped us rediscover them. This multidisciplinary anthropological (ethnohistorical) analysis has produced a different reading of the Eden tale; it has also revealed many otherwise invisible aspects of women's everyday lives and experiences in Israelite households. This expanded knowledge about the lives of Israelite women in turn helps us confront the problematic stereotypes projected onto the biblical past in popular culture and biblical scholarship, both of which follow the long tradition of reading later ideas about women into Israelite contexts. Recovering the household context of women's lives also means challenging the validity of patriarchy as a designation for Israelite society. Facile use of that model not only contributes to the negative stereotypes about women in the period of the Hebrew Bible but also is less accurate than heterarchy in depicting the complexities of household life and general sociopolitical organization in the Israelite past. This alternative model makes the power and agency of women—senior women and also professionals—more visible.

Epilogue

Beyond the Hebrew Bible

WHAT HAPPENED TO Eden Eve and Everywoman Eve? The Eve of Eden is rescued in chapters 4 and 5 from the negative press of early Christian and Jewish tradition. Similarly, Everywoman Eve of the agrarian settlements of ancient Israel emerges in chapters 7, 8, and 10 as a woman with considerable agency and power, a complement to her spouse in carrying out the myriad tasks of an agrarian household—hardly a subservient, passive, and inferior housewife. Chapter 9 adds professional roles: prophet, sage, judge, singer, landowner, skilled women, general, and more.

Although women are far less visible than men in the androcentric Hebrew Bible, they are not presented as inferior. To be sure, they may seem sexually dangerous, as in Proverbs. Yet even the one seemingly misogynist statement (Eccl 7:26) probably does not apply to women in general but rather is the same kind of seductive imagery portraying the temptresses of Proverbs.[1] Male control of female sexuality in the Hebrew Bible is particularly troubling in relation to contemporary values, but it has a functional role in a patrilineal system that must deal with problems of adultery, divorce, betrothal, inheritance, etc. (see chapter 10, pp. 200–201). Otherwise, women are nowhere portrayed as less intelligent or capable than men; rather, they often appear as clever, competent, and sometimes heroic figures.[2] As in the Iron Age society in which many biblical materials took shape, biblical women move about freely; and female professionals serve a variety of community needs. Labeling the Hebrew Bible misogynist is unwarranted.

What happened to Eden Eve and Everywoman Eve and the notable women of the Hebrew Bible in the post-Israelite world? Sacred texts have a continuing vitality. Later generations inevitably and continually appropriate, interpret, rewrite, and transmit sacred traditions. Their views appear in music, art, film, and literature as well as in religious and theological texts. The reception history or "afterlife" of Eve begins with the general negativity of early Jewish and Christian traditions described in chapter 4. Subsequent texts continue the disparaging perspectives and scathing rhetoric of those early writings, although Christian sources show more interest in Eve than do Jewish ones. For example, the thirteenth-century writer Thomas Aquinas, whose work influenced Christian thinking about women for centuries, sees Eve as naturally subordinate, intellectually inferior, susceptible to temptation, and more sinful than Adam (*Summa Theologia* II-II, 163-165). Some views, especially beginning in the Reformation, are more moderate; but the negative ones beginning with Paul and Augustine dominate until the rise of critical biblical studies. Fascination with Eve's disconcerting afterlife has produced many scholarly and popular works chronicling her presentation in Jewish, Christian, and Islamic texts.[3]

The afterlife of biblical women isn't much better. At best, the sources are ambivalent about them, acknowledging positive traits but presenting them in an overall negative if not harsh manner. Hierarchical claims make all women subordinate.

Jewish rabbinic literature of the first five to six centuries CE recognizes worthy qualities in some biblical women but also finds ways to censure or demonize them. Traditions about Sarah, for example, praise her as mother of generations but also call her a deceptive eavesdropper and complainer (*Gen. Rab.* 45:5). Deborah, an outstanding biblical woman because of her roles as judge, prophet, and military leader, is considered a braggart who defies her husband and immodestly sings her own praises (e.g., *b. Meg.* 14a,b). Even worse, rabbinic texts often sexualize the deeds of exemplary biblical women and thus of all later women, depicting them as threatening, dangerous, and in need of strict male control.[4] Rabbinic legal texts thus seek to restrict the movements of women and their participation in community affairs, making them completely subject to their husband's authority. Male dominance is constructed on claims that women are mentally, emotionally, and morally inferior. The affection of men for their wives and an appreciation of their generosity and compassion do appear in rabbinic anecdotes and tales—along with exceptionally derogatory, harsh, and misogynous comments.

Postbiblical Christian literature pays little attention to Hebrew Bible women other than Eve, but when these women appear, they are usually depicted negatively. For example, in criticizing deeds of the Genesis patriarchs, patristic texts blame their wives for leading them astray or deceiving them into committing blameworthy acts.[5] Otherwise, interest in biblical women focuses on New Testament figures, many of whom suffer the same fate in patristic sources that Hebrew Bible women suffer in rabbinic texts. A notable example is Mary Magdalene. In a process of vilification that may begin in the New Testament, she is transformed, especially in the Western church, from a faithful follower of Jesus to a repentant whore.[6] Misogyny abounds except for virgins and perhaps widows, and gender hierarchy is considered natural.

These brief comments barely touch on the many appearances of Eve and other women in the vast array of Jewish and Christian sources. Women are often depicted as different, inferior, and sometimes dangerous in postbiblical sources but not in the Hebrew Bible. What caused this sea change? What led to the transformation of the less visible but not necessarily inferior women of the Hebrew Bible (and ancient Israel) into these problematic female figures?

The Bible was surely the most important text in the Jewish and Christian communities in the early postbiblical period and for centuries afterward. That it influenced the development of Jewish and Christian culture and beliefs is obvious. What is often overlooked is that the social-historical conditions and ways of thinking of later generations influenced how the Bible was interpreted. The context of the interpreters determined to a great extent how they read sacred texts.

The profound shift in the way women were viewed and portrayed began in the early centuries of Judaism in the last centuries BCE and continued in both Judaism and Christianity in the first several centuries CE. Major changes in the east Mediterranean were under way during this period. Beginning late in the fourth century BCE, when Alexander the Great conquered Palestine and Syria along with much of the Near East and North Africa, Greco-Roman influence penetrated the Semitic cultures of the Iron Age and Persian periods. This Hellenization of the biblical world brought new political forms and also general cultural change. New languages, artistic genres and architectural styles, economic patterns, religious beliefs, philosophies, and even new technologies altered to a greater or lesser degree the way of life that had endured for millennia in the east Mediterranean. Many of these changes impacted gender roles and relationships and, consequently, the way women were portrayed in Jewish and Christian literature.

The influence of these cultural developments in creating the alarmingly negative attitudes and regulations in texts of the Hellenistic-Roman period (ca. 330 BCE to 350 CE) has been explored in recent scholarship and can only be highlighted here.[7] I will focus on changes in the Jewish community, for those changes directly or indirectly affected the earliest Christians and the development of Christianity. The Jewish community was diverse, but a number of factors leading to the transformation of gender patterns likely affected most groups.

One factor was the *development of urban centers*. The postexilic (post-Iron Age) community was relatively small for the first few centuries after the Babylonian conquest (587 BCE), when many people died, fled, or were exiled. Jerusalem was reduced to a tiny fraction of its late Iron Age size. But by the Hellenistic-Roman period Jerusalem had expanded, and other urban centers and large towns emerged in the Levant. Hellenistic (Greek) and then Roman control of the east Mediterranean was accompanied by efforts to divide the area into *poleis* (city-states) and develop city life.

The development of large settlements with features of urban life meant that increasing numbers of households were sustained economically by (male) wage labor rather than self-supporting agriculture. This probably had begun in a limited way in the Iron Age in Jerusalem and several other large settlements but without an accompanying widespread market economy (see chapter 6, p. 132). But in the Hellenistic-Roman period, the emergence of trades and enterprises requiring paid labor meant the growth of markets and the availability of consumer goods (augmented by the technological change described below). Sometimes women were wage earners in urban contexts, but male wage labor was more common. (In a popular second-century BCE Jewish book, Tobit, a woman supports her family by selling cloth to a shop, but only when her husband becomes incapacitated; and her work arouses suspicion and marital discord.[8])

The rise of (male) wage labor meant the erosion of self-sufficient households. As women's work became less essential to the household economy, their voice in economic decisions weakened, as did their power. Also, agricultural work in the Iron Age had favored the formation of joint families (see chapter 6, pp. 110–111); but wage labor meant that smaller, nuclear-family households became more common. The managerial roles of senior women were thus diminished.

A second factor was the greater *intrusion of governing powers into household life*. The destruction and disruption of exile weakened the kinship-based clan structures in which households were embedded and which had tempered the control of the central government throughout the Iron Age (see chapter 6, pp. 115–117). As anthropologists have noted, reducing the kinship base triggers "important changes in gender status and gender relations."[9] Government control was also abetted by the extensive road system built by the Romans.[10] Small towns and villages were more easily reached by military or political authorities, and economic exchanges were also facilitated. Both reduced the independence of individual households. So did the increased tax burden imposed by the imperial rulers (Persians, then Greeks, then Romans) and also Jewish priestly authorities. Under these conditions male decision-making increases, and female power and prestige likely recede.

A third relevant feature was *increased priestly importance*. In the absence of a monarchy in the postexilic period, the Jerusalem temple (destroyed by the Babylonians and rebuilt in the late sixth century BCE) and its priesthood gained power, consolidating extensive economic as well as political control.[11] Priestly power meant an emphasis on celebrating festivals in Jerusalem at the temple rather than in local or regional shrines. This may have reduced somewhat the participation of women from households far from Jerusalem and thus weakened an important aspect of their religious roles (described in chapter 8).

A fourth and related factor was *the increased importance of sacred writings*, including an early form of the Pentateuch. The authority vacuum in the absence of monarchic power (except for Hasmonean and Herodian kingship from ca. 140 BCE to ca. 90 CE) was not only filled by the priesthood but was also supported by the texts preserved and promulgated by literate priests, who replaced the monarchic scribes as guardians of national documents. The priestly importance in the postexilic period gave authority to these documents in a process called the textualization of authority. At least for some Jewish sects, legal provisions in the Pentateuch, many with gender differentials favoring males, gradually became authoritative policy rather than resources for adjudication among elites. The postexilic community was becoming a "people of the Book."[12] Although this was a positive development in many ways, it also contributed to the shift of the locus of power from household life to a central institution: the male priesthood, whose members served as guardians and teachers of authoritative texts.

A fifth and little recognized but highly significant factor was *technological change*. Technological innovations in the Hellenistic-Roman period affected two major components of women's maintenance activities (described in chapter 7)—bread production and textile production.

Cereal products, as mentioned several times, were the mainstay of the Israelite diet. Women devoted much time, energy, and expertise to converting grains to edible forms; and grinding grains to produce flour was the most time-consuming part of the process. A revolutionary change in flour-production technology took place in the last centuries BCE. The millennia-old method of grinding with handstone and quern or slab was replaced by milling with machines, which were far more efficient than the old grinding tools. Olynthus mills, rotary mills, and donkey mills appeared throughout the Mediterranean basin.[13] Donkey mills using animal power were the most efficient of the new devices. According to ancient Roman sources, one donkey mill could produce a hundred times more flour per day than could a person using a handstone and slab or quern.[14]

Two of the new devices—Olynthus and donkey mills—found their way into the towns and cities of the Jewish community in Palestine by the Roman period. (Rotary mills were used only by the Roman occupying forces.) Both were more expensive to make and operate than were the old grinding tools. According to ancient sources Olynthus mills were found mainly in wealthier households or commercial mills; and donkey mills were used almost exclusively in commercial settings—flour shops or commercial bakeries.[15] Archaeological data indicate that, although households in small villages of the Greco-Roman period continued to use grinding tools, the new mills dominated in the many urban centers, making flour and bread available in markets.[16] Commercially produced bread may have been available in Jerusalem in the late Iron Age (Jer 37:21 mentions a "bakers' street"), but the advent of milling many centuries later dramatically increased the scale and extent of such production.

The impact on women's lives of the availability of flour and bread in the markets of the cities and towns would have been considerable. First the good news. The body position and movements involved in grinding produced repetitive stress injuries and painful arthritic deformities that have been identified in studies of skeletal remains.[17] Women's physical health probably improved when they no longer spent hours bent over a grinding slab. But there was a downside. With women no longer solely responsible for a basic household commodity, their overall contribution to the household economy was reduced and the Iron Age gender balance in household economic activities diminished. The reduction in women's bread production tipped the gender balance in favor of male power and also reduced the empowering social interaction of women working together.

And to make matters worse, there was also a shift in the technology of textile production, with similar consequences for women. In the first

and second centuries CE the single-beam loom used in Iron Age household textile production was gradually replaced by a two-beam loom,
which produced material of higher quality.[18] Like the new milling technology, this innovation was more efficient and less physically taxing; and
the old loom technology virtually disappeared. Textiles were still produced at home, but workshops using the new technology and employing
both women and men became common. Cloth may have been commercially available in earlier periods (see Prov 31:24), but a more developed
textile market in the Roman period meant that household cloth production diminished. In this way too an economic and social component of
women's maintenance activities was reduced, again negatively impacting
their household power.

An even more insidious negative effect can be attributed to the
new technologies and the increased availability of commercial products.
Women no longer spent long hours grinding or spinning, giving many of
them more leisure time than before. Presumably elite women (wives of
royal bureaucrats or temple officials) had household servants and access to
commercial bread and textiles already in the Iron Age in the urban center of Jerusalem. With leisure time, some women were inevitably "loose,"
perhaps giving rise to images of seductive women in sections of Proverbs
addressed to young elite males (e.g., 7:5-15).

In the Hellenistic-Roman period, more urban contexts, a larger range
of commercial goods, and technological changes reducing women's workload increased tendencies already present. Adultery "in all societies tends
to be an indulgence" of people with leisure time.[19] Rabbinic sources,
mostly arising in urban contexts, explicitly link leisure time with sexual
wantonness: "idleness leads to unchastity" (*m. Ketub.* 5.5). Statements in
ancient Roman literature suggest that work protects women from the
sexual temptations resulting from leisure.[20] A striking parallel occurred
millennia later in a Mesoamerican community: men opposed commercial milling, preferring their wives to use the old grinding techniques in
the belief that women who could buy flour would have more leisure and
more opportunity to be unfaithful.[21] All of these sources, of course, blame
women for infidelity and contributed to the perception that women
needed to be controlled.[22]

This negative perception was facilitated by a sixth factor, *the penetra-
tion of Greco-Roman culture, especially Greek philosophy, into the Semitic
east.*[23] Many Jewish leaders, including rabbinic sages from aristocratic families, spoke Greek and were familiar with Greek intellectual traditions.[24]

For some, earlier holistic notions of the person as an integrated mind and body gave way to dualistic concepts, which separated mind and body.

In Greek philosophy this mind-body dualism became a more general perception of binary categories or opposites. For example, the mind or soul was aligned with enduring life, rationality, and goodness, whereas the body was connected with death, irrationality, and evil. With disastrous consequences, gender was sometimes aligned with these categories: men were linked to the soul and its positive qualities, and women to the body with its bestial and even evil qualities (e.g., Plato, *Tim.* 21c). This dualism influenced some Jewish intellectuals, including the renowned Jewish thinker Philo Judaeus (20 BCE–50 CE). Philo was mentioned in chapter 4, and more must be said.

He lived in the Greek-speaking Jewish community in Alexandria. Many of his writings have survived, attesting to their popularity and providing an invaluable source for analyzing the impact of Greco-Roman thought on Jews and Christians. In fact, he was probably more influential on early Christian thinkers (e.g., Clement of Alexandria, Justin Martyr, Tertullian, Origen, perhaps even Paul) than on Jewish sages. Well versed in Greek philosophy, Philo had a gentile audience in mind; he wanted to "explain" Judaism to non-Jews. He wrote commentaries in Greek about biblical texts, including Genesis. His dualistic reading includes these statements[25]:

- Man should rule over immortality and everything good but woman over death and everything vile. In the allegorical sense, however, woman is a symbol of sense, and man, of mind. (*Questions and Answers on Genesis* 1.37, about Gen 3:6)
- And woman becomes for him [Adam] the beginning of blameworthy life. (*On the Creation* 151)
- Mind corresponds to man, the senses to woman; and pleasure encounters and holds parley with the senses first, and through them cheats with her quackeries the sovereign mind itself. (*On the Creation* 165)
- For pre-eminence always pertains to the masculine, and the feminine always comes short of and is lesser than it. (*On Flight and Finding* 51)

These and similar sentiments, together with the other factors described above, led to the belief that women were inherently different from men in their cognitive and moral faculties as well as their physical (sexual) characteristics.[26] Conceptualized as a breed apart, women were not only different, they were also inferior and even dangerous.

Finally, another aspect of Greco-Roman culture was the increased use of Bible translations, especially Greek and Latin ones. Translations have to "resonate with the surrounding world,"[27] and the shift from a Semitic language (Hebrew) to Indo-European ones (Greek and Latin) inevitably introduced the prevailing cultural values. Many of the nuances of the Hebrew of Genesis 3:16, as discussed in chapter 5, were distorted by the "quantum leap"[28] to different language systems in a world far removed from the culture of the original. Similarly, other aspects of gender in the opening chapters of Genesis were adversely affected by the ancient translation process, which influenced many later Bible translations and contributed to the biblical justifications for the subordination of women.

THE TRANSFORMATION FROM the generally positive views about women in the Hebrew Bible to the negative ones in Greco-Roman period texts was a complex process involving multiple variables. And it is uncertain how pervasive were the views expressed by Philo and others. The Jewish and Christian communities of the early centuries CE were diverse and were not equally affected by Greco-Roman culture. In small villages and hamlets distant from urban centers and transportation routes, some of the Iron Age patterns likely continued in household life.

Still, it is hard to ignore that the rabbinic texts taking shape in the second and third centuries CE differ greatly from the Hebrew Bible with respect to gender. They are replete with negative narrative depictions and legal rulings, some explicitly misogynist and others presenting unflattering stereotypes. In their own time these texts probably affected the lives of wealthy residents of the larger settlements but not necessarily the general Jewish populace.[29] But in later generations these texts, emanating from an urban, upper-class minority, become normative for most Jews.[30] Community roles for women largely disappeared. And, although the social reality of daily life may have differed to some extent from what the texts imply, an ideology of patriarchy was developing, with households becoming more like the patriarchal structures erroneously projected onto Israelite society.

A somewhat similar trajectory can be posited for early Christianity. The earliest Christian gatherings were in people's homes, and the role of women as household managers boded well for egalitarian leadership and a positive regard for women. But the emergence of an institutionalized Church, empowered as the official religion of the Roman Empire in the fourth century CE, meant that the influential views of patristic writers, influenced by Philo and similar sources, became normative.[31] Community roles diminished, and the domination of men in household life became more common, notwithstanding the likely gap between patristic writings and social reality.

Given these developments in Judaism and Christianity, admittedly oversimplified and generalized, it is no wonder that misogynist readings of the Eden story are found in Jewish and Christian literature. An Eve associated with death and sin replaced the Eve of the Genesis narrative. It is sometimes difficult to see the Israelite agrarian women embedded in the Edenic depiction because of these subsequent readings. But recovering Eve's Iron Age context, as the chapters of this book have attempted to do, has allowed us to rediscover in some measure the Eve of Eden along with the experiences of real women. If one of the ways we understand our gendered present is to trace the long cultural history that produced it, it behooves us to strive continually, despite the constraints of inadequate sources, to learn as much as we can about gender in the biblical past. Eve and her sisters remain important figures in our culture as we look to the future, for they hover in the background of the never-ending effort to comprehend and transcend the gender and social inequities in the Bible and other valued cultural productions.

Notes

Chapter 1 Eve and Israelite Women: Understanding the Task

1. *Newsweek*, January 11, 1988.
2. Bohmbach (2000), 34–35.
3. The books without women are Obadiah, Jonah, Habakkuk, Zephaniah, and Haggai.
4. K. Hopkins (1983), 41–42.
5. Classically stated by Rogers (1975) and more recently by Gilchrist (1999), 32–36.
6. See Bellis (2000b), 24–25.
7. Pilarski (2011), 19–22; Milne (1997), 40–43, 48–60.
8. See, e.g., the essays—especially those attempting to define feminism—in Hermann and Stewart (2001). Stansell (2010) provides a history of feminism.
9. See the essays in Ginsberg (2008).
10. See, e.g., the essays on sex, sexuality, and gender in: Hendel, Kronfeld, and Pardes (2010); Sofaer (2006), 9–116; Hermann and Stewart (2001), 131–270. A convenient summary appears in Løland (2008), 59–63.
11. Fischer et al. (2011), 5.
12. Chaves (2011). 1.
13. See Gifford (1985).
14. Schüssler Fiorenza (2001), 89.
15. K. M. O'Connor (2006), 12–15.
16. E.g., Fontaine (1997); Trible (1984).
17. See Meyers (2003d) and Kray (2002).
18. Shectman (2009), 11–54, provides an extensive summary. See also Bellis (2007), 20–23; Phillips (2004); McKay (1997), 69–78.
19. E.g., Daly (1968) and (1973).

20. See Sakenfeld (1989), 165–168.

21. Cf. Wacker (1998), 63–82, who also briefly mentions depth psychology, history of religions, and social science approaches.

22. E.g., Fuchs (2008) and (2000); but cf. Berlinerblau (1999) and also the critique of patriarchy in chapter 10 of this book.

23. Sakenfeld (1989), 161.

24. E.g., Brenner and Van Dijk-Hemmes (1996); Pardes (1992).

25. E.g., Lapsley (2005).

26. See Ackerman (2003), 172–174.

27. Exum (2010), 2.

28. Features and problems of second-wave feminism are summarized in Meyers (1988), 27–37.

29. E.g., W. R. Smith (1889).

30. E.g., Wellhausen (1885).

31. Weber (1952; originally published, 1917–1919).

32. For examples, see Carter and Meyers (1996). See also Meyers (2006) and Steinberg (2004).

33. Especially Gottwald (1979).

34. E.g., Gottwald's study (1979) of tribes, Frick's book (1985) on state formation, and Wilson's work (1980) on prophecy.

35. A useful synthesis appears in McNutt (1999).

36. Banks (2006) provides an overview of Israelite historiography; see also, inter alia, Grabbe (2011) and Moore and Kelle (2011).

37. Pfoh (2010b), 7.

38. Iron technology probably developed in Cyprus and Palestine; so Muhly (1997), 13–14.

39. See Mazar (1997), 218 for different chronological schemes.

40. On identifying ethnicity in the archaeological record, see Faust (2006).

41. The difficulties of naming this region are discussed in Ben-Tor (1992b), 2.

Chapter 2 Resources for the Task

1. Gilchrist (1999), 52.

2. Flanagan (1985), 309.

3. See Meyers (2011), 63–67.

4. Brenner and van Dijk-Hemmes (1996). On the Song, see Brenner (1989), 63–67, 89–90; for Proverbs, see Bellis (1996) and also chapter 7, pp. 137–138, of this book.

5. Davies (1998), 82.

6. Rollston (2010), 127–135.

7. According to a 2007 survey; see: http://www.catholicnews.com/data/stories/cns/0802435.htm (accessed April 7, 2012).

8. D. E. S. Stein (2008).

9. Faust (2010).

10. Similar records were apparently kept in Samaria, the northern kingdom's capital (e.g., 1 Kgs 22:39).

11. Hiecke (2011); cf. McNutt (1999), 76–79.

12. Westbrook and Wells (2009), 5.

13. B. Wells (2008).

14. See Démare-Lafont (2011), 118.

15. Knight (2000). The Covenant Code was thought to be the oldest legal corpus in the Bible because it supposedly reflected village life, which in turn was (erroneously) considered characteristic mainly of the premonarchic period.

16. Patekile Holomisa, quoted in S. LaFraniere (2005), 1.

17. Leach (1982), 130.

18. Wilfong (2002).

19. Ibid., 87.

20. Riegelhaupt (1967), 124.

21. See Borowski (2009) and (1998).

22. Lesko (1989), xvi.

23. For Mesopotamian cities, see Frick (1997), 17 and for Palestinian ones, Fritz (1997), 20. See also Finkelstein (2007), 153–154 and Barkay (1992), 330.

24. See Meyers (2003a) and (1997).

25. For an overview of biblical archaeology, see Dever (1997b).

26. http://www.jpost.com/Magazine/Features/Article.aspx?id=115615 (accessed April 11, 2012).

27. https://sites.google.com/site/megiddoexpedition/the-site/introduction (accessed May 14, 2012; http://megiddo.tau.ac.il/history.html (accessed January 20, 2011).

28. Roberts (1993), 18.

29. E.g., Hardin (2010).

30. E.g., Finkelstein (1986).

31. E.g., Brody (2009).

32. Such projects provide the data for Stager (1985).

33. See Renfrew and Bahn (2008), 40–41 and Sabloff (2005). The impact of the New Archaeology on Palestinian archaeology is summarized by Dever (1997b), 316–318.

34. So Levy and Hall (1995), 4.

35. Described by Hodder (2005).

36. So Allison (1999b), 10–11.

37. Nelson (2005). For an overview of the extensive literature on gender archaeology, see Meyers (2003a), 191–195; Nelson (2004) and Gilchrist (1999) are especially useful.

38. Sorenson (2005); see also Hayes-Gilpin (2000).
39. E.g., Renfrew (1984); see also Renfrew and Bahn (2008), 177–230.
40. Meskell et al. (2001), 5.
41. Murdock and Provost 1973.
42. For overview of the potentials and problems, see Watson (1999) and Carter (1997); see also Hardin (2011), 19–22 and Parker (2011), 604–605.
43. Singer-Avitz (2011), 277.
44. Holladay (1997) and (1992).
45. See Stockett and Geller (2006).
46. E.g., Reiter (1975); Rosaldo and Lamphere (1974).
47. See Renfrew and Bahn (2008), 227.
48. See Nelson (2006) for an overview and Nelson (2004) for interpretive possibilities.
49. See Meyers (forthcoming a); cf. Harkin 2010.
50. Classically explained by Harris (1979), 32–41.

Chapter 3 Setting the Scene: The Ancient Environment

1. Friedl (1975), 7–8.
2. This discussion does not include the small forts and defensive towers erected sporadically in the Iron Age. For a complete hierarchy of eighth-century BCE sites, see Dever (2012), 47–104.
3. Summarized by Broshi (1997); cf. Zorn (1994).
4. See Dever (2003); cf. Stager (1998).
5. Dever (2003), 99.
6. These estimates are based on Dever (1997a), 183, Table I and Finkelstein (1993), 61, Table 2.
7. Fritz (1997), 24; Holladay (1995), 392–393.
8. Meyers (2005c), 553–554; Barkay (1992), 329, 372; cf. Finkelstein (2007), 153–154.
9. See Dever (2012), 84; Mazar (2003), 167; Dever (1997a), 183, Table II; Fritz (1997), 24.
10. So Knight (2000), 171–172.
11. See Faust (2003), 97–98; Otto (2001); B. A. Levine (1999), 423–426.
12. Portugali (1983).
13. Lenski (1984), 199–200.
14. Garnsey (1999), 25.
15. Orni and Efrat (1980), 270.
16. E.g., Barkay (1992), 329.
17. See Holladay (1995), 392 and Finkelstein (1993), 61, Table 2.
18. Lenski (2005), 84, Fig. 5.1, and 96–97; Womack (2001), 104–105.
19. See Nolan and Lenski (2009), 124.

20. http://www.beatlesbible.com/people/john-lennon/albums/milk-and-honey/ (accessed April 11, 2012).

21. E.g., Lev 26:19-20; Deut 28:15-24; Jer 11:3-5; 32:22-23; Ezek 20:6-8.

22. Inter alia, see Dever (2003); Joffe (2002); Bloch-Smith and Nakhai (1999); Meyers (1998); Stager (1998).

23. Orni and Efrat (1980), 148.

24. See Tsuk (1997); Barkay (1992), 332–333.

25. E.g., Zorn (1993), 1098–1099.

26. See the discussions in Borowski (2009), 14–18 and D. C. Hopkins (1985), 173–187.

27. Stager (1985), 6, 9.

28. Borowski (2009), 17–18.

29. Edelstein and Gat (1980), 73; see also Borowski (2009), 31–44.

30. The soils are described in Singer (2007), 85–123, 179–206, and Col. Fig. 9.1(a); D. C. Hopkins (1985), 126–129; Orni and Efrat (1980), 57–58.

31. A. Sasson (2010), 11, 120. See Waters (2007), 1 for a definition of subsistence agriculture.

32. J. R. Jackson (2005), 62–66.

33. D. C. Hopkins (1997), 26. For a discussion of what is meant by "Mediterranean," see H. Allen (2001), 3–10.

34. See Borowski (2009), 85–139; MacDonald (2008b), 17–40; Borowski (2004); King and Stager (2001), 93–107.

35. Grigg (1999), 401.

36. Reported in Counihan (1999), 29.

37. MacDonald (2008b), 19; cf. Gallant (1991), 67–68.

38. Du Boulay (1974), 56.

39. Borowski (2009), 124–125.

40. Broshi (2001), 129, 162. (This estimate is probably based on classical sources.)

41. A. Sasson (1998), 3.

42. Pimentel and Pimentel (2003), 660S.

43. The estimates here come from Finkelstein (1993).

44. http://www.census.gov/ipc/www/idb/worldpop.php (accessed April 12, 2012).

45. McNeill (1975), 284.

46. D. C. Hopkins (1997), 27.

47. Summarized in D. C. Hopkins (2007).

48. Hareuveni (1980), 37.

49. So D. C. Hopkins (1985), 189.

50. Faust (2000), 22–23.

51. E.g., Seger (1981), 102–103, Pls. 119, 146, 147; du Boulay (1974), 33.

52. Gavrielides (1976), 269.

53. Amiry and Tamari (1989), 35–36.

54. Whittaker (2000), 63.

55. As in rural Greece until the 1950s, when most children were sent to school; ibid., 100.
56. Bradley (1993), 72.
57. Rossi (1977), 22.
58. Cited in Garnsey (1999), 110–111.
59. J. K. Campbell (1964), 165.
60. Assmuth (1997), 74.
61. Trichopoulou and Lagiou (1999), 519, Fig. 1.
62. See MacDonald (2008b), 91–92 and Garnsey (1999), 19–21, 43–48.
63. Garnsey (1999), 21.
64. McNeill (1975), 13–14.
65. Hare (1954), 37, 66.
66. Documented in D. C. Hopkins (1985), 77–108.
67. Ibid., 91–94.
68. T. Allen (2001), 22; D. C. Hopkins (1985), 245.
69. Garnsey (1999), 2, 30, 34–35.
70. Forbes (1976), 258.
71. Lutfiyya (1966), 112.
72. Avalos (1995), 121–139, 241–245.
73. Atrahasis Epic I:352 f.; cf. II:1-8. Translation of Lambert and Millard (1969). This epic poem dates to the second millennium BCE.
74. Gallant (1991), 34–59, 113–142.
75. As at Tell en Nasbeh; see Brody (2009), 52.
76. Borowski (1998), 186–187; and see ibid., 149–158 for a discussion of birds as food.
77. Garnsey (1999), 36–41; Gallant (1991), 115–121; Forbes (1976).
78. D. C. Hopkins (1987), 188. See also ibid., 248; Garnsey (1999), 40; Gallant (1991), 121–127.
79. H. Allen (2001), 19; A. Sasson (2010), 11.
80. Domeris (2007), 9–26, also notes the social construction of poverty in the biblical terminology.
81. Du Boulay (1974), 57.
82. Dimen (1986), 63, 64.

Chapter 4 Eve in Eden: Genesis 2–3

1. Noted by Rendsburg (2003), 23.
2. Hendel (1997), 160; Niditch (1993), 46.
3. Although the definite article is lacking before 'adam in Gen 2:5, 20 and 3:17, many scholars understand those instances to mean "man" (not Adam); see the NRSV and Kraus (2011), 20, and n. 22. (Eve's name is discussed in the next chapter.)

4. Bellis (2000a), 80.
5. Malina (1969), 22–24.
6. Translations are by Johnson (1983).
7. Collins (2004).
8. Cited in Brown (1967), 63.
9. Stark (2007), 28–29.
10. Bronner (1994), 22–36.
11. Anderson (2009), col. 348; Reuling (2006), 331–335.
12. Summarized for the visual arts by Jefferson (2009), for music by Peterson (2009), for film by Plate (2009), and for literature by Swindell (2009).
13. McColgan (1994); Swindell (2009), col. 354.
14. O'Brien and Major (1982), 95; see also Whitfield (2007).
15. Amply documented by Higgins (1976).
16. von Rad (1961). 87.
17. Nickel (2009), 252.
18. See Kraus (2011), 7–15; see also the discussion in the epilogue.
19. Barr (1990), 122; cf. Lohr (2011), 234 and Clark (1986).
20. Trible (1978), 73.
21. Ibid.
22. For a small sample of feminist studies of Gen 2–3, see Bellis (2007), 37–56 and Brenner (1993), 39–193. For copious references to other scholarship, see two recent monographs and an older classic: Mettinger (2007); Stordalen (2000); Westermann (1984).
23. Bellis (2007), 51; Bird (1994), 523.
24. Niditch (1993), 3–47, 89–90.
25. Clifford (1994) provides an overview of ancient Near Eastern creation accounts.
26. Even if Gen 2–3 is exilic in date, as some argue, it would be addressing those same concerns.
27. J. Sasson (2008), 498.
28. J. Sasson (2001), 211.
29. Examined in detail in Meyers (2012a), 146–151.
30. Newsom (2000), 65.
31. See van der Kooij (2010).
32. See D. E. S. Stein (2008).
33. Hiebert (1996), 34–36.
34. "Clods" and "ground" often appear together; see Wächter (2001), 259–260.
35. D. E. S. Stein (2006), 393. One exception might be the reference to a progenitor in Josh 14:15.
36. Although *'adam* lacks the definite article in 3:17, it can still have an indefinite reference; see ibid. and n. 3.
37. Asher-Greve (2002), 11.

38. Kadari (2006); Bronner (1994), 26–28.
39. Gelpi (1974).
40. Asher-Greve (2002), 21.
41. In the *Woman's Bible*: Stanton (1895), Part I, 14–15.
42. See Shectman (2009), 130–134; Bird (1994; 1997); Clines (1990), 41–44.
43. Freedman (1983). See Deut 33:29, where *'ezer* also means power rather than help.
44. Fabry (2003), 403–404.
45. Translation by R. Marcus (1953).
46. These words are explained in D. E. S. Stein (2006), xxiv-xxv, 394–395.
47. Arnold (2009), 61.
48. Clifford (1994), 144–145.
49. A. Sasson (2010), 15–16; see also Meyers (2012a).
50. Gottwald (1979), 437–439.
51. Amiry and Tamari (1989), 11.
52. Garnsey (1999), 61–71.
53. Bar-Efrat (1992), 212–215; Alter (1981), 92–95.
54. Gunn and Fewell (1993), 148.
55. Cited and translated by Alter (1981), 93.
56. Pagels (1991).
57. Kraus (2011), 28; Niehr (2001).
58. Sarna (1989), 19.
59. Day (2006).
60. Ibid., 116.

Chapter 5 Eve out of Eden: Genesis 3:16

1. Translation is mine; cf. Hiebert (1996), 32–33.
2. See Ottosson (1974), 393–399.
3. See Gordon (2010).
4. J. Sasson (2001), 216.
5. Cf. Ramsey (1988).
6. Oden (2000).
7. Translation is by Reuling (2006), 30.
8. Author's translation.
9. In *Liber Hebraicarum Quaestionum in Genesim* (*Hebrew Questions on Genesis*); cited in Kraus (2011), 91.
10. Cf. Barr (1990).
11. According to the Christian Bookseller Association: http://www.cbaonline.org/ nm/documents/BSLs/Bible_Translations.pdf (accessed April 8, 2012).
12. These differences are often discussed in the scholarship (see chapter 4, n. 22) on the Eden story.

13. For an overview of poetic parallelism, see Weiss (2007), 256–258.

14. Ottosson (1978), 458.

15. Terms for birth and labor are discussed in Bauman (1980); see also Ottosson (1978), 459.

16. Meyers (2001), 279.

17. That root is related to an Arabic word for "cut"; so ibid. and Seow (1997), 316. The verse in Ecclesiastes would read: "Whoever quarries stones may be cut by them."

18. See Meyers (2001), 278.

19. *Ponos* is used for normal childbirth pains and *odyne* for especially severe ones; so Demand (1994), 20 and cf. Reuling (2006), 31.

20. Du Boulay (1974), 54.

21. See D. E. S. Stein (2006), 394–395.

22. Reuling (2006), 32.

23. So Lohr (2011), 233–234.

24. Lohr (2011).

25. Ibid.

26. For examples of those problematic commentaries see ibid.

27. von Rad (1961), 90.

28. Vawter (1977), 85.

29. E.g., Fuchs (2000), 143, 175; Trible (1978), 128.

30. See Arnold and Choi (2003), 168.

31. Ullendorf (1978, 428–429) also cites the Talmud (*b. 'Erub.* 100b); cf. LaCoque (2006), 222. Simkins too notes that the context implies male control over procreation (2009, 50).

32. Faust (2004), 175–176; Bloch-Smith (1992), 25–29.

33. Reported in "The Other Afghanistan" on National Public Radio, http://thestory.org/archive/the_story_041012.mp3/view (accessed April 10, 2012).

34. Demand (1994), 22; Gallant (1991), 20–21.

35. Golden (2004), 147–148.

36. See Wilcox et al. (1988).

37. Demand (1994), 21.

38. Giles (1958), 318; the Iron Age osteological report of the site does not provide specific age estimates.

39. P. Smith (1993), 10.

40. Alesan, Malgos, and Simo (1999).

41. See Brewer and Teeter (2007), 114, for Egypt; Gallant (1991), 20, for Greece; and Frier (1982), 249, for Rome.

42. United Nation's statistics are given in Table 17 in: http://www.un.org/esa/population/publications/wpp2006/WPP2006_Highlights_rev.pdf (accessed April 8, 2012).

43. Schofield (1986), 235.

44. Demand (1994), 71–86.
45. Garnsey (1999), 21.
46. UNICEF (2011), 22.
47. King and Stager (2001), 37; van der Toorn (1994), 59.
48. French feminists supported this but insisted on better conditions for women in many areas of life; see Offen (1984).
49. LeVine and LeVine (1985), 30.
50. Kilmer (1972, 171–172) is discussing Atrahasis III.vi.1.
51. Mettinger (2007), 85.
52. Cf. Geertz (2000), 89–90, 166–169.
53. English syntax entails adding "many" before pregnancies to deal with the elliptical "make great [the number of] your pregnancies." Also, "pregnancies" is singular in Hebrew, but the verbal form implies a collective plurality requiring the plural in English.

Chapter 6 Eve's World: The Household

1. Gallant (1991), 12–13. See also Netting, Wilk, and Arnould (1984b), xii; Yanagisako (1979), 199.
2. So Rapoport (1994), 461; cf. Souvatzi (2008), 1–8 and Rapp, Ross, and Bridenthal (1979), 176.
3. Hendon (1996), 48; see also chapter 7, pp. 139–143.
4. Illustrations appear, inter alia, in Faust and Bunimovitz (2003) and Holladay (1997).
5. E.g., by Faust (2006), 71–84; Faust and Bunimovitz (2003); Holladay (1997), 337; and Shiloh (1973); cf. Finkelstein (1996), 204–205 and Stager (1985), 17.
6. E.g., Amiry and Tamari (1989), 22, 30, 32; Jäger (1912), 24–26.
7. As noted for a highland community in southern Greece by Bialor (1976), 231; cf. Domeris (2007), 62.
8. Faust (2011), 263–265.
9. Lipiński (1998), 326.
10. Hudson (1999), 489.
11. Redfield (1956), 26–30.
12. See Rapp, Ross, and Bridenthal (1979), 176, 181, 183.
13. Zorn (1994), 33. Stager (1985, 18) suggests a four-person nuclear family, or a maximum of seven.
14. See Wilk and Rathje (1982), 631.
15. Brody (2011) and Stager (1985), 18–20; contra Faust (2000), 19–22 and (1999).
16. Goody (1972), 122.
17. Faust (1999), 96.
18. See n. 15.

19. See Dever (2012), 151.
20. See Hirschfeld (1995), Table 5 and Burch (1972).
21. Suggested by Faust (1999); cf. Routledge (2009) and Reviv (1993), 49–51.
22. Yorburg (1975), 9.
23. McNutt (1999), 76–77; Wilson (1992), 930–931.
24. For a detailed discussion see Meyers (1991).
25. Camp (2000), 550.
26. For a convenient summary of the household in its larger context, see Block (2003), 35–40.
27. More accurately, Jacob's son Joseph is not the eponymous ancestor of a tribe, but his sons (Ephraim and Manasseh) count as two of the tribes for a total of thirteen, and another of Jacob's sons (Levi) has no land and doesn't count as one of the twelve territorial tribes.
28. Domeris (2007), 45; R. Miller (2005); Gottwald (2001), 171.
29. For archaeological evidence of public works, see Mazar (1992), 380–387, 406–414, 420–421, 424–432.
30. Gottwald (2001), 92–94.
31. Ibid., 392.
32. Na'aman (1986), 17. Cf. Lipschitz, Sergi, and Koch (2011) and Mazar (1992), 455–458.
33. See McNutt (1999), 88–90 and Gottwald (1979), 257–278.
34. Faust (2011), 269–273.
35. Ibid., 265.
36. Amiry and Tamari (1989), 13, 38.
37. D. C. Hopkins (1985), 274–275.
38. Faust (2011), 271–272; Weiss and Kislev (2004).
39. A. Sasson (2010), 123; cf. Holladay (1995), 392.
40. MacDonald (2008b), 79; E. F. Campbell (1998), 313–316; Cogan (1998), 334–340.
41. Domeris (2007), 52–53.
42. Routledge (2009).
43. McNutt (1999), 174.
44. E.g., Steinberg (1991), 168.
45. Faust (2011), 266; McNutt (1999), 174.
46. Conkey and Spector (1984), 5.
47. Di Vito (1999), 221, 223; see also van der Toorn (1996), 3.
48. van der Toorn (2004), 423.
49. Rogerson (1989), 5.
50. Pedersen (1926), 256–263.
51. Hendon (2006), 176.
52. Salamone (1987), 207, 216; see also Hart (1992), 172 and Dimen (1986), 53.
53. J. K. Campbell (1964), 186.

54. Counihan (1999), 25–26.
55. Osterud (1988), pp. 77–79.
56. Simpson and Wilson (1992).
57. S. Lawrence (1999), 121.
58. Nelson (2004), 1–8, 66.
59. Brumfiel (1991), 224–225.
60. Souvatzi (2008), 15.
61. Stockett and Geller (2006), 6–7; see also Gilchrist (1999), 24 and Spencer-Wood (1996).
62. Assmuth (1997), 74.
63. See Whyte's classic study (1978).
64. Rosaldo and Lamphere (1974), mentioned in chapter 2, n. 46.
65. Rosaldo (1974).
66. Rosaldo (1980); see also Reverby and Helly (1992) and Sharistanian (1987).
67. Conkey and Spector (1984), 19.
68. Stockett and Geller (2006), 7.
69. Hegland (1991), 216–218, 228–229.
70. Cf. Bowser and Patton (2004), 158–159; Hendon (1996), 47; Ross (1986), 844; Yanagisako (1979), 191.
71. Bodel and Olyan (2008a), 278; see also Stowers (2008), 6.

Chapter 7 Women and Household Maintenance, Part I: Economic, Reproductive, and Sociopolitical Activities

1. E.g., Wilk and Netting (1984), 5–15; Goody (1972), 106.
2. Conkey and Gero (1991), 3: cf. Hendon (1996), 49.
3. Aranda, Montón-Subías, Sánchez-Romero, and Alarcón (2009), 42; Romero (2002), 178.
4. González-Marcén, Montón-Subías, and Picazo (2008), 3; see also Conkey and Spector (1984), 25.
5. See Picazo (1997), 59.
6. Wilk and Netting (1984), 5.
7. Lenski (2005), 55.
8. Resources for gender attribution are described in Costin (1996), 117–120.
9. Cf. Gelb (1967), 6.
10. Bridenthal and Koontz (1977), 6.
11. See the classic study of Murdock and Provost (1973).
12. E.g., Amiry and Tamari (1989), 34; Seger (1981), 102, 113, 116.
13. For a detailed discussion of the evidence, see Meyers (2007b), 72–75.
14. See Exod 11:5; Num 11:8; Deut 24:6; Isa 47:1–2. NRSV translations vary and don't adequately represent the ancient objects.

15. Broshi (2001), 123–124.
16. Lutfiyya (1966), 112.
17. E.g., Garfinkel (2009), 175; Finkelstein (1986), 93–94; cf. Rosenberg (2008).
18. Cited in Meyers (2007b), 75.
19. Wilk and Rathje (1982), 622.
20. Holladay (1997), 339 and Mazar (1992), 488; cf. Singer-Avitz (2011), 285–287.
21. Parker (2011), 614–617; McQuitty (1984), 265.
22. Baadsgaard (2008) provides a comprehensive study of oven locations at Iron Age sites; cf. McQuitty (1984), 35.
23. Hart (1992), 28, 61–65; Dimen (1986), 61.
24. McQuitty (1993–1994), 70; Amiry and Tamari (1989), 20; Seger (1981), 107; Lutfiyya (1966), 31.
25. Parker (2011), 611.
26. P. Wells (1986); Casper (2007).
27. Murdock and Provost (1973), Table I:42.
28. Ebeling and Homan (2008).
29. E.g., Amiry and Tamari (1989), 38, 40.
30. For detailed discussions see Cassuto (2008), 66–69 and Meyers (2003c), 432–434; see also O'Brian (1999), 31.
31. E.g., Amiry and Tamari (1989), 46–47.
32. Barber (1994), Figs. 3.5, 3.6, 9.4, 9.5, 10.2.
33. See Cassuto (2004) and (2008).
34. Strand (2010), 12–13.
35. Amiry and Tamari (1989), 47.
36. See Romero (2002), 180–181; McQuitty (1993–1994), 57; Murdock and Provost (1973), 212.
37. Hendon (1996), 51; cf. Dever (2012), 139.
38. London (2000), 104; Tekkök-Bicken (2000), 97.
39. Salem (1999), 69–71; Amiry and Tamari (1989), 43–44; K. Seger (personal communication based on ethnographic observation). A. Berlin (personal communication) reports ceramic production in Hellenistic- and Roman-period households.
40. Salem (1999), 71.
41. Amiry and Tamari (1989), 42–43; Lutfiyya (1966), 118–119.
42. Ebeling (2002) provides examples; cf. Romero (2002), 180–181.
43. Parker (2011), 606–608; see also McQuitty (1993–1994), 57 and (1981), 122–125.
44. McQuitty (1993–1994), 20; Seger (1981), 109; J. K. Campbell (1964), 33.
45. See Eskenazi (2000).
46. Souvatzi (2008), 18; see also Romero (2002), 178 and Dimen (1986), 53.
47. Picazo (1997), 60.
48. Noted by Tilly (1978), 167.

49. Bradley (1993), 76–77.
50. Ibid., 79–80.
51. Connerton (1989), 39.
52. Finegan (1970), 375.
53. Bellis (1996).
54. Cited in Snowden (1921), 7.
55. See Dell (2006), 52–56; Westermann (1995), 60, 142; Fontaine (1990), 155–163.
56. See Camp (2000), 548–549.
57. For different opinions about the existence of schools see Rollston (2010), 91–92, 94–95.
58. Maher (1976), 52–53.
59. Assmuth (1997), 75.
60. Maher (1976), 52, 71.
61. A detailed discussion appears in Meyers (2003b).
62. See Bohmbach (2000), 37–38; Pardes (1992), 39–59.
63. E.g., Counihan (1999), 53; Assmuth (1997), 72, 75; Dimen (1986), 66; du Boulay (1974), 214, 217.
64. March and Taqqu (1986), 20, 58.
65. Kennedy (1986), 130; see also J. K. Campbell (1964), 275.
66. Dimen (1986), 61.
67. Gallant (1991), 143; cf. D. C. Hopkins (1985), 269.
68. Amiry and Tamari (1989), 25, 47.
69. Sutton (2001), 131.
70. Parker (2011), 612–613, 623.
71. Counihan (1999), 51.
72. Gottwald (1979), 257–284, 315–318, and passim.
73. Zonabend (1996), 25–39.
74. See Parker (2011), 622.
75. Ross (1986), 843–844.
76. Yanagisako (1979), 191.
77. Sweely (1999a), 168.
78. Riegelhaupt (1967), 124.
79. Maher (1976), 52.
80. As at Beersheba, so Singer-Avitz (2011), 294; see also Nakhai (2011), 347–348.
81. Nevett (2010), 49 and cf. 41.
82. Ross (1986).
83. See Bowser and Patton (2004).
84. Hendon (1996), 56.
85. Hegland (1991).
86. Ibid., 223.
87. Niditch (2008), 5, 40–41, 65, 154, 191.

88. See Ross (1986), 851.
89. Ortner (1996), 136.

Chapter 8 Women and Household Maintenance, Part II: Religious Activities

1. Albertz (1994).
2. Dever (2005).
3. See Bird (1996), 515–517.
4. Perlitz (1898), 114.
5. Wellhausen (1897), 89–90.
6. Bird (1996) and similarly Bird (1991).
7. See, e.g., M. S. Smith (2008) and (2004); Gnuse (1997).
8. See, e.g., Stowers (2008), 8–10; Zevit (2001), 11–17.
9. Chaves (2011).
10. van der Toorn (2004).
11. Armstrong (2009), xii.
12. Gudme (2010), 79.
13. E.g., many of the articles in Albertz et al. (forthcoming); Meyers (forthcoming b) and (2010); Bodel and Olyan (2008b).
14. Dubisch (1986a), 197.
15. Schmitt (forthcoming).
16. Nakhai (2011), 347, 350–353.
17. See Meyers (2010), 121–122; Fogelin (2007), 55, 60–61.
18. So Stavrakopoulou (2010), 37–39; Gudme (2010), 85.
19. Stavrakopoulou (2010), 50; Gudme (2010).
20. E.g., Schmitt (2004).
21. Meyers (2005b), 19–22.
22. Meyer and Mirecki (1995).
23. Meyers (1999); cf. Gerstenberger (2002), 35–36.
24. Avalos (1992), 457; see also ibid., 452–453, 457 and idem (1995), 172–182, 251–258.
25. Geller (2010), 19–21.
26. Zohary (1982), 183; cf. Amar (1996), 53*-54*.
27. Fontaine (2002), 76.
28. Dayagi-Mendels (1989), 89–100.
29. Fontaine (2002), 71; Sharp (1986).
30. Du Boulay (1974), 65–66.
31. Meyers (2000).
32. So Fontaine (2002), 78.
33. Geller (2010), 26, 81, 96.

34. For references, see Meyers (2005b), 44–45.

35. Garnett (1890–91). Her book is the source of the ethnographic examples in this section.

36. See Olyan (2010).

37. Meyers (2007c).

38. Stol (2000), 35, 49–74.

39. For a fuller discussion see Meyers (2005b).

40. Klein (2000), 205.

41. Elliott (1991); cf. du Boulay (1974), 67–68.

42. Sabar (2007), 109.

43. Meyers (2007d).

44. Darby (2011).

45. Online Etymological Dictionary: http://www.etymonline.com/index.php?term=feast (accessed April 10, 2012).

46. Clarke (2001), 145.

47. See the articles in Dieter and Hayden (2001).

48. E.g., kings hold large-scale feasts to mark special events, like accession to kingship or temple dedication (1 Kgs 1:40-41; 8:62-66); see MacDonald (2008a).

49. See Albertz (2006).

50. Brenner and van Dijk-Hemmes (1996), 93–94.

51. See Meyers (2005a), 64–66.

52. Ibid., 63–64, 66–67. See also Gerstenberger (2002), 37.

53. Albertz (2006).

54. Bohmbach (2000), 37–38.

55. See Burnett-Bletsch (2000).

56. See Milgrom (1991), 759–760.

57. B. S. Jackson (2011), 221–230, 232–240.

58. Ibid., 244–252.

59. Tyldesley (1994), 52–53; Westbrook and Wells (2009), 57; cf. van der Toorn (1994), 59–69.

60. Coontz (2005), 106.

61. Alexiou (2002), 12, 14–23.

62. Garnett (1890–91), I:31, 258–259, 491, II:91.

63. Danforth and Tsiaras (1982), 39, 71–74, 110, 132, 135.

64. Dubisch (1986a), 207; cf. du Boulay (1986), 143.

65. van der Toorn (2004), 424.

66. Lewis (1989), 49–51, 115–116.

67. Bloch-Smith (2009), 128.

68. Nemet-nejat (1998), 144.

69. Garnett (1890–91), I:17, 101; Dubisch (1986a), 207.

70. See Borowski (2009), 21–44.

71. See Hallo (1977).
72. For further discussion of the antiquity and household observance of these festivals see Meyers (forthcoming b).
73. Schmitt (forthcoming).
74. van der Toorn (2008), 26; cf. Albertz (2008), 98–99.
75. D. E. S. Stein (2006), 403; cf. Brettler (2000).
76. For a full discussion, with sources cited, see Meyers (2012b).
77. Gudme (2010), 78.
78. Dubisch (1986a), 207–208.
79. Sutton (2001), 9.
80. See Counihan (1999), 37.
81. Wilkins (2000), 122–123.
82. Dubisch (1986a), 208.
83. Counihan (2000), 1513.
84. Wellhausen (1885), 76.
85. Cited in Sutton (2001), 20.
86. Douglas (1972), 71.
87. Hastorf and Weisenmantel (2007).
88. Stowers (2008), 12.
89. See B. A. Levine (1993), 393–394 and Milgrom (1990), 121.
90. Blackman (1924), 229.
91. Lutfiyya (1966), 112.
92. Cf. Lesko (2008), 202.
93. E.g., Douglas (1966, 1972); see the critique by Lemos (2009) and cf. MacDonald (2008b), 67–68, 70.
94. See Wapnish and Hesse (1998).
95. Hendel (2007), 140–142.
96. On the latter, see Meyers (2005a), 203.
97. See Hardin (2010), 133–143.
98. Amiry and Tamari (1989), 29.
99. van der Toorn (2008), 26 and (1994), 36; see also Schmitt (forthcoming).
100. See Albertz (2008), 97.
101. J. Z. Smith (2004), 327.
102. Dubisch (1986a), 207.
103. So du Boulay (1974), 54–55.
104. Cf. Caravelli (1986), 171.
105. Franzman, (2000), 69–72; cf. Sered (1992), 6–8, 87–88.
106. Albertz (1994), 194; his views have since changed.
107. Ackerman (2008), 149.
108. Knight (2011), 82, 230-231.
109. Sered (1988); cf. Baadsgaard (2008), 43.

Chapter 9 Excursus: Professional Women

1. For more information (including bibliographical references) about the professionals mentioned in this chapter see Meyers, Craven, and Kraemer (2000), ad loc. The following notes provide several additional sources.
2. Avigad and Sass (1997), 30–31.
3. Meyers (2011), 91–93.
4. See Stol (2000), 115–116; Beckman (1983), 234–235.
5. Albertz (2006).
6. See Sabar (2007), 125–140.
7. Fischer (2004), 50–62.
8. Meyers (2008a), 289–290; Zevit (2001), 558–559.
9. Sköl (2010); Williamson (2010), 74.
10. Meyers (2008a), 290–292; Bowen (1999), 417–419; Korpel (1996).
11. Tyldesley (1994), 132.
12. Gray (1964), pls. 56–57.
13. Feld and Fox (1994), 39.
14. Kalmanofsky (2007), 63.
15. Brenner and van Dijk-Hemmes (1996), 86.
16. Frymer-Kensky (1990), 275–278.
17. See L. Day (2006).
18. See Solvang (2003).
19. Jordan and Kalčik (1985), xii.
20. E.g., Joseph (1980) and Abrahams (1968).

Chapter 10 Gender and Society: Reconstructing Relationships, Rethinking Systems

1. Fuchs (2000), 12. For other examples of derogatory assumptions, see Block (2003), 61.
2. Ruether (1985), 119.
3. Marsman (2003), 26, 733, 738.
4. E.g., Bach (1999), xiv.
5. Ringe (1998), 5.
6. Frymer-Kensky (2002), xiv.
7. O'Connor (2006), 13–14.
8. http://www.religioustolerance.org/ofe_bibl.htm (accessed April 12, 2012).
9. Rogers (1975), 727.
10. Spencer-Wood (1999), 175.
11. Ibid.
12. Friedl (1967).
13. Salamone (1987), 204.

14. Rogers (1975), 728–729.
15. Assmuth (1997), 17.
16. Sweely (1999b), 2.
17. Spencer-Wood (1999), 179.
18. Goody (1982), 70.
19. Cassuto (2011).
20. Salem (1999), 70.
21. Counihan (1998), 2, 4.
22. Whyte (1978), 68.
23. Hirschfeld (1995), 152, 182.
24. See Friedl (1967), 106
25. Assmuth (1997), 92.
26. Ibid. and Hendon (1996), 46.
27. Salamone (1987), 205.
28. See Counihan (1999), 29.
29. Ibid., 37. See also Hart (1992), 127, 191; J. K. Campbell (1964), 153.
30. See Kohl (1988) and Myres (1982), 164–167.
31. Fontaine (1990), 161.
32. D. E. S. Stein (2006), 403.
33. For further information about the passages discussed here, see the relevant entries and their bibliographies in Meyers, Craven, and Kraemer (2000) in addition to the sources cited below.
34. See Schroer (2000), 80, 82
35. Contra NRSV, which understands only one object although the Hebrew mentions two.
36. Shields (2010), 83
37. Camp (1998), 113.
38. Cogan and Tadmor (1988), 56.
39. Suggested by Frymer-Kensky (2002), 71–73.
40. B. Lawrence (2010), 343.
41. Pomeroy (1994), 34, 36, 247.
42. Knight (2000), 177.
43. Westbrook and Wells (2009), 73.
44. Greenfield (1982) and D. Lambert (personal communication).
45. Guenther (2005), 403–406.
46. Meyers (1988), 41–43 and passim.
47. Sweely (1999b).
48. Meagher (2011), 441.
49. Lerner (1986), 240.
50. E.g., Kray (2002); Lesko (1989), xiv.
51. Meagher (2011), 441–442; Sered (1994).
52. Nash (2009), 103.

53. Gilchrist (1999), xvi.

54. Schloen (2001), 52. See also King and Stager (2001), 38.

55. For a fuller discussion of these issues see Meyers (2007a).

56. E.g., Saller (1994), 74–132.

57. Frymer-Kensky (2002), 324.

58. See G. Stein (1998).

59. Schroer (1998), 90.

60. Block (2003), 41.

61. Meyers (1988), 37–40.

62. Schüssler Fiorenza (2001), 211, 118.

63. Crumley (1979), 144.

64. Crumley (1995), 3.

65. The term's origins and development are summarized in Meyers (2007a), 95.

66. Crumley (1979), 144–145.

67. Hayes-Gilpin (2000), 98.

68. Brumfiel (1995), 125.

69. See the examples in Ehrenreich, Crumley, and Levy (1995).

70. J. E. Levy (2006).

71. Crumley (2005), 40.

72. Gottwald (2001), 171.

73. Zevit (2001, 648) draws on the analysis of Iron Age kingdoms east of the Jordan; see LaBianca (1999).

74. Nakhai (2011), 358.

75. Cf. Esler (2005), 4.

76. See Womack (2001), 26–27.

77. Tilley (2000) offers a trenchant critique of relativism.

78. So Avalos (2011).

79. See chapter 6, pp. 119–120; cf. D. E. S. Stein (2006), 401–402.

80. As in a Greek mountain village; J. K. Campbell (1964), 187.

81. See Meyers (2009), 890.

82. Brayford (1999), 166.

83. Kawashima (2011), 6.

84. See Fulkerson (2001), 49, 119–120, 229.

85. Fischer et al. (2011), 5–6, citing the Eden story as an example.

Epilogue: Beyond the Hebrew Bible

1. Seow (1997), 262–263.

2. See Frymer-Kensky (2002).

3. E.g., Becking and Hennecke (2011); Caspi and Jiyad (2004); Anderson (2001); Kvam, Schearing, and Ziegler (1999). See also Kraus (2011) and Reuling (2006).

4. See the examples in Bronner (1994); see also Baskin (2002) and Wegner (1998).
5. I thank Maria Doerfler for this observation.
6. See, inter alia, Schaberg (2004).
7. See Baskin (2002), 36–40 for a summary of the scholarship on rabbinic sources.
8. Craven (2000).
9. Conkey and Spector (1984), 6.
10. Roll (1983).
11. See Watts (2007).
12. Schniedewind (2004), inter alia, explores this process.
13. Meyers (2008b), 65–67 provides a detailed description of the new milling machines.
14. Curtis (2001), 348.
15. See Frankel (2003).
16. Meyers (2008b), 87–70.
17. See Molleson (1994).
18. See Peskowitz (1997), 81–84.
19. Williams (1996), 133.
20. So Peskowitz (1997), 99.
21. Bauer (1990), 16.
22. Baskin (2002), 8–9, 13–43.
23. See Meyers and Meyers (2011), 5; cf. P. Miller (2011).
24. See, inter alia, L. I. Levine (1989).
25. Translations by Marcus (1953).
26. Wegner (1998), 82.
27. Kraus (2011), 10.
28. Ibid., 188.
29. Ilan (1995), 228–229.
30. See Lapin (2006).
31. See Torjeson (1993); cf. the cautionary approach in Kraemer (2011).

Bibliography

Abrahams, R. D.

    1968. Introductory Remarks to a Rhetorical Theory of Folklore. *Journal of American Folklore* 81:143–148.

Ackerman, S.

    2003. Digging up Deborah: Recent Hebrew Bible Scholarship on Gender and the Contribution of Archaeology. *Near Eastern Archaeology* 66:172–184.

    2008. Household Religion in Ancient Israel. In Bodel and Olyan (2008b), 126–158.

Albertz, R.

    1994. *A History of Israelite Religion in the Old Testament Period* (trans. J. Bowden). 2 volumes. Louisville, Ky.: Westminster/John Knox.

    2006. Ritual Setting and Religious Significance of Birth in Ancient Israel. Paper presented at the European Association of Biblical Studies annual meeting. Piliscaba and Budapest: August 6–9.

    2008. Family Religion in Ancient Israel. In Bodel and Olyan (2008b), 89–112.

Albertz, R., Nakhai, B. A., Olyan, S. M., and Schmitt, R., eds.

    forthcoming. *Family and Household Religion—Towards a Synthesis of Old Testament Studies, Archaeology, Epigraphy, and Cultural Studies*. Winona Lake, Ind.: Eisenbrauns.

Alesan, A., Malgosa, A., and Simo, C.

    1999. Looking into the Demography of an Iron Age Population in the Western Mediterranean. I. Mortality. *American Journal of Physical Anthropology* 110:285–301.

Alexiou, M.

    2002. *The Ritual Lament in Greek Tradition*. 2nd edition. Lanham, Md.: Rowman & Littlefield.

Allen H.

    2001. *Mediterranean Ecogeography*. Harlow, England: Prentice Hall.

Allen, T.

    2001. Food Production in the Middle East. In *A Taste of Thyme: Culinary Cultures of the Middle East*, eds. S. Zubaida and R. Tapper, 219–232. London: Tauris Parke.

Allison, P. M.

    1999a ed., *The Archaeology of Household Activities*. New York: Routledge.

    1999b. Introduction. In Allison (1999a), 1–18.

Alter, R.

    1981. *The Art of Biblical Narrative*. New York: Basic Books.

Amar, Z.

    1996. Medicinal Substances in Eretz-Israel in the Times of the Bible, the Mishnah, and the Talmud in Light of Written Sources. In *Illness and Healing in Ancient Times* (trans. M. Rosovsky), ed. O. Rimon, 52*–61.* Haifa: University of Haifa.

Amiry, S. and Tamari, V.

    1989. *The Palestinian Village Home*. London: British Museum Publications.

Anderson, G. A.

    2001. *The Genesis of Perfection: Adam and Eve in Jewish and Christian Imagination*. Louisville, Ky.: Westminster John Knox.

    2009. Adam and Eve, Story of. III. Christianity. *Encyclopedia of the Bible and Its Reception* 1:348–349. Berlin: de Gruyter.

Aranda, G., Montón-Subías, S., Sánchez-Romero, M., and Alarcón, E.

    2009. Death and Everyday Life: The Argaric Societies from Southeast Iberia. *Journal of Social Archaeology* 9:139–162.

Armstrong, K.

    2009. *The Case for God: What Religion Really Means*. New York: Knopf.

Arnold, B. T.

    2009. *Genesis*. New York: Cambridge University Press.

Arnold, B. T. and Choi, J. H.

    2003. *A Guide to Biblical Hebrew Syntax*. Cambridge: Cambridge University Press.

Asher-Greve, J. M.

    2002. Decisive Sex, Essential Gender. In *Sex and Gender in the Ancient Near East: Proceedings of the 47th Rencontre Assyriologique Internationale, Helsinki, July 2–6, 2001*, eds. S. Parpola and R. M. Whiting, 11–26. Helsinki: Neo-Assyrian Text Corpus Project, University of Helsinki.

Assmuth, L.

    1997. *Women's Work, Women's Worth: Changing Lifecourses in Highland Sardinia*. Saarijärvi, Finland: Gummerus Kirjapaino Oy.

Avalos, H.

    1992. Medicine. *Anchor Bible Dictionary* 3:450–459. New York: Doubleday.

    1995. *Illness and Health Care in the Ancient Near East: The Role of the Temple in Greece, Mesopotamia, and Israel*. Atlanta: Scholars Press.

2011. *Slavery, Abolitionism, and the Ethics of Biblical Scholarship*. Sheffield: Sheffield Phoenix.

Avigad, N. and Sass, B.

1997. *Corpus of West Semitic Seals*. Jerusalem: Israel Academy of Sciences and Humanities, Israel Exploration Society, and Institute of Archaeology, Hebrew University of Jerusalem.

Baadsgaard, A.

2008. A Taste of Women's Sociality: Cooking as Cooperative Labor in Iron Age Syro-Palestine. In Nakhai (2008), 13–44.

Bach, A.

1999. Introduction: Man's World, Women's Place: Sexual Politics in the Hebrew Bible. In *Women in the Hebrew Bible: A Reader*, ed. A. Bach, xiii–xxvi. New York: Routledge.

Banks, D.

2006. *Writing the History of Israel*. New York: T&T Clark.

Barber, E. W.

1994. *Women's Work: The First 20,000 Years: Women, Cloth and Society in Early Times*. New York: W. W. Norton.

Bar-Efrat, S.

1992. *Narrative Art in the Bible*. Sheffield: Almond Press.

Barkay, G.

1992. The Iron Age II-III. In Ben-Tor (1992a), 302–373.

Barr, J.

1990. The Vulgate Genesis and St. Jerome's Attitude to Women. In *Equally in God's Image: Women in the Middle Ages*, ed. J. B. Holloway, C. S. Wright, and J. Bechtold, 122–128. New York: Peter Lang.

Baskin, J. R.

2002. *Midrashic Women: Formations of the Feminine in Rabbinic Literature*. Hanover, N.H.: Brandeis University Press.

Bauer, A. J.

1990. Millers and Grinders: Technology and Household Economy in Meso-America. *Agricultural History* 64:10–17.

Bauman, A.

1980. *ḥyl*; *chîl*; *chîlâh*; *chalchâlâh*. *Theological Dictionary of the Old Testament* 4 (trans. D. E. Green): 344–347. Grand Rapids, Mich.: Eerdmans.

Becking, B. and Hennecke, S., eds.

2011. *Out of Paradise: Eve and Adam and Their Interpreters*. Sheffield: Sheffield Phoenix.

Beckman, G.

1983. *Hittite Birth Rituals*. Wiesbaden: Harrassowitz.

Bellis, A. O.

1996. The Gender and Motives of the Wisdom Teacher in Proverbs. *Bulletin for Biblical Research* 6:15–22.

2000a. Eve in the Apocryphal/Deuterocanonical Books (Tob 8:6; Sir 25:24; 40:1; 42:13; 4 Macc 18:7). In Meyers, Craven, and Kraemer (2000), 82–83.

2000b. Feminist Biblical Scholarship. In Meyers, Craven, and Kraemer (2000), 24–32.

2007. *Helpmates, Harlots, and Heroes: Women's Stories in the Hebrew Bible.* 2nd edition. Louisville, Ky.: Westminster John Knox.

Ben-Tor, A.

1992a. ed., *The Archaeology of Ancient Israel* (trans. R. Greenberg). New Haven: Yale University Press.

1992b. Introduction. In Ben-Tor (1992a), 1–9.

Berlinerblau, J.

1999. Ideology, Pierre Bourdieu's Doxa, and the Hebrew Bible. *Semeia* 87:193–214.

Bialor, P. A.

1976. The Northwest Corner of the Peloponnesos: Mavrikon and Its Region. In *Regional Variation in Modern Greece and Cyprus: Toward a Perspective on the Ethnography of Greece*, eds. M. Dimen and E. Friedl, 222–235. New York: New York Academy of Sciences.

Bird, P.

1991. Israelite Religion and the Faith of Israel's Daughters. In Jobling, Day, and Sheppard (1991), 97–108, 311–317.

1994. Bone of My Bones and Flesh of My Flesh. *Theology Today* 50:521–534.

1996. The Place of Women in the Israelite Cultus. In Carter and Meyers (1996), 515–536.

1997. "Male and Female He Created Them": Gen. 1:27b in the Context of the Priestly Account of Creation. In P. Bird, *Missing Persons and Mistaken Identities: Women and Gender in Ancient Israel,* 123–154. Minneapolis: Fortress.

Blackman, W. S.

1924. *The Fellahin of Upper Egypt.* London: Harrap.

Block, D. I.

2003. Marriage and Family in Ancient Israel. In *Marriage and Family in the Biblical World*, ed. K. M. Campbell, 33–102. Downers Grove, Ill.: InterVarsity.

Bloch-Smith, E.

1992. *Judahite Burial Practices and Beliefs about the Dead.* Sheffield: JSOT Press.

2009. From Womb to Tomb: The Israelite Family in Death as in Life. In Dutcher-Walls (2009), 122–131.

Bloch-Smith, E. and Nakhai, B. A.

1999. A Landscape Comes to Life: The Iron Age I. *Near Eastern Archaeology* 62:62–92.

Bodel, J. and Olyan, S. M.

2008a. Comparative Perspectives. In Bodel and Olyan (2008b), 276–282.

2008b. eds., *Household and Family Religion in Antiquity.* Malden, Mass.: Blackwell.

Bohmbach, K. G.

2000. Names and Naming in the Biblical World. In Meyers, Craven, and Kraemer (2000), 33–39.

Borowski, O.

1998. *Every Living Thing: The Daily Use of Animals in Ancient Israel.* Walnut Creek, Calif.: AltaMira.

2004. Eat, Drink, and Be Merry: The Mediterranean Diet. *Near Eastern Archaeology* 67:96–107.

2009. *Agriculture in Iron Age Israel.* Winona Lake, Ind.: Eisenbrauns. First published, 1987.

du Boulay, J.

1974. *Portrait of a Greek Mountain Village.* Oxford: Clarendon Press.

1986. Women—Images of Their Nature and Destiny in Rural Greece. In Dubisch (1986b), 139–168.

Bowen, N. R.

1999. The Daughters of Your People: Female Prophets in Ezekiel 13:17–23. *Journal of Biblical Literature* 118:417–433.

Bowser, B. J. and Patton, J. Q.

2004. Domestic Spaces as Public Places: An Ethnoarchaeological Case Study of Houses, Gender, and Politics in the Ecuadorian Amazon. *Journal of Archaeological Method and Theory* 11:157–181.

Bradley, C.

1993. Women's Power, Children's Labor. *Cross-Cultural Research* 27:70–96.

Brayford, S.

1999. To Shame or Not to Shame: Sexuality in the Mediterranean Diaspora. *Semeia* 87:163–176.

Brenner, A.

1989. *The Song of Songs.* Sheffield: Sheffield Academic Press.

1993. ed., *A Feminist Companion to Genesis.* Sheffield: Sheffield Academic Press.

Brenner, A. and Fontaine, C. R., eds.

1997. *A Feminist Companion to Reading the Bible: Approaches, Methods, and Strategies.* Sheffield: Sheffield Academic Press.

Brenner, A. and van Dijk-Hemmes, F.

1996. *On Gendering Texts: Female and Male Voices in the Hebrew Bible.* Leiden: Brill.

Brettler, M.

2000. Women in the Decalogue. In Meyers, Craven, and Kraemer (2000), 191–200.

Brewer, D. J. and Teeter, E.
    2007. *Egypt and the Egyptians*. 2nd edition. Cambridge: Cambridge University
        Press.
Bridenthal, R. and Koonz, C.
    1977. Introduction. In *Becoming Visible: Women in European History*, eds. R.
        Bridenthal and C. Koonz, 1–11. Boston: Houghton Mifflin.
Brody, A. J.
    2009. "Those Who Add House to House": Household Archaeology and the Use
        of Domestic Space in an Iron II Residential Compound at Tell en-Naṣbeh.
        In *Exploring the Long Durée: Essays in Honor of Lawrence E. Stager*, ed. J.
        D. Schloen, 45–56. Winona Lake, Ind.: Eisenbrauns.
    2011. The Archaeology of the Extended Family: A Household Compound from
        Iron II Tell en-Naṣbeh. In Yassur-Landau, Ebeling, and Mazow (2011),
        237–354.
Bronner, L. L.
    1994. *From Eve to Esther: Rabbinic Reconstructions of Biblical Women*. Louisville:
        Westminster John Knox.
Broshi, M.
    1997. Demography. *Oxford Encyclopedia of Archaeology in the Near East* 2:142–
        144. New York: Oxford University Press.
    2001. *Bread, Wine, Walls, and Scrolls*. London: Sheffield Academic Press.
Brown, P.
    1967. *Augustine of Hippo: A Biography*. Berkeley: University of California Press.
Brumfiel, E. M.
    1991. Weaving and Cooking: Women's Production in Aztec Mexico. In Gero
        and Conkey (1991), 224–251.
    1995. Heterarchy and the Analysis of Complex Societies: Comments. In
        Ehrenreich, Crumley, and Levy (1995), 125–131.
Burch, J. K.
    1972. Some Demographic Determinants of Average Household Size: An
        Analytic Approach. In Laslett and Wall (1972), 91–102.
Burnett-Bletsch, R.
    2000. Women after Childbirth (Lev 12:1–9). In Meyers, Craven, and Kraemer
        (2000), 204.
Camp, C. V.
    1998. 1 and 2 Kings. In Newsom and Ringe (1998), 102–116.
    2000. Woman Wisdom in the Hebrew Bible (Job 28:1–28; Prov 1:20–33;
        3:13–18; 4:1–9; 7:1–5; 8:1–36; 9:1–6; 14:1). In Meyers, Craven, and
        Kraemer (2000), 548–550.
Campbell, E. F., Jr.
    1998. A Land Divided: Judah and Israel from the Death of Solomon to the
        Fall of Samaria. In Coogan (1998), 270–319.

Campbell, J. K.

    1964. *Honour, Family, and Patronage: A Study of Institutions and Moral Values in a Greek Mountain Community.* Oxford: Clarendon Press.

Caravelli, A.

    1986. The Bitter Wounding: The Lament as Social Protest. In Dubisch (1986b), 169–195.

Carter, C. E.

    1997. Ethnoarchaeology. *Oxford Encyclopedia of Archaeology in the Near East* 2:280–284. New York: Oxford University Press.

Carter, C. E. and Meyers, C., eds.

    1996. *Community, Identity, and Ideology: Social Science Approaches to the Hebrew Bible.* Winona Lake, Ind.: Eisenbrauns.

Casper, L. R.

    2007. Wines of Spain, 2007. *The Splendid Table*, October 6, 2007. http://splendid-table.publicradio.org/about/slide/2007/spain/13.html (accessed April 19, 2012).

Caspi, M. with Jiyad, M.

    2004. *Eve in Three Traditions and Literatures: Judaism, Christianity, and Islam.* Lewiston, N.Y.: Edwin Mellen.

Cassuto, D.

    2004. The Social Context of Weaving in the Land of Israel: Investigating the Contexts of Iron Age II. M.A. thesis, Bar-Ilan University.

    2008. Bringing Home the Artifacts: A Social Interpretation of Loom Weights in Context. In Nakhai (2008), 63–77.

    2011. Domestic vs. Non-Domestic: Identification and Interpretation of Weaving Workshops in the Archaeological Record. Paper given at the American Schools of Oriental Research Annual Meeting. San Francisco.

Chaves, M.

    2011. *American Religion: Contemporary Trends.* Princeton: Princeton University Press.

Clark, E.

    1986. Heresy, Asceticism, Adam, and Eve: Interpretations of Genesis 1–3 in the Later Latin Fathers. In E. Clark, *Ascetic Piety and Women's Faith*, 353–385. Lewiston, N.Y.: Edwin Mellen.

Clarke, M. J.

    2001. Akha Feasting: An Ethnoarchaeological Perspective. In *Feasts: Archaeological and Ethnographic Perspectives on Food, Politics, and Power*, eds. M. Dietler and B. Hayden, 144–184. Washington, D.C.: Smithsonian.

Clifford, R. J.

    1994. *Creation Accounts in the Ancient Near East and in the Bible.* Washington, D.C.: Catholic Biblical Association of America.

Clines, D. J. A.

    1990. *What Does Eve Do to Help? and Other Readerly Questions in the Old Testament.* Sheffield: Sheffield Academic Press.

Cogan, M.

1998. Into Exile: From the Assyrian Conquest of Israel to the Fall of Babylon. In Coogan (1998), 320–365.

Cogan, M. and Tadmor, H.

1988. *II Kings: A New Translation with Introduction and Commentary*. Garden City, N.Y.: Doubleday.

Collins, J. J.

2004. Before the Fall: The Earliest Interpretations of Adam and Eve. In *The Idea of Biblical Interpretation: Essays in Honor of James L. Kugel*, eds. H. Najman and J. H. Newman, 293–308. Leiden: Brill.

Conkey, M. W. and Gero, J. M.

1991. Tensions, Pluralities, and Engendering Archaeology: An Introduction to Women and Prehistory. In Gero and Conkey (1991), 3–30.

Conkey, M. W. and Spector, J. D.

1984. Archaeology and the Study of Gender. In *Advances in Archaeological Method and Theory*, vol. 7, ed. M. Schiffer, 1–38. New York: Academic Press.

Connerton, P.

1989. *How Societies Remember*. Cambridge: Cambridge University Press.

Coogan M. D., ed.

1998. *The Oxford History of the Biblical World*. New York: Oxford University Press.

Coontz, S.

2005. *Marriage, a History: From Obedience to Intimacy, or How Love Conquered Marriage*. New York: Viking.

Coote, R. B. and Gottwald, N. K., eds.

2007. *To Break Every Yoke: Essays in Honor of Marvin L. Chaney*. Sheffield: Sheffield Phoenix.

Costin, C.

1996. Exploring the Relationship Between Gender and Craft in Complex Societies: Methodological and Theoretical Issues of Gender Attribution. In *Gender and Archaeology*, ed. R. P. Wright, 111–140. Philadelphia: University of Pennsylvania Press.

Counihan, C. M.

1998. Introduction—Food and Gender: Identity and Power. In *Food and Gender: Identity and Power*, eds. C. M. Counihan and S. L. Kaplan, 1–10. Amsterdam: Harwood.

1999. Bread as World: Food Habits and Social Relations in Modernizing Sardinia. In C. Counihan, *The Anthropology of Food and the Body: Gender, Meaning, and Power*, 25–42, 216–217. New York: Routledge.

2000. The Social and Cultural Uses of Food: Food and Community. In *The Cambridge World History of Food*, ed. K. F. Kiple and K. C. Ornelas, 1513–1523 in vol. 1. 2 volumes. Cambridge: Cambridge University Press.

Craven T.
> 2000. Anna 1. In Meyers, Craven, and Kraemer (2000), 49–50.

Crumley, C. L.
> 1979. Three Locational Models: An Epistemological Assessment of Anthropology and Archaeology. In *Advances in Archaeological Method and Theory* 2, ed. M. B. Schiffer, 141–173. New York: Academic Press.
> 1995. Heterarchy and the Analysis of Complex Societies. In Ehrenreich, Crumley, and Levy (1995), 1–5.
> 2005. Remember How to Organize: Heterarchy across Disciplines. In *Nonlinear Models for Archaeology and Anthropology: Continuing the Revolution*, eds. C. S. Beekman and W. W. Baden, 35–50. Aldershot: Ashgate.

Curtis, R. L.
> 2001. *Ancient Food Technology*. Leiden: Brill.

Daly, M.
> 1968. *The Church and the Second Sex*. New York: Harper & Row.
> 1973. *Beyond God the Father: Toward a Philosophy of Women's Liberation.* Boston: Beacon.

Danforth, L. and Tsiaras, A.
> 1982. *The Death Rituals of Rural Greece*. Princeton: Princeton University Press.

Darby, E.
> 2011. Interpreting Judean Pillar Figurines: Gender and Empire in Judean Apotropaic Ritual. Ph.D. Dissertation, Duke University.

Davies, P. R.
> 1998. *Scribes and Schools: The Canonization of the Hebrew Scriptures*. Louisville, Ky.: Westminster John Knox.

Day, J.
> 2010. *Prophecy and the Prophets in Ancient Israel: Proceedings of the Oxford Old Testament Seminar*. New York: T&T Clark.

Day, L.
> 2006. Wisdom and the Feminine in the Hebrew Bible. In Day and Pressler (2006), 114–127.

Day, L. and Pressler, C., eds.
> 2006. *Engaging the Bible in a Gendered World: An Introduction to Feminist Biblical Interpretation in Honor of Katharine Sakenfeld*. Louisville: Westminster John Knox.

Dayagi-Mendels, M.
> 1989. *Perfumes and Cosmetics in the Ancient World*. Jerusalem: Israel Museum.

Dell, K. J.
> 2006. *The Book of Proverbs in Social and Theological Context*. New York: Cambridge University Press.

Demand, N.
> 1994. *Birth, Death, and Motherhood in Classical Greece*. Baltimore: The Johns Hopkins University Press.

Démare-Lafont. S.

    2011. The Status of Women in the Legal Texts of the Ancient Near East. In Fischer, Puerto, with Taschl-Erbele (2011), 109–132.

Dever, W. G.

    1997a. Archaeology, Urbanism, and the Rise of the Israelite State. In *Urbanism in Antiquity: From Mesopotamia to Crete*, eds. W. E. Aufrecht, N. A. Mirau, and S. W. Gauley, 172–193. Sheffield: Sheffield Academic Press.

    1997b. Biblical Archaeology. *Oxford Encyclopedia of Archaeology in the Near East* 1:315–319. New York: Oxford University Press.

    2003. *Who Were the Early Israelites and Where Did They Come From?* Grand Rapids, Mich.: Eerdmans.

    2005. *Did God Have a Wife? Archaeology and Folk Religion in Ancient Israel.* Grand Rapids, Mich.: Eerdmans.

    2012. *The Lives of Ordinary People: What the Bible and Archaeology Tell Us about Everyday Life in Ancient Israel.* Grand Rapids, Mich.: Eerdmans.

Dieter, M. and Hayden, B., eds.

    2001. *Feasts: Archaeological and Ethnographic Perspectives on Food, Politics, and Power.* Washington, D.C.: Smithsonian.

Dimen, M.

    1986. Servants and Sentries: Women, Power, and Social Reproduction in Kriovrisi. In Dubisch (1986b), 53–67.

Di Vito, R. A.

    1999. Old Testament Anthropology and the Construction of Personal Identity. *Catholic Biblical Quarterly* 61:217–238.

Domeris, W. R.

    2007. *Touching the Heart of God: The Social Construction of Poverty Among Biblical Peasants.* New York: T&T Clark.

Douglas, M.

    1966. *Purity and Danger: An Analysis of Concepts of Pollution and Taboo.* London: Routledge and K. Paul.

    1972. Deciphering a Meal. *Daedalus* 101:61–81.

Dubisch, J.

    1986a. Culture Enters through the Kitchen: Women, Food, and Social Boundaries in Rural Greece. In Dubisch (1986b), 195–214.

    1986b. ed., *Gender and Power in Rural Greece.* Princeton: Princeton University Press.

Dutcher-Walls, P., ed.

    2009. *The Family in Life and in Death: The Family in Ancient Israel: Sociological and Archaeological Perspectives.* New York: T&T Clark.

Ebeling, J. R.

    2002. Bread Making as Women's Technology in Ancient Israel. Paper given at the American Schools of Oriental Research Annual Meeting. Toronto.

Ebeling, J. R. and Homan, M. M.

    2008. Baking and Brewing Beer in the Israelite Household: A Study of Women's Cooking Technology. In Nakhai (2008), 45–62.

Edelstein, G. and Gat, Y.

    1980. Terraces around Jerusalem. *Israel—Land and Nature* 6:72–78.

Ehrenreich, R. M., Crumley, C. L, and Levy, J. E., eds.

    1995. *Heterarchy and the Analysis of Complex Societies*. Arlington, Va.: American Anthropological Association.

Elliott, J. H.

    1991. The Evil Eye in the First Testament: The Ecology and Culture of a Pervasive Belief. In Jobling, Day, and Sheppard (1991), 147–159.

Esler, P. F.

    2005 Social-Scientific Models in Biblical Interpretation. In *Ancient Israel: The Old Testament in Its Social Context*, ed. P. F. Esler, 3–32. Minneapolis: Fortress.

Eskenazi, T.

    2000 Daughters of Shallum (Neh 3:12). In Meyers, Craven, and Kraemer (2000), 287.

Exum, J. C.

    2010. Where Have All the Feminists Gone? Reflections on the Impact of Feminist Biblical Exegesis on the Scholarly Community and Women's Lives. *lexio difficilior* 2/2010. Available: http://www.lectio.unibe.ch/10_2/exum_feminists.html (accessed April 19, 2012).

Fabry, H.-J.

    2003 *ṣēlāʿ*. *Theological Dictionary of the Old Testament* 12 (trans. D. W. Stott): 400–405. Grand Rapids, Mich.: Eerdmans.

Faust, A.

    1999. Differences in Family Structure between Cities and Villages in the Iron Age II. *Tel-Aviv* 26:233–252.

    2000. The Rural Community in Ancient Israel during Iron Age II. *Bulletin of the American Schools of Oriental Research* 317:17–39.

    2003. The Farmstead in the Highlands of Iron Age II Israel. In *The Rural Landscape of Ancient Israel*, eds. A. M. Maeir, S. Dar, and Z. Safrai, 91–104. Oxford: Archaeopress.

    2004. "Mortuary Practices, Society, and Ideology:" The Lack of Iron Age I Burials in the Highlands in Context. *Israel Exploration Journal* 54:174–190.

    2006. *Israel's Ethnogenesis: Settlement, Interaction, Expansion and Resistance*, London: Equinox.

    2010. The Archaeology of the Israelite Cult: Questioning the Consensus. *Bulletin of the American Schools of Oriental Research* 310:23–35.

    2011. Household Economics in the Kingdoms of Israel and Judah. In Yasur-Landau, Ebeling, and Mazow (2011), 255–273.

Faust, A. and Bunimovitz, S.
    2003. The Four-Room House: Embodying Iron Age Israelite Society. *Near Eastern Archaeology* 66:22–31.
Finegan, R.
    1970. *Oral Literature in Africa*. Oxford: Oxford University Press.
Finkelstein, I.
    1986. *'Izbet Sartah: An Early Iron Age Site near Rosh Ha'ayin, Israel*. Oxford: British Archaeological Reports.
    1993. Environmental Archaeology and Social History: Demographic and Economic Aspects of the Monarchic Period. In *Biblical Archaeology Today, 1990: Proceedings of the Second International Congress on Biblical Archaeology*, eds. A. Biran and J. Aviram, 56–66. Jerusalem: Israel Exploration Society and the Israel Academy of Sciences and Humanities.
    1996. Ethnicity and the Origin of the Iron Age I Settlers in the Highlands of Canaan: Can the Real Israel Stand Up? *Biblical Archaeologist* 59:198–212.
    2007. The Two Kingdoms: Israel and Judah. In I. Finkelstein and A. Mazar, *The Quest for the Historical Israel: Debating Archaeology and the History of Early Israel*, ed. B. B. Schmidt, 147–157. Atlanta: Society of Biblical Literature.
Fischer, I.
    2004. *Gender-faire Exegese: Gesammelte Beiträge zur Reflexion des Genderbias und seiner Auswirkungen in der Übersetzung und Auslegung von biblischen Texten*. Münster: Lit.
Fischer, I., Økland, J., Puerto, M. N., and Valerio. A.
    2011. Introduction—Women, Bible, and Reception History. In Fischer, Økland, and Taschl-Erbele (2011), 1–30.
Fischer, I. and Puerto, M. N., with Taschl-Erbele, A., eds.
    2011. *Hebrew Bible—Old Testament: Torah*, Vol. 1.1 of *The Bible and Women: An Encyclopedia of Exegesis and Cultural History*, eds. J. Økland, I. Fischer, M. N. Puerto, and A. Valerio. Atlanta: Society of Biblical Literature.
Flanagan, J. W.
    1985. History as Hologram: Integrating Literary, Archaeological, and Comparative Sociological Evidence. In *Society of Biblical Literature Seminar Papers*, 291–314. Atlanta: Scholars Press.
Fogelin, L.
    2007. The Archaeology of Religious Ritual. *Annual Review of Anthropology* 36:55–71.
Fontaine, C. R.
    1990. The Sage in Family and Tribe. In Gammie and Perdue (1990), 155–164.
    1997. The Abusive Bible: The Use of Feminist Methods in Pastoral Contexts. In Brenner and Fontaine (1997), 84–113.
    2002. *Smooth Words, Proverbs and Performance in Biblical Wisdom*. London: Sheffield Academic Press.

Forbes, M. H. C.

　1976. Gathering in the Argolid: a Subsistence Subsystem in a Greek Agricultural Community. In *Regional Variation in Modern Greece and Cyprus: Toward a Perspective on the Ethnography of Greece*, eds. M. Dimen and E. Friedl, 251–264. New York: New York Academy of Sciences.

Feld, S. and Fox, A.

　1994. Music and Language. *Annual Review of Anthropology* 23:25–53.

Frankel, R.

　2003. Mills and Querns in Talmudic Literature–A Reappraisal in Light of Archaeological Evidence. *Cathedra* 110:43–60. [Hebrew]

Franzman, M.

　2000. *Women and Religion*. New York: Oxford University Press.

Freedman, R. D.

　1983. Woman, a Power Equal to Him. *Biblical Archaeology Review* 9:56–58.

Frick, F. S.

　1985. *The Formation of the State in Ancient Israel*. Sheffield: Almond Press.

　1997. Cities: An Overview. *Oxford Encyclopedia of Archaeology in the Near East* 2:15–19. New York: Oxford University Press.

Friedl, E.

　1967. The Position of Women: Appearance and Reality. *Anthropological Quarterly* 40:47–108.

　1975. *Women and Men: An Anthropologist's View*. New York: Holt, Rinehart and Winston.

Frier, B. W.

　1982. Roman Life Expectancy: Ulpian's Evidence. *Harvard Studies in Classical Philology* 86:213–252.

Fritz, V.

　1997. Cities of the Bronze and Iron Ages. *Oxford Encyclopedia of Archaeology in the Near East* 2:19–25. New York: Oxford University Press.

Frymer-Kensky, T.

　1990. The Sage in the Pentateuch. In Gammie and Perdue (1990), 275–287.

　2002. *Reading the Women of the Bible*. New York: Schocken.

Fuchs, E.

　2000. *Sexual Politics in the Biblical Narrative: Reading the Hebrew Bible as a Woman*. Sheffield: Sheffield Academic Press.

　2008. Reclaiming the Hebrew Bible for Women: The Neoliberal Turn in Contemporary Feminist Scholarship. *Journal of Feminist Studies in Religion* 24:45–65.

Fulkerson, M. McC.

　2001. *Changing the Subject: Women's Discourses and Feminist Theology*. Eugene, Ore.: Wipf and Stock.

Gallant, T. W.

    1991. *Risk and Survival in Ancient Greece: Reconstructing the Rural Domestic Economy*. Stanford: Stanford University Press.

Gammie, J. G. and Perdue, L. G., eds.

    1990. *The Sage in Israel and the Ancient Near East*. Winona Lake, Ind.: Eisenbrauns.

Garfinkel, Y.

    2009. Stone and Metal Artifacts. In Y. Garfinkel and S. Ganor, *Khirbet Qeiyafa Vol. I: Excavation Report 2008–2008*, 175–194. Jerusalem: Israel Exploration Society and the Institute of Archaeology, The Hebrew University of Jerusalem.

Garnett, L. M. S.

    1890–1891. *The Women of Turkey and Their Folklore*. 2 volumes. London: David Nutt.

Garnsey, P.

    1999. *Food and Society in Classical Antiquity*. Cambridge: Cambridge University Press.

Gavrielides, N.

    1976. The Cultural Ecology of Olive Growing in the Fourni Valley. In *Regional Variation in Modern Greece and Cyprus*, eds. M. Dimen and E. Friedl, 265–274. New York: New York Academy of Sciences.

Geertz, C.

    2000. *The Interpretation of Cultures*. 2nd edition. New York: Basic Books.

Gelb, I. J.

    1967. Approaches to the Study of Ancient Society. *Journal of the American Oriental Society* 87:1–7.

Geller, M.

    2010. *Ancient Babylonian Medicine: Theory and Practice*. Chichester, U.K.: Wiley-Blackwell.

Gelpi, B. C.

    1974. The Politics of Androgyny. *Women's Studies* 2:151–160.

Gero, J. M. and Conkey, M. W., eds.

    1991. *Engendering Archaeology: Women and Prehistory*. Oxford: Basil Blackwell.

Gerstenberger, E. S.

    2002. *Theologies in the Old Testament* (trans. J. Bowden). Minneapolis: Fortress.

Gifford, C. DeS.

    1985. American Women and the Bible: The Nature of Women as Hermeneutical Issue. In *Feminist Perspectives in Biblical Scholarship*, ed. A. Y. Collins, 11–34. Chico, Calif.: Scholars Press.

Gilchrist, R.

1999. *Gender and Archaeology:* Contesting the Past. London: Routledge.

Giles, M.

1958. The Human and Animal Remains. In *Lachish IV: The Bronze Age,* ed. O. Tufnell, Appendix B, 318–322. London: Oxford University Press.

Ginsberg, A. E., ed.

2008. *The Evolution of American Women's Studies: Reflections on Triumphs, Controversies, and Change.* New York: Palgrave Macmillan.

Gnuse, R. K.

1997. *No Other Gods: Emergent Monotheism in Israel.* Sheffield: Sheffield Academic Press.

Golden, M.

2004. Mortality, Mourning, and Mothers. In *Naissance et petite enfance dans l'Antiquité: Actes du colloque de Fribourg, 28 novembre–1ᵉʳ décembre 2001,* ed. V. Dasen, 145–157. Fribourg: Academic Press.

González-Marcén, P., Montón-Subías, S., and Picazo, M.

2008. Towards an Archaeology of Maintenance Activities. In *Engendering Social Dynamics: The Archaeology of Maintenance Activities,* ed. S. Montón-Subías, 3–8. Oxford: Archaeopress.

Goody, J.

1972. The Evolution of the Family. In Laslett and Wall (1972), 103–124.

1982. *Cooking, Class, and Cuisine: A Study in Comparative Sociology.* Cambridge: Cambridge University Press.

Gordon, R. P.

2010. The Ethics of Eden: Truth-Telling in Genesis 2–3. In *Ethical and Unethical in the Old Testament,* ed. K. J. Dell, 11–33. New York: T&T Clark.

Gottwald, N. K.

1979. *The Tribes of Yahweh: A Sociology of the Religion of Liberated Israel, 1250–1050 B.C.E.* Maryknoll, N.Y.: Orbis.

2001. *The Politics of Ancient Israel.* Louisville, Ky.: Westminster John Knox.

Grabbe, L. L., ed.

2011. *Enquire of the Former Age: Ancient Historiography and Writing the History of Israel.* New York: Y&T Clark.

Gray, J.

1964. *The Canaanites.* London: Thames and Hudson.

Greenfield, J.

1982. Adi balṭu—Care for the Elderly and Its Rewards. *Vorträge gehalten auf der 28. Rencontre Assyriologique Internationale in Wien, 6.-10. Juli 1981,* 309–316. Horn, Austria: Berger & Söhne.

Grigg, D.

1999. Food Consumption in the Mediterranean Region. *Journal of Economic and Social Geography* 90:391–409.

Gudme, A. K. de H.

2010. Modes of Religion: An Alternative to "Popular/Official" Religion. In Pfoh (2010a), 77–104.

Guenther, A.

2005. A Typology of Israelite Marriage: Kinship, Socio-Economic, and Religious Factors. *Journal for the Study of the Old Testament* 29:387–407.

Gunn, D. M. and Fewell, D. N.

1993. *Narrative in the Hebrew Bible*. New York: Oxford University Press.

Hallo, W.

1977. New Moons and Sabbaths: A Case-Study in the Contrastive Approach. *Hebrew Union College Annual* 48:1–18.

Hardin, J. W.

2010. *Households and the Use of Domestic Space at Iron II Tell Halif: An Archaeology of Destruction*. Winona Lake, Ind.: Eisenbrauns.

2011. Method and Theory for Understanding Houses, Households, and the Levantine Archaeological Record. In Yasur-Landau, Ebeling, and Mazow (2011), 9–25.

Hare, R.

1954. *Pomp and Pestilence: Infectious Disease, Its Origins and Conquest*. London: Victor Gollancy.

Hareuveni, N.

1980. *Nature in Our Biblical Heritage*. Kiryat Ono, Israel: Neot Kedumim.

Harkin, M. E.

2010. Ethnohistory's Ethnohistory: Creating a Discipline from the Ground Up. *Social Science History* 34:113–128.

Harris, M.

1979. *Cultural Materialism: The Struggle for a Science of Culture*. New York: Vintage.

Hart, L. K.

1992. *Time, Religion, and Social Experience in Rural Greece*. Lanham, Md.: Rowman & Littlefield.

Hastorf, C. A. and Weismantel, M.

2007. Food: Where Opposites Meet. In *The Archaeology of Food and Identity*, ed. K. C. Twiss, 308–331. Carbondale: Center for Archaeological Investigation, Southern Illinois University.

Hayes, J. H., ed.

2004. *Methods of Biblical Interpretation*. Nashville: Abingdon.

Hayes-Gilpin, K.

2000. Feminist Scholarship in Archaeology. *Annals of the American Academy of Political and Social Science* 571:89–106.

Hegland, M. E.

1991. Political Roles of Aliabad Women: The Public-Private Dichotomy Transcended. In *Women in Middle Eastern History: Shifting Boundaries in*

Sex and Gender, eds. N. R. Kiddie and S. Baron, 215–230. New Haven: Yale University Press.

Hendel, R.

1997. The Poetics of Myth in Genesis. In *The Seductiveness of Jewish Myth*, ed. S. D. Breslauer, 157–170. Albany: SUNY Press.

2007. Table and Altar: The Anthropology of Food in the Priestly Torah. In Coote and Gottwald (2007), 131–148.

Hendel, R., Kronfeld, C., and Pardes, I.

2010. Gender and Sexuality. In *Reading Genesis: Ten Methods*, ed. R. Hendel, 71–91. New York: Cambridge University Press.

Hendon, J.

1996. Archaeological Approaches to the Organization of Domestic Labor: Household Practice and Domestic Relations. *Annual Review of Anthropology* 22:45–61.

2006. The Engendered Household. In Nelson (2006), 171–198.

Hermann, A. C. and Steward, A. J., eds.

2001. *Theorizing Feminism: Parallel Trends in the Humanities and Social Sciences*. 2nd edition. Boulder, Colo.: Westview.

Hiebert, T.

1996. *The Yahwist's Landscape: Nature and Religion in Early Israel*. New York: Oxford University Press.

Hiecke, T.

2011. Genealogy as a Means of Presenting History in the Torah and the Role of Women in the Genealogical System. In Fischer and Puerto, with Taschl-Erber (2011), 151–192.

Higgins, J.

1976. The Myth of Eve the Temptress. *Journal of the American Academy of Religion* 44:639–647.

Hirschfeld, Y.

1995. The Traditional Palestinian House: Results of a Survey in the Hebron Hills. In *The Palestinian Dwelling in the Roman-Byzantine Period*, 109–215. Jerusalem: Franciscan Printing Press and Israel Exploration Society.

Hodder, I.

2005. Post-Processual Archaeology. In Renfrew and Bahn (2005), 207–212.

Holladay, J. S., Jr.

1992. House, Israelite. *Anchor Bible Dictionary* 3:308–318. New York: Doubleday.

1995. The Kingdoms of Israel and Judah: Political and Economic Centralization in the Iron IIA-B (ca. 1000–750 BCE). In T. E. Levy (1995), 368–398.

1997. Four-room House. *Oxford Encyclopedia of Archaeology in the Near East* 2:336–342. New York: Oxford University Press.

Hopkins, D. C.

1985. *The Highlands of Canaan*. Sheffield: Almond Press.

1987. Life on the Land: The Subsistence Struggles of Early Israel. *Biblical Archaeologist* 30:178–191.

1997. Agriculture. *Oxford Encyclopedia of Archaeology in the Near East* 1:22–30. New York: Oxford University Press.

2007. "All Sorts of Field Work:" Agricultural Labor in Ancient Palestine. In Coote and Gottwald (2007), 149–172.

Hopkins, K.

1983. *Death and Renewal*. Cambridge: Cambridge University Press.

Hudson, M.

1999. Summary Review: From Open Land to Private Ownership. In Hudson and Levine (1999), 481–489.

Hudson, M. and Levine, B. A., eds.

1999. *Urbanization and Land Ownership in the Ancient Near East*, vol. 2. Cambridge, Mass.: Peabody Museum of Archaeology and Ethnology, Harvard University.

Ilan, T.

1995. *Jewish Women in Greco-Roman Palestine: An Inquiry into Image and Status*. Tübingen: Mohr Siebeck.

Jackson, B. S.

2011. The "Institutions" of Marriage and Divorce in the Hebrew Bible. *Journal of Semitic Studies* 56:221–251.

Jackson, J. R.

2005. Enjoying the Fruits of One's Labor: Attitudes toward Male Work and Workers in the Hebrew Bible. Ph.D. diss., Duke University.

Jäger, K.

1912. *Das Bauernhaus in Palästina*. Göttingen, Germany: Vandenhoeck and Ruprecht.

Jefferson, L. M.

2009. Adam and Eve, Story of. VI. Visual Arts. *Encyclopedia of the Bible and Its Reception* 1:356–360. Berlin: de Gruyter.

Jobling, D., Day, P., and Sheppard, G. T., eds.

1991. *The Bible and the Politics of Exegesis: Essays in Honor of Norman K. Gottwald on His Sixty-Fifth Birthday*. Cleveland: Pilgrim.

Joffe, A.

2002. The Rise of Secondary States in the Levant. *Journal of the Economic and Social History of the Orient* 45:425–467.

Johnson, M. D.

1983. Life of Adam and Eve: A New Translation and Introduction. In *The Old Testament Pseudepigrapha* ed. J. H. Charlesworth, 249–295 in vol. 2. 2 volumes. Garden City, N.Y.: Doubleday.

Jordan, R. A. and Kalčik, S. J.

1985. Introduction. In *Women's Folklore, Women's Culture,* eds. R. A. Jordan and S. J. Kalčik, ix–xiv. Philadelphia: University of Pennsylvania Press.

Joseph, T. B.

1980. Poetry as a Strategy of Power: The Case of Riffian Berber Women. *SIGNS* 5:418–434.

Kadari, T.

2006. Eve: Midrash and Aggadah. *Jewish Women: A Comprehensive Historical Encyclopedia,* eds. P. E. Hyman and D. Ofer. Philadelphia: Jewish Publication Society. <http://jwa.org/encyclopedia/article/eve-midrash-and-aggadah> (accessed April, 2012).

Kalmanofsky, A.

2007. "Their Heart Cried Out to God:" Gender and Prayer in the Book of Lamentations. In Rooke (2007), 53–65.

Kapitan, T., ed.

1999. *Archaeology, History and Culture in Palestine and the Near East: Essays in Memory of Albert E. Glock.* Atlanta: Scholars Press.

Kawashima, R. S.

2011. Could a Woman Say "No" in Biblical Israel? On the Genealogy of Legal Status in Biblical Law and Literature. *Association for Jewish Studies Review* 35:1–22.

Kennedy, R.

1986. Women's Friendships in Crete. In Dubisch (1986b), 121–138.

Kilmer, A.

1972. The Mesopotamian Concept of Overpopulation and Its Solution as Represented in the Mythology. *Orientalia* 41:160–177.

King, P. J. and Stager, L. E.

2001. *Life in Biblical Israel.* Louisville, Ky.: Westminster John Knox.

Klein, M.

2000. *A Time To Be Born: Customs and Folklore of Jewish Birth.* Philadelphia: Jewish Publication Society.

Knight, D. A.

2000. Village Law and the Book of the Covenant. In *"A Wise and Discerning Mind": Essays in Honor of Burke O. Long,* eds. S. M. Olyan and R. C. Culley, 163–179. Providence: Brown Judaic Studies.

2011. *Law, Power, and Justice in Ancient Israel.* Louisville, Ky.: Westminster John Knox.

Kohl, S.

1988. Women's Participation in North American Family Agricultural Enterprises. In *Women and Farming: Changing Roles, Changing Structures,* eds. W. G. Haney and J. N. Knowles, 89–108. Boulder, Colo.: Westview.

van der Kooij, A.

2010. The Story of Paradise and Mesopotamian Culture. In *Genesis, Isaiah and Psalms: A Festschrift to honour Professor John Emerton for his eightieth birthday*, eds. K. J. Dell, G. Davies, and Y. V. Koh, 3–22. Leiden: Brill.

Korpel, M. C. A.

1996. Avian Spirits in Ugarit and Ezekiel 13. In *Ugarit, Religion, and Culture*, eds. N. Wyatt, W. G. E. Watson, and J. B. Loyd, 99–113. Münster: Ugarit-Verlag.

Kraemer, R. S.

2011. *Unreliable Witnesses: Religion, Gender, and History in the Greco-Roman Mediterranean*. Oxford: Oxford University Press.

Kraus, H.

2011. *Gender Issues in Ancient and Reformation Translations of Genesis 1–4*. Oxford: Oxford University Press.

Kvam, K. E., Schearing, L. S., and Ziegler, V. H., eds.

1999. *Eve & Adam: Jewish, Christian, and Muslim Readings on Genesis and Gender*. Bloomington: Indiana University Press.

Kray, S.

2002. "New Mode of Feminist Historical Analysis"—Or Just Another Collusion with "Patriarchal" Bias? *SHOFAR* 2:66–90.

LaBianca, O. S.

1999. Salient Features of Iron Age Tribal Kingdoms. In *Ancient Ammon*, eds. B. MacDonald and R. W. Younker, 19–23. Leiden: Brill.

LaCoque, A.

2006. *The Trial of Innocence: Adam, Eve, and the Yahwist*. Eugene, Ore.: Cascade.

LaFraniere, S.

2005. Women's Rights Laws and African Custom Clash. *New York Times*, December 30, 2005. Available: http://www.nytimes.com/2005/12/30/international/africa/30africa.html?_r=1&scp=1&sq=wiomen%27s%20rights%20laws%20and%20african%20customs&st=cse (accessed April 20, 2012).

Lambert, W. G. and Millard, A. R.

1969. *Atrahasis: The Babylonian Story of the Flood*. Oxford: Clarendon.

Lapin, H.

2006. The Origins and Development of the Rabbinic Movement in the Land of Israel. In *The Cambridge History of Judaism*, ed. S. T. Katz, 206–229 in vol. 4. New York: Cambridge University Press.

Lapsley, J.

2005. *Whispering the Wind: Strategies for Reading Women's Stories in the Old Testament Theologically*. Louisville, Ky.: Westminster John Knox.

Laslett, P. and Wall, R. eds.

1972. *Household and Family in Past Time*. London: Cambridge University Press.

Lawrence, B.
2010 Gender Analysis: Gender and Method in Biblical Studies. In *Method Matters: Essays on the Interpretation of the Hebrew Bible in Honor of David. L. Petersen*, ed. J. M. LeMon and K. H. Richards, 333–348. Leiden: Society of Biblical Literature.

Lawrence, S.
1999. Towards a Feminist Archaeology of Households: Gender and Household Structure in the Australian Goldfields. In Allison (1999a), 121–141.

Leach, E. R.
1982. *Social Anthropology*. Glasgow: Fontana.

Lemos, T.
2009. The Universal and the Particular: Mary Douglas and the Politics of Impurity. *Journal of Religion* 89: 236–251.

Lenski, G. E.
1984. *Power and Privilege: A Theory of Social Stratification*. Chapel Hill: University of North Carolina Press.
2005. *Ecological-Evolutionary Theory: Principles and Applications*. Boulder, Colo.: Paradigm.

Lerner, G.
1986. *The Creation of Patriarchy*. New York: Oxford University Press.

Levine, B. A.
1993. *Numbers 1–20: A New Translation with Introduction and Commentary*. New York: Doubleday.
1999. The Biblical "Town" as Reality and Typology: Evaluating Biblical References to Towns and Their Functions. In Hudson and Levine (1999), 421–453.

Levine, L. I.
1989. *The Rabbinic Class of Roman Palestine in Late Antiquity*. New York: Jewish Theological Seminary of America.

LeVine, S. and LeVine, R. A.
1985. Age, Gender, and the Demographic Transition: The Life Course in Agrarian Societies. In *Gender and the Life Course*, ed. A.S. Rossi, 29–42. New York: Aldine.

Lesko, B. S.
1989. Preface. In *Women's Earliest Records: From Ancient Egypt and Western Asia*, ed. B.S. Lesko, xiii–xviii. Atlanta: Scholars Press.
2008. Household and Domestic Religion in Ancient Egypt. In Bodel and Olyan (2008b), 197–209.

Lewis, T.
1989. *Cults of the Dead in Ancient Israel and Ugarit*. Atlanta: Scholars Press.

Levy, J. E.
2006. Gender, Heterarchy, and Hierarchy. In Nelson (2006), 219–246.

Levy, T. E., ed.

> 1995. *The Archaeology of Society in the Holy Land*, ed. T. E. Levy. New York: Facts on File.

Levy, T. E. and Hall, A. F. C.

> 1995. Social Change and the Archaeology of the Holy Land. In Levy (1995), 2–8.

Lipiński, E.

> 1998. *nāḥal*; *naḥᵃlâ*. *Theological Dictionary of the Old Testament* 9 (trans. D. E. Green): 319–335. Grand Rapids, Mich.: Eerdmans.

Lipschitz, O., Sergi, O., and Koch, I.

> 2011. Judahite Stamped and Incised Jar Handles: A Tool for Studying the History of Late Monarchic Judah. *Tel Aviv* 38:5–41.

Lohr, J. N.

> 2011. Sexual Desire? Eve, Genesis 3:16, and הקושת. *Journal of Biblical Literature* 130: 227–246.

Løland, H.

> 2008. *Silent or Salient Gender? The Interpretation of Gendered God-Language in the Hebrew Bible, Exemplified in Isaiah 42, 46 and 49*. Tübingen: Mohr Siebeck.

London, G.

> 2000. Continuity and Change in Cypriot Pottery Production. *Near Eastern Archaeology* 63:101–110.

Lutfiyya, A. M.

> 1966. *Baytīn, A Jordanian Village: A Study of Social Institutions and Social Change in a Folk Community*. The Hague: Mouton.

McNeill, W. H.

> 1975. *Plagues and Peoples*. Garden City, N.Y.: Doubleday.

MacDonald, N.

> 2008a. Feasting Fit for a King: Food and the Rise of the Monarchy. In *Not Bread Alone: The Uses of Food in the Old Testament*, 134–166. Oxford: Oxford University Press.

> 2008b. *What Did the Ancient Israelites Eat?: Diet in Biblical Times*. Grand Rapids, Mich.: Eerdmans.

Maher, V.

> 1976. Kin, Clients, and Accomplices: Relationships among Women in Morocco. In *Sexual Divisions and Society: Process and Change*, eds. D. L. Barber and S. Allen, 52–75. London: Tavistock.

Malina, B. J.

> 1969. Some Observations of the Origin of Sin in Judaism and St. Paul. *Catholic Biblical Quarterly* 31:18–34.

March, K. S. and Taqqu, R. L.

> 1986. *Women's Informal Associations in Developing Countries*. Boulder, Colo.: Westview.

Marcus, R., trans.

   1953. *Philo: Questions and Answers on Genesis.* Cambridge, Mass.: Harvard
   University Press.

Marsman, H. J.

   2003. *Women in Ugarit and Israel: Their Social and Religious Position in the
   Context of the Ancient Near East.* Leiden: Brill.

Mazar, A.

   1992. *Archaeology of the Land of the Bible: 10,000–586 B.C.E.* New York:
   Doubleday.

   1997. Palestine: Palestine in the Iron Age. *Oxford Encyclopedia of Archaeology
   in the Near East* 4:217–222. New York: Oxford University Press.

   2003. The Divided Monarchy: Comments on Some Archaeological Issues. In
   I. Finkelstein and A. Mazar. *The Quest for the Historical Israel: Debating
   Archaeology and the History of Early Israel*, ed. B. B. Schmidt, 159–179.
   Atlanta: Society of Biblical Literature.

McColgan, K. P.

   1994. Abundant Gifts: Hierarchy and Reciprocity in "Paradise Lost." *South
   Central Review* 11:75–86.

McKay, H.

   1997. On the Future of Feminist Biblical Criticism. In Brenner and Fontaine
   (1997), 61–83.

McNutt, P. M.

   1999. *Reconstructing the Society of Ancient Israel.* Louisville, Ky.: Westminster
   John Knox.

McQuitty, A.

   1984. An Ethnographic and Archaeological Study of Clay Ovens in Jordan.
   Annual of the Department of Antiquities in Jordan 28:259–257.

   1993–1994. Ovens in Town and Country. *Berytus Archaeological Studies*
   41:53–76.

Meagher, M.

   2011. Patriarchy. *Concise Encyclopedia of Sociology*, eds. G. Ritzier and J. M.
   Ryan, 441–442. Hoboken, N.J.: Wiley-Blackwell.

Meskell, L., Gosden, C., Hodder, I., Joyce, R. A., and Preucel, R.

   2001. Editorial Statement. *Journal of Social Archaeology* 1:5–12.

Mettinger, T. N. D.

   2007. *The Eden Narrative: A Literary and Religio-Historical Study of Genesis
   2–3.* Winona Lake, Ind.: Eisenbrauns.

Meyer, M. and Mirecki, P.

   1995. Introduction. In *Ancient Magic and Ritual Power*, eds. M. Meyer and P.
   Mirecki. Boston: Brill.

Meyers, C.

   1988. *Discovering Eve: Ancient Israelite Women in Context.* New York: Oxford
   University Press.

1991. "To Her Mother's House"—Considering a Counterpart to the Israelite *Bêt 'āb.* In Jobling, Day, and Sheppard (1991), 39–52, 304–307.

1997. Recovering Objects, Re-Visioning Subjects: Archaeology and Feminist Biblical Study. In Brenner and Fontaine (1997), 270–284.

1998. Kinship and Kingship: The Early Monarchy. In Coogan (1998), 165–205.

1999. Wellness and Holiness in the Bible. In *Illness and Health in the Jewish Tradition: Writings from the Bible to Today,* eds. D. L. Freeman and J. Z. Abrams, 129–133. Philadelphia: Jewish Publication Society.

2000. Female Images of God in the Hebrew Bible. In Meyers, Craven, and Kraemer (2000), 525–528.

2001. *'aṣab; 'eṣeb; 'ōṣeb; 'āṣeb; 'iṣṣābôn; 'aṣṣebet; ma'aṣēbâ. Theological Dictionary of the Old Testament* 11 (trans. D. E. Green): 278–280. Grand Rapids. Mich.: Eerdmans.

2003a. Engendering Syro-Palestinian Archaeology: Reasons and Resources. *Near Eastern Archaeology* 66:185–197.

2003b. Everyday Life in Biblical Israel: Women's Social Networks. In *Life and Culture in the Ancient Near East,* ed. R. E. Averbeck, M. W. Chavalas, and D. B. Weisberg, 185–204. Bethesda, Md.: CDL Press.

2003c. Material Remains and Social Relations: Women's Culture in Agrarian Households of the Iron Age. In *Symbiosis, Symbolism, and the Power of the Past: Canaan, Ancient Israel, and Their Neighbors from the Late Bronze Age through Roman Palestina,* eds. W. G. Dever and S. Gitin, 425–444. Winona Lake, Ind.: Eisenbrauns.

2003d. Rape or Remedy: Sex and Violence in Prophetic Marriage Metaphors. In *Prophetie in Israel* (Beiträge des Symposiums "Das Altes Testament und die Kultur der Moderne," anlässlich des 100. Geburtstags Gerhard von Rads [1901–1971], Heidelberg, 18.21. Oktober 2001), eds. H. Williamson, K. Schmid, and I. Fischer, 185–198. Münster: Lit-Verlag.

2005a. *Exodus.* New York: Cambridge University Press.

2005b. *Households and Holiness: The Religious Culture of Israelite Women.* Minneapolis: Fortress.

2005c. Jerusalem. In *Dictionary of the Old Testament: Historical Books,* eds. B. T. Arnold and H. G. M. Williamson, 547–556. Downers Grove, Ill.: InterVarsity.

2006. Anthropology, Cultural (OT). *New Interpreter's Dictionary of the Bible* 1:170–171. Nashville: Abingdon.

2007a. Contesting the Notion of Patriarchy: Anthropology and the Theorizing of Gender in Ancient Israel. In Rooke (2007), 84–105.

2007b. From Field Crops to Food: Attributing Gender and Meaning to Bread Production in Iron Age Israel. In *The Archaeology of Difference: Gender, Ethnicity, Class and the "Other" in Antiquity: Studies in Honor of Eric M. Meyers,* eds. D. R. Edwards and C. T. McCollough, 67–84. Boston: American Schools of Oriental Research.

2007c. Mandrake. *Encyclopaedia Judaica* 13:466. 2nd edition. Detroit: Macmillan Reference.

2007d. Terracottas without Texts: Judean Pillar Figurines in Anthropological Perspective. In Coote and Gottwald (2007), 115–130.

2008a. Engendering Ezekiel: Female Figures Reconsidered. In *Birkat Shalom: Studies in the Bible, Ancient Near Eastern Literature, and Postbiblical Judaism Presented to Shalom M. Paul on the Occasion of His Seventieth Birthday*, eds. C. Cohen, V. A. Hurowitz, A. Hurvitz, Y. Muffs, B. J. Schwartz, and J. H. Tigay, 281–297 in vol. 1. 2 volumes. Winona Lake, Ind.: Eisenbrauns.

2008b. Grinding to a Halt: Gender and the Changing Technology of Flour Production in Roman Galilee. In *Engendering Social Dynamics: The Archaeology of Maintenance Activities*, eds. S. Montón-Subías and M. Sánchez-Romero, 65–74. Oxford: ArchaeoPress.

2009. Women in the OT. *New Interpreter's Dictionary of the Bible* 5: 888–892. Nashville, Tenn.: Abingdon.

2010. Household Religion. In Stavrakopoulou and Barton (2010), 118–134.

2011. Archaeology—A Window to the Lives of Israelite Women. In Fischer and Puerto, with Taschl-Erbele (2011), 61–108.

2012a. Food and the First Family: A Socioeconomic Perspective. In *The Book of Genesis: Composition, Reception, and Interpretation*, eds. C. A. Evans, J. N. Lohr, and D. L. Petersen, 137–157. Leiden: Brill.

2012b. The Function of Feasts: An Anthropological Perspective on Israelite Religious Festivals. In *Social Theory and the Study of Israelite Religion: Retrospect and Prospect*, ed. S. M. Olyan, 140–168. Atlanta: Society of Biblical Literature.

forthcoming a. Beyond the Bible: Archaeology, Ethnohistory, and the Study of Israelite Women. In *Daughters of Zillah: A Retrospective of the Influence of Feminist Hermeneutics on Methodology of the Hebrew Bible*, ed. F. R. Madalene. Vol. 3 of *The Feminist Hermeneutics of the Hebrew Bible Retrospective Project*. Sheffield: Sheffield Phoenix.

forthcoming b. Feast Days and Foodways: The Religious Dimensions of Household Life. In Albertz et al. (forthcoming).

Meyers, C., Craven, T., and Kraemer, R. S., eds.

2000. *Women in Scripture: A Dictionary of the Named and Unnamed Women in the Hebrew Bible, the Apocrypha/Deuterocanonical Books, and the New Testament*. Boston: Houghton Mifflin.

Meyers, E. and Meyers, C.

2011. The Material Culture of Late Hellenistic—Early Roman Palestinian Judaism: What It Can Tell Us about Earliest Christianity and the New Testament. In *Neues Testament und hellenistische-jüdische Alltagskultur: Wechselseitige Wahrnehmungen. III. Internationales Symposium zum*

Corpus Judaeo-Hellenisticum Novi Testamenti 21.-24. Mai 2009, Leipzig,
eds. R. Deines, J. Herzer, and K.-W. Niebuhr, 3–23. Tübingen: Mohr
Siebeck.

Milgrom, J.

1990. *The JPS Torah Commentary: Numbers.* Philadelphia: Jewish Publication
Society.

1991. *Leviticus 1–16: A New Translation with Introduction and Commentary.*
New York: Doubleday.

Miller, P. L.

2011. Greek Philosophical Dualism. In *Light Against Darkness: Dualism in
Ancient Mediterranean Religion and the Contemporary World,* eds. A. Lange,
E. M. Meyers, B. H. Reynolds III, and R. Styers, 106–144. Göttingen:
Vandenhoeck & Ruprecht.

Miller, R.

2005. *Chieftains of the Highland Clans: A History of Israel in the 12th and 11th
Centuries.* Grand Rapids, Mich.: Eerdmans.

Milne, P. J.

1997. Toward Feminist Companionship: The Future of Feminist Biblical Studies
and Feminism. In Brenner and Fontaine (1997), 39–60.

Molleson, T.

1994. The Eloquent Bones of Abu Hureyra. *Scientific American* 271:70–75.

Moore, M. B. and Kelle, B. E.

2011. *Biblical History and Israel's Past: The Changing Study of the Bible and
History.* Grand Rapids, Mich: Eerdmans.

Muhly, J. D.

1997. Metals: Artifacts of the Neolithic, Bronze, and Iron Ages. In *The Oxford
Encyclopedia of Archaeology in the Near East* 4:5–15. New York: Oxford
University Press.

Murdock, G. P., and Provost, C.

1973. Factors in the Division of Labor by Sex: A Cross-Cultural Analysis.
Ethnology 12:203–225.

Myres, S. L.

1982. *Westering Women and the Frontier Experience 1800–1915.* Albuquerque:
University of New Mexico Press.

Na'aman, N.

1986. Hezekiah's Fortified Cities and the "LMLK" Stamps. *Bulletin of the
American Schools of Oriental Research* 261:5–21.

Nakhai, B. A.

2008. ed., *The World of Women in the Ancient and Classical Near East.* Newcastle
upon Tyne: Cambridge Scholars.

2011. Varieties of Religious Expression in the Domestic Setting. In Yasur-
Landau, Ebeling, and Mazow (2011), 347–360.

Nash, G. J.
    2009. Patriarchy. In *International Encyclopedia of Human Geography*, eds. R. Kitchen and N. Thrift, 102–107. Amsterdam: Elsevier.

Nelson, S. M.
    2004. *Gender in Archaeology: Analyzing Power and Prestige*. 2nd edition. Walnut Creek, Calif.: AltaMira.
    2005. Gender Archaeology. In Renfrew and Bahn (2005), 27–33.
    2006. ed., *Handbook of Gender in Archaeology*. Lanham, Md.: AltaMira.

Nemet-Nejat, K. R.
    1998. *Daily Life in Ancient Mesopotamia*. Westport, Conn.: Greenwood.

Netting, R. McC., Wilk, R. R., and Arnould, E. J.
    1984a. eds., *Households: Comparative and Historic Studies of the Domestic Group*. Berkeley: University of California Press.
    1984b. Introduction. In. R. McC. Netting, R. R. Wilk, and E. J. Arnould (1984a), xiii–xxxviii.

Nevett, L. C.
    2010. *Domestic Space in Classical Antiquity*. Cambridge: Cambridge University Press.

Newsom, C. A.
    2000. Common Ground: An Ecological Reading of Genesis 2–3. In *The Earth Story in Genesis*, eds. N. C. Habel and S. Wurst, 60–72. Sheffield: Sheffield Academic Press.

Newsom, C. A. and Ringe, S. H., eds.
    1998. *Women's Bible Commentary*. Revised edition. Louisville, Ky.: Westminster John Knox.

Nickel, G.
    2009. Adam and Eve, Story of. IV. Islam. *Encyclopedia of the Bible and Its Reception* 1:350–352. Berlin: de Gruyter.

Niditch, S.
    1993. *Folklore and the Hebrew Bible*. Minneapolis: Fortress.
    2008. *Judges: A Commentary*. Louisville: Westminster John Knox.

Niehr, H.
    2001. *'āram*; *'ārûm*; *'ormâ*. *Theological Dictionary of the Old Testament* 11 (trans. D. E. Green): 361–366. Grand Rapids, Mich.: Eerdmans.

Nolan, P. and Lenski, G.
    2009. *Human Societies: An Introduction to Macrosociology*. 11th edition. Herndon, Va.: Paradigm.

O'Brian, R.
    1999. Who Weaves and Why? Weaving, Loom Complexity, and Trade. *Cross-Cultural Research* 33:30–42.

O'Brien, J. and Major, W.
    1982. *In the Beginning*. Chico, Calif.: Scholars Press.

O'Connor, K. M.

    2006. The Feminist Movement Meets the Old Testament: One Woman's Perspective. In Day and Pressler (2006), 3–24.

Oden, R. A.

    2000. Grace or Status? Yahweh's Clothing of the First Humans. In *The Bible without Theology: The Theological Tradition and Alternatives to It*, 92–105. Champaign: University of Illinois Press.

Offen, K.

    1984. Depopulation, Nationalism, and Feminism in Fin-de-siècle France. *American Historical Review* 89:648–674.

Olyan, S. M.

    2010. What Do We Really Know about Women's Rites in the Israelite Family Context? *Journal of Ancient Near Eastern Religions* 10:55–67.

Orni, E. and Efrat, E.

    1980. *Geography of Israel*. 4th revised edition. Jerusalem: Israel Universities Press.

Ortner, S. B.

    1996. *Making Gender: The Politics and Erotics of Culture*. Boston: Beacon.

Osterud, N. G.

    1988. Land, Identity, and Agency in the Oral Autobiographies of Farm Women. In *Women and Farming: Changing Roles, Changing Structures*, eds. W. H. Haney and J. B. Knowles, 73–87. Boulder, Colo.: Westview.

Otto, E.

    2001. 'ir. *Theological Dictionary of the Old Testament* 11 (trans. D. E. Green): 51–67. Grand Rapids, Mich.: Eerdmans.

Ottosson, M.

    1974. 'erets. *Theological Dictionary of the Old Testament* 1 (trans. J. T. Willis): 390–405. Grand Rapids, Mich.: Eerdmans.

    1978. hārāh; hāreh; hērāyôn; hēron. *Theological Dictionary of the Old Testament* 3 (trans. J. T. Willis, 1–358, and D. E. Green, 359–464): 458–461. Grand Rapids, Mich.: Eerdmans.

Pagels, E.

    1991. The Social History of Satan, the "Intimate Enemy": A Preliminary Sketch. *Harvard Theological Review* 84:105–128.

Pardes. I.

    1992. *Countertraditions in the Bible: A Feminist Approach*. Cambridge, Mass.: Harvard University Press.

Parker, B. J.

    2011. Bread Ovens: Social Networks and Gendered Space: An Ethno-archaeological Study of *Tandir* Ovens in Southeastern Anatolia. *American Antiquity* 76:603–627.

Pedersen, J.

    1926. *Israel: Its Life and Culture* (trans. A. Møller). 2 volumes. London: Oxford University Press.

Perlitz, I. J.

1898. Women in the Ancient Hebrew Cult. *Journal of Biblical Literature* 17:111–148.

Peskowitz, M. B.

1997. *Spinning Fantasies: Rabbis, Gender and History*. Berkeley: University of California Press.

Peterson, N. H.

2009. Adam and Eve, Story of. VII. Music. *Encyclopedia of the Bible and Its Reception* 1:361–363. Berlin: de Gruyter,

Pfoh, E.

2010a. ed., *Anthropology and the Bible: Critical Perspectives*. Piscataway, N.J.: Gorgias.

2010b. Introduction: Anthropology and the Bible Revisited. In Pfoh (2010a), 3–12.

Phillips, V. C.

2004. Feminist Biblical Scholarship. In Hayes (2004), 371–384.

Picazo, M.

1997. Hearth and Home: The Timing of Maintenance Activities. In *Invisible People and Processes: Writing Gender and Childhood into European Archaeology*, eds. J. Moore and E. Scott, 59–67. Leicester: Leicester University Press.

Pilarski, A. E.

2011. The Past and Future of Feminist Biblical Hermeneutics. *Biblical Theology Bulletin* 41:16–23.

Pimentel D. and Pimentel, M.

2003. Sustainability of Meat-based and Plant-based Diets and the Environment. *American Journal of Clinical Nutrition* 78:660S–663S.

Plate, S. B.

2009. Adam and Eve, Story of. VIII. Film. *Encyclopedia of the Bible and Its Reception* 1:364. Berlin: de Gruyter.

Pomeroy, S. B.

1994. *Xenophon, Oeconomicus: A Social and Historical Commentary*. Oxford: Clarendon.

Portugali, Y.

1983. 'Arim, Banot, Migrashim, and Ḥaṣerim: The Spatial Organization of Eretz-Israel in the 12th–10th Centuries BCE according to the Bible. *Eretz Israel* 17:282–290. [Hebrew]

von Rad, G.

1961. *Genesis* (trans. J. H. Marks). Philadelphia: Westminster (originally published in 1956).

Ramsey, G. W.

1988. Is Name-Giving an Act of Domination in Genesis 2:23 and Elsewhere? *Catholic Biblical Quarterly* 50:224–235.

Rapoport, A.

1994. Spatial Organization and the Built Environment. *Companion Encyclopedia of Archaeology*, ed. T. Ingold, 460–502. London: Routledge.

Rapp, R., Ross, E., and Bridenthal, R.

1979. Examining Family History: Household and Family. *Feminist Studies* 5:174–200.

Redfield, R.

1956. *Peasant Society and Culture: An Anthropological Approach to Civilization*. Chicago: University of Chicago Press.

Reiter, R. R., ed.

1975. *Toward an Anthropology of Women*. New York: Monthly Review.

Rendsburg, G.

2003. Unlikely Heroes: Women as Israel. *Bible Review* 19:16–23, 52–53.

Renfrew, C.

1984. *Approaches to Social Anthropology*. Cambridge, Mass.: Harvard University Press.

Renfrew, C. and Bahn, P.

2005. eds., *Archaeology: The Key Concepts*. London: Routledge.

2008. *Archaeology: Theories, Methods, and Practice*. 5th edition. New York: Thames and Hudson.

Reuling, H.

2006. *After Eden: Church Fathers and Rabbis on Genesis 3:16–21*. Leiden: Brill.

Reverby, S. M. and Helly, D. O.

1992. Introduction: Converging on History. In *Gendered Domains: Rethinking Public and Private in Women's History*, eds. D. O. Helly and S. M. Reverby, 1–24. Ithaca, N.Y.: Cornell University Press.

Reviv, H.

1993. *The Society in the Kingdoms of Israel and Judah*. Jerusalem: Mosad Bialik. [Hebrew]

Riegelhaupt, J. F.

1967. Saloio Women: An Analysis of Informal and Formal Political and Economic Roles of Portuguese Peasant Women. *Anthropological Quarterly* 40:109–126.

Ringe, S. H.

1998. When Women Interpret the Bible. In Newsom and Ringe (1998), 1–9.

Roberts, C.

1993. A Critical Approach to Gender as a Category of Analysis in Archaeology. In *Women in Archaeology: A Feminist Critique*, eds. H. du Clos and L. Smith, 16–21. Canberra: Research School of Pacific Studies, Australian National University.

Rogers, S. C.

1975. Female Forms of Power and the Myth of Male Dominance: A Model of Female/Male Interaction in Peasant Society. *American Ethnologist* 2:727–756.

Rogerson, J. W.

1989. Anthropology of the Old Testament. In *The World of Ancient Israel: Sociological, Anthropological and Political Perspectives*, ed. R. E. Clements, 17–38. New York: Cambridge University Press.

Roll, I.

1983. The Roman Road System in Judaea. In *The Jerusalem Cathedra: Studies in the History, Archaeology, Geography and Ethnography of the Land of Israel*, ed. L. I. Levine, 136–161 in vol. 3. 3 volumes. Jerusalem: Yad Izhak Ben-Zvi.

Rollston, C. A.

2010. *Writing and Literacy in the World of Ancient Israel: Epigraphic Evidence from the Iron Age*. Atlanta: Society of Biblical Literature.

Romero, M. S.

2002. Women, Maintenance Activities, and Space. *Proceedings of the Symposium on Mediterranean Archaeology: SOMA 2001: Proceedings of the Fifth Annual Meeting of Postgraduate Researchers, the University of Liverpool, 23–25 February 2001*, eds. G. Muskett, A. Koltsida, M. Georgiadis, 178–182. Oxford: Archaeopress.

Rooke, D. W., ed.

2007. *A Question of Sex? Gender and Difference in the Hebrew Bible and Beyond*. Sheffield: Sheffield Phoenix.

Rosaldo, M. Z.

1974. Women, Culture, and Society: A Theoretical Overview. In Rosaldo and Lamphere (1974), 17–42.

1980. The Use and Abuse of Anthropology: Reflections on Feminism and Cross-Cultural Understanding. *SIGNS* 5:389–417.

Rosaldo, M. Z. and Lamphere, L., eds.

1974. *Women, Culture, and Society*. Stanford, Calif.: Stanford University Press.

Rosenberg, D.

2008. Spatial Distribution of Food Processing Activities at Late Iron I Megiddo. *Tel Aviv* 35:96–113.

Ross, M. H.

1986. Female Political Participation: A Cross-Cultural Explanation. *American Anthropologist*, new series 88:843–858.

Rossi, A.

1977. A Biosocial Perspective on Parenting. *Daedalus* 106:1–31.

Routledge, B.

2009. Average Families? House Size Variability in the Southern Levantine Iron Age. In Dutcher-Walls (2009), 42–60.

Ruether, R. R.

1985. Feminist Interpretation: A Method of Correlation. In *Feminist Interpretations of the Bible*, ed. L. M. Russell, 111–124. Philadelphia: Westminster.

Sabar, Y.

2007. Agonies of Childbearing and Child Rearing in Iraqi Kurdistan: A Narrative in Jewish Neo-Aramaic and in English Translation. In *Studies in Semitic and General Linguistics in Honor of Gideon Goldenberg*, eds. T. Bar and E. Cohen, 107–145. Münster: Ugarit-Verlag.

Sakenfeld, K. D.

1989. Feminist Biblical Interpretation. *Theology Today* 46:154–168.

Sabloff, J.

2005. Processual Archaeology. In Renfrew and Bahn (2005), 212–219.

Salamone, S. D.

1987. Tradition and Gender: The *Nikokyrio*: The Economics of Sex Role Complementarity in Rural Greece. *Ethos* 15:203–225.

Salem, H. J.

1999. Implications of Cultural Tradition: The Case of Palestinian Traditional Pottery. In Kapitan (1999), 66–82.

Saller, R. P.

1994. *Patriarchy, Property, and Death in the Roman Family Economy*. Cambridge: Cambridge University Press.

Sarna, N.

1989. *The JPS Torah Commentary: Genesis*. Philadelphia: Jewish Publication Society.

Sasson, A.

1998. The Pastoral Component in the Economy of Hill Country Sites in the Intermediate Bronze and Iron Ages: Archaeo-ethnographic Case Studies. *Tel Aviv* 25:3–51.

2010. *Animal Husbandry in Ancient Israel: A Zooarchaeological Perspective on Livestock Exploitation, Herd Management and Economic Strategies*. London: Equinox.

Sasson, J.

2001. "The Mother of All... " Etiologies. In *"A Wise and Discerning Mind": Essays in Honor of Burke O. Long*, eds. S. M. Olyan and R. C. Culley, 205–220. Providence: Brown Judaic Studies.

2008. Time and Mortality: Creation Narratives in Ancient Israel and Mesopotamia. In *Papers on Ancient Literatures: Greece, Rome and The Near East: Proceedings of the "Advanced Seminar in the Humanities" Venice International University 2004–2005*, eds. E. Cingano and L. Milano, 489–509. Padua: S.A.R.G.O.N. Editrice e Libreria.

Schaberg, J.

2004. *Resurrection of Mary Magdalene: Legends, Apocrypha, and the Christian Testament*. New York: Continuum.

Schloen, J. D.

2001. *The House of the Father as Fact and Symbol: Patrimonialism in Ugarit and the Ancient Near East*. Winona Lake, Ind.: Eisenbrauns.

Schmitt, R.

    2004. *Magic im Alten Testament*. Münster: Ugarit-Verlag.

    forthcoming. A Typology of Iron Age Cult Places. In Albertz et al. (forthcoming).

Schniedewind, W. M.

    2004. *How the Bible Became a Book: The Textualization of Ancient Israel*. Cambridge: Cambridge University Press.

Schofield, R.

    1986. Did the Women Really Die? Three Centuries of Maternal Mortality in "The World We Have Lost." In *The Worlds We Have Gained: Histories of Population and Social Structure: Essays Presented to Peter Laslett on His Seventieth Birthday*, eds. L. Bonfield, R. M. Smith, and K. Wrightson, 231–260. Oxford: Basil Blackwell.

Schotroff, L., Schroer, S., and Wacker, M.-T.

    1998. *Feminist Interpretation: The Bible in Women's Perspective* (trans. M. and B. Rumscheidt). Minneapolis: Fortress.

Schroer, S.

    1998. Toward a Feminist Reconstruction of the History of Israel. In Schotroff, Schroer, and Wacker (1998), 83–176.

    2000. Abigail: A Wise Woman Works for Peace. In S. Schroer, *Wisdom Has Built Her House: Studies on the Figure of Sophia in the Bible* (trans. L. M. Mahoney and W. McDonough), 78–83. Collegeville, Minn.: Liturgical.

Schüssler Fiorenza, E.

    2001. *Wisdom Ways: Introducing Feminist Biblical Interpretation*. Maryknoll, N.Y.: Orbis.

Seger, K., ed. (and author of the text)

    1981. *Portrait of a Palestinian Village: The Photographs of Hilma Granqvist*. London: Third World Centre for Research and Publishing.

Seow, C.-L.

    1997. *Ecclesiastes: A New Translation with Introduction and Commentary*. New York: Doubleday.

Sered, S. S.

    1988. Food and Holiness: Cooking as a Sacred Act among Middle Eastern Jewish Women. *Anthropological Quarterly* 61:129–140.

    1992. *Women as Ritual Experts: The Religious Lives of Elderly Jewish Women in Jerusalem*. New York: Oxford University Press.

    1994. *Priestess, Mother, Sacred Sister: Religions Dominated by Women*. New York: Oxford University Press.

Sharistanian, J., ed.

    1987. *Beyond the Public/Domestic Dichotomy: Contemporary Perspectives on Women's Public Lives*. New York: Greenwood.

Sharp, Sharon A.

    1986. Folk Medicine Practices: Women as Keepers and Carriers of Knowledge. *Women's Studies International Forum* 9:243–249.

Shectman, S.

2009. *Women in the Pentateuch: A Feminist and Source-critical Analysis.* Sheffield: Sheffield Phoenix.

Shields, M.

2010. A Feast Fit for a King: Food and Drink in the Abigail Story. In *The Fate of King David: The Past and Present of a Biblical Icon*, eds. T. Linafelt, C. V. Camp, and T. Beal, 38–54. New York: T&T Clark.

Shiloh, Y.

1973. The Four-Room House—The Israelite Type House. *Eretz-Israel* 11:277–285.

Simkins, R. A.

2009. Gender, the Environment, and Sin in Genesis. In *Women, Gender, and Religion*, ed. S. Calef and R. A. Simkins. Omaha: Creighton University Kripke Center.

Simpson, I. H. and Wilson, J.

1992. Proprietary Family Orientations of Black and White Farm Couples. Paper presented at the Fourth National Conference on American Rural and Farm Women in Historical Perspective. University of California-Davis, June 26–28.

Singer, A.

2007. *The Soils of Israel.* New York: Springer.

Singer-Avitz, L.

2011. Household Activities at Tel Beersheba. In Yasur-Landau, Ebeling, and Mazow (2011), 275–301.

Sköl, J.

2010. Female Prophets in the Ancient Near East. In J. Day. (2010), 47–61.

Smith, J. Z.

2004. Here, There, and Anywhere. In J.Z. Smith, *Relating Religion: Essays in the Study of Religion*, 323–339. Chicago: University of Chicago Press.

Smith, M. S.

2004. *The Memoirs of God: History, Memory, and the Experience of the Divine in Ancient Israel.* Minneapolis: Fortress.

2008. *God in Translation: Deities in Cross-Cultural Discourse in the Biblical World.* Tübingen: Mohr Siebeck.

Smith, P.

1993. An Approach to the Paleodemographic Analysis of Human Skeletal Remains from Archaeological Sites. In *Biblical Archaeology Today, 1990: Proceedings of the Second International Congress on Biblical Archaeology* (Pre-Congress Symposium Supplement), eds. A. Biran and J. Aviram, 1–13. Jerusalem: Israel Exploration Society.

Smith, W. R.

1889. *Lectures on the Religion of the Semites.* Edinburgh: A. & C. Black.

Snowden, J. H.

1921. *The Meaning of Education.* New York: Abingdon.

Sofaer, J. R.

2006. *The Body as Material Culture: A Theoretical Osteoarchaeology*. New York: Cambridge University Press.

Solvang, E. K.

2003. *A Woman's Place is in the House: Royal Women of Judah and their Involvement in the House of David*. Sheffield: Sheffield Academic Press.

Sorenson, M. L. S.

2005. Feminist Archaeology. In Renfrew and Bahn (2005), 116–121.

Souvatzi, S. D.

2008. *A Social Archaeology of Households in Neolithic Greece: An Anthropological Approach*. Cambridge: Cambridge University Press.

Spencer-Wood, S. M.

1996. Toward the Further Development of Feminist Historical Archaeology. *World Archaeology Bulletin* 7:118–136.

1999. Gendering Power. In Sweely (1999c), 175–183.

Stager, L. A.

1985. The Archaeology of the Family in Ancient Israel. *Bulletin of the American Schools of Oriental Research* 260:1–36.

1998. Forging an Identity: The Emergence of Ancient Israel. In Coogan (1998), 122–175.

Stansell, C.

2010. *The Feminist Promise: 1792 to the Present*. New York: Modern Library.

Stanton, E. C.

1895, 1898. *The Woman's Bible* (2 parts). New York: European Publishing Company (reprinted 1974, as *The Original Feminist Attack on the Bible*, with introduction by B. Welter). New York: Arno.

Stark, J. C.

2007. Introduction. In *Feminist Interpretations of Augustine*, ed. J. C. Stark, 1–42. University Park: Pennsylvania University Press.

Stavrakopoulou, F.

2010. "Popular" Religion and "Official" Religion: Practice, Perception, and Portrayal. In Stavrakopoulou and Barton (2010), 37–58.

Stavrakopoulou, F. and Barton, J., eds.

2010. *Religious Diversity in Ancient Israel and Judah*. London: T&T Clark.

Stein, D. E. S.

2006. ed., *The Contemporary Torah: A Gender-Sensitive Adaptation of the JPS Translation*. Philadelphia: Jewish Publication Society.

2008. The Grammar of Social Gender in Biblical Hebrew. *Hebrew Studies* 49:7–26.

Stein, G.

1998. Heterogeneity, Power, and Political Economy: Some Current Research Issues in the Archaeology of Old World Complex Societies. *Journal of Archaeological Research* 6:1–44.

Steinberg, N.

    1991. The Deuteronomic Law Code and the Politics of State Centralization. In Jobling, Day, and Sheppard (1991), 161–170.

    2004. Social Science Criticism. In Hayes (2004), 270–275.

Stockett, M. K. and Geller, P. L.

    2006. Feminist Anthropology: Perspectives on Our Past, Present, and Future. In *Feminist Anthropology: Past Present, and Future*, ed. P. L. Geller and M. K. Stockett, 1–19. Philadelphia: University of Pennsylvania Press.

Stol, M.

    2000. *Birth in Babylonia and the Bible: Its Mediterranean Setting*. Groningen: STYX.

Stordalen, T.

    2000. *Echoes of Eden: Genesis 2–3 and Symbolism of the Eden Garden in Biblical Hebrew Literature*. Leuven: Peeters.

Stowers, S. K.

    2008. Theorizing the Religions of Ancient Households and Families. In Bodel and Olyan (2008b), 5–19.

Strand, E. A.

    2010. The Basics of Textile Tools and Textile Terminology: From Fiber to Fabric. In *Textile Terminologies of the Ancient Near East and Mediterranean from the Third to the First Millennia BC*, eds. C. Michel and M.-L. Nosch, 10–22. Oxford: Oxbow.

Sutton, D. E.

    2001. *Remembrance of Repasts: An Anthropology of Food and Memory*. Oxford: Berg.

Sweely, T. L.

    1999a. Gender, Space, People, and Power at Cerén, El Salvador. In Sweely (1999c), 155–171.

    1999b. Introduction. In Sweely (1999c), 1–14.

    1999c. ed., *Manifesting Power: Gender and Interpretation of Power in Archaeology*, London: Routledge.

Swindell, A.

    2009. Adam and Eve, Story of. V. Literature. *Encyclopedia of the Bible and Its Reception* 1:352–356. Berlin: de Gruyter.

Tekkök-Bicken, B.

    2000. Pottery Production in the Troad: Ancient and Modern Akköy. *Near Eastern Archaeology* 63:94–101.

Tilley, J. T.

    2000. Cultural Relativism. *Human Rights Quarterly* 22:501–547.

Tilly, L.

    1978. The Social Sciences and the Study of Women: A Review Article. *Comparative Studies in Society and History* 20:163–173.

van der Toorn, K.

1994. *From Her Cradle to Her Grave: The Role of Religion in the Life of the Israelite and the Babylonian Woman* (trans. S. J. Denning-Bolle). Sheffield: Sheffield Academic Press.

1996. *Family Religion in Babylonia, Syria and Israel: Continuity and Change in the Forms of Religious Life*. Leiden: Brill.

2004. Religious Practices of the Individual and Family: Introduction. In *Religions of the Ancient World: A Guide*, ed. S. I. Johnston, 423–424. Cambridge, Mass.: Belknap.

2008. Family Religion in Second Millennium West Asia (Mesopotamia, Emar, Nuzi). In Bodel and Olyan (2008b), 20–36.

Torjeson, K. J.

1993. *When Women Were Priests: Women's Leadership in the Early Church and the Scandal of their Subordination in the Rise of Christianity*. San Francisco: HarperSanFrancisco.

Trible, P.

1978. *God and the Rhetoric of Sexuality*. Philadelphia: Fortress.

1984. *Texts of Terror: Literary-Feminist Readings of Biblical Narratives*. Philadelphia: Fortress.

Trichopoulou, A. and Lagiou, P.

1999. Dietary Guidelines for Adults in Greece. *Archives of Hellenic Medicine* 16:516–524.

Tsuk, T.

1997. Cisterns. *Oxford Encyclopedia of Archaeology in the Near East* 2:12–13. New York: Oxford University Press.

Tyldesley, J.

1994. *Daughters of Isis*. London: Viking/Penguin.

Ullendorf, E.

1978. *The Bawdy Bible*. Oxford: Oxford Centre for Postgraduate Hebrew Studies.

UNICEF

2011. *The State of the World's Children 2011: Adolescence, and Age of Opportunity*. New York: United Nations Children's Fund.

Vawter, B.

1977. *On Genesis: A New Reading*. Garden City, N.Y.: Doubleday.

Wacker, M.-T.

1998. Historical, Hermeneutical, and Methodological Foundations. In Schotroff, Schroer, and Wacker, (1998), 1–82.

Wächter, L.

2001. *ʿāpār; ʿpr; ʿēper*. *Theological Dictionary of the Old Testament* 11 (trans. D. E. Green): 257–265. Grand Rapids, Mich.: Eerdmans.

Wapnish, P. and Hesse, B.

1998. Pig Use and Abuse in the Ancient Levant: Ethnoreligious Boundary-Building and Swine. In *Ancestors for the Pigs: Pigs in Prehistory*, ed.,

S. M. Nelson, 123–136. Philadelphia: University of Pennsylvania Museum of Archaeology and Anthropology.

Waters, T.

2007. *The Persistence of Subsistence Agriculture: Life Beneath the Level of the Marketplace*. Lanham, Md.: Lexington.

Watson, P. J.

1999. Ethnographic Analogy and Ethnoarchaeology. In Kapitan (1999), 47–65.

Watts, J. W.

2007. The Torah as the Rhetoric of Priesthood. In *The Pentateuch as Torah: New Models for Understanding Its Promulgation and Acceptance*, eds. G. N. Knoppers and B. M. Levinson, 319–332. Winona Lake, Ind.: Eisenbrauns, 2007.

Weber, M.

1952. *Ancient Judaism* (trans. and ed. H. H. Gerth and D. Martindale). Glencoe, Ill.: Free Press (originally published 1917–1919).

Wegner, J. R.

1998. Women in Classical Rabbinic Judaism. In *Jewish Women in Historical Perspective,* ed. J. Baskin, 73–100. Detroit: Wayne State University Press.

Weiss, A.

2007. Biblical Poetry. *Encyclopaedia Judaica* 16:254–262. 2nd edition. Detroit: Macmillan Reference.

Weiss, E. and Kislev, M. E.

2004. Plant Remains as Indicators for Economic Activity: Iron Age Ashkelon, a Case Study. *Journal of Archaeological Science* 31:1–13.

Wellhausen, J.

1885. *Prolegomena to the History of Ancient Israel* (trans. J. S. Black and A. Menzies). Edinburgh: A. & C. Black (originally published in German in 1878).

1897. *Israelitische und Jüdische Geschichte*. 3rd edition. Berlin: Georg Reimer.

Wells, B.

2008. What is Biblical Law? A Look at Pentateuchal Rules and Near Eastern Practice. *Catholic Biblical Quarterly* 70:223–243.

Wells, P.

1986. Fare of the Country; France's Vintage Village Ovens. *New York Times,* March 2, 1986. Available: http://query.nytimes.com/gst/fullpage.html?res=9A0DE3DA1030F931A35750C0A960948260&sec=travel&spon=&pagewanted=1 (accessed April 21, 2012).

Westbrook R. and Wells, B.

2009. *Everyday Law in Biblical Israel: An Introduction*. Louisville, Ky.: Westminster John Knox.

Westermann, C.

1984. *Genesis 1–11: A Commentary* (trans. J. J. Scullion). Minneapolis: Augsburg.

1995. *The Roots of Wisdom: The Oldest Proverbs of Israel and Other Peoples* (trans. J. D. Charles). Louisville: Westminster John Knox.

Whitfield, J. L.

2007. The Invisible Woman: Eve's Self Image in Paradise Lost. *Oshkosh Scholar* 2:57–61.

Whittaker, J. C.

2000. Alonia and Dhoukanes: The Ethnoarchaeology of Threshing in Cyprus. *Near Eastern Archaeology* 63:62–69.

Whyte, M. K.

1978. *The Status of Women in Pre-industrial Societies*. Princeton, N.J.: Princeton University Press.

Wilcox, A. J., Weinberg, C. R., O'Connor, J. F., Baird, D. D., Schlatterer, J. P., Canfield, R. E., Armstrong, E. G., and Nisula, B. C.

1988. Incidence of Early Loss of Pregnancy. *New England Journal of Medicine* 319:189–194.

Wilfong, T. G.

2002. *Women of Jeme: Lives in a Coptic Town in Late Antique Egypt*. Ann Arbor: University of Michigan Press.

Wilk, R. R. and Netting, R. McC.

1984. Households: Changing Forms and Functions. In Netting, Wilk, and Arnould (1984a), 1–28.

Wilk, R. R. and Rathje, W. L.

1982. Household Archaeology. *American Behavioral Scientist* 25:617–639.

Wilkins, J.

2000. Food Preparation and Gender Roles: Representations of Gender Roles in the Literary Evidence. In *Representations of Gender from Prehistory to the Present*, eds. M. Donald and L. Hurcombe, 118–134. London: Macmillan.

Williams, G.

1996. Representations of Women in Literature. In *I, Claudia: Women in Ancient Rome*, eds. D. E. E. Kleiner and S. B. Matheson, 126–138. New Haven: Yale University Art Gallery.

Williamson, H. G. M.

2010. Prophetesses in the Hebrew Bible. In J. Day (2010), 65–80.

Wilson, R. W.

1980. *Prophecy and Society in Ancient Israel*. Philadelphia: Fortress.

1992. Genealogy, Genealogies. In *Anchor Bible Dictionary* 2:929–932. New York: Doubleday.

Womack, M.

2001. *Being Human: An Introduction to Cultural Anthropology*. 2nd edition. Upper Saddle River, N.J.: Prentice Hall.

Yanagisako, S. J.

1979. Family and Household: The Analysis of Domestic Groups. *Annual Review of Anthropology* 8:161–205.

Yasur-Landau, A., Ebeling, J., and Mazow L., eds.
    2011. *Household Archaeology in the Ancient Israel and Beyond.* Leiden: Brill.
Yorburg, B.
    1975. The Nuclear and the Extended Family: An Area of Conceptual Confusion. *Journal of Comparative Family Studies* 6:5–14.
Zevit, Z.
    2001. *The Religions of Ancient Israel: A Synthesis of Parallactic Approaches.* New York: Continuum.
Zohary, M.
    1982. *Plants of the Bible.* Cambridge: Cambridge University Press.
Zonabend, F.
    1996. An Anthropological Perspective on Kinship and the Family. In *Distant Worlds, Ancient Worlds* (trans. S. H. Tenison, R. Morris, and A. Wilson), eds. A. Burghière, C. Klapisch-Zuber, and F. Zonabend, 9–68. *A History of the Family*, vol. 1. Cambridge, Mass.: Belknap Press.
Zorn, J. R.
    1993. Nasbeh, Tell en-. *New Encyclopedia of Archaeological Excavations in the Holy Land* 3:1098–1102. Jerusalem: The Israel Exploration Society and Carta.
    1994. Estimating the Population Size of Ancient Settlements: Methods, Problems, Solutions, and a Case Study. *Bulletin of the American Schools of Oriental Research* 295:31–48.

Index of Biblical and Other Ancient Texts

Index

taxation, taxes, 50, 55, 58, 114, 116, 117, 207
technology, 15, 31
  change of, 132, 135, 207–208
  developments of, 49
  female-gendered, 132, 135, 142, 170
  household, 184–185
  imaging, 17
  iron, 214n38
  subsistence, 38
  terracing, 45–46
temple (Jerusalem), 20, 105, 148, 172, 174, 176, 178, 197, 228n48
temple cult, 148
temple prostitute, 173
terminology, 14–16, 41
terraces, 45–46, 50, 51, 107, 108
terracotta figurines, 129, 130, 156, 176
textiles, 49, 105, 107, 209
  production, 133, 139, 167, 191, 207, 208–209
  work, 172–173, 184
theologians, 176
theological language, 12
theophoric names, 158
third-world countries, 145
Tobit, 61, 206
toil, 91, 93, 94
tools, 15, 29, 33, 105, 131, 133, 135. *See also* grinding; mills
traditional publications, 30
translation, 84–87, 211
  bias, 64–65
transverse room, 107
tree of knowledge, 61
tribes, 11, 103, 114
Trible, Phyllis, 65
turning, 94
typological groupings, 29

unclean animals, 166
underground shafts, 44
urban centers. *See* settlements, urban

values, 170
  cultural, 101, 211
  egalitarian, 202
  gender equality and, 65
  judgments, 10, 199
  of land, 201
  patriarchal, 180, 195
  texts and, 8
  of women's work, 33, 34, 36, 121–122, 187
vegetables, 48
Victorian gender ideology, 183
village society, 23
von Rad, Gerhard, 95
Vulgate, 64, 85, 86, 89, 92

wage labor, 121, 206
water, 43–44. *See also* rain
weaving, 133, 141. *See also* textiles
Weber, Max, 11, 193
Wellhausen, Julius, 11, 148, 165, 194
Wilk, Robert., 127
wine, 47, 48, 132
wisdom, 80, 138
Woman Wisdom, 80, 113, 138, 177
women-centered analysis, 5
women's networks, 139–143, 198
word-motif, 78

Xenophon, 191

Yahweh, 108, 148, 172
Year of Our Lord (AD), 15

Zephaniah, 213n3
Zevit, Ziony, 198, 232n73

Printed in Great Britain
by Amazon

35304140R00176